"Ever wondered how baptism 'w [...] answers that question. Both a humble charity toward those holding other positions and yet a crystal clarity mark this book. The book is full of cogent exegesis, simple summaries, and excellent illustrations. Clear, concise, more constructive than argumentative, Bobby Jamieson's prose is smooth, his reasoning is simple, his reading of the contemporary scene is careful. Invest in reading this book so that you (and others you help) can better follow Christ."

Mark Dever
Pastor, Capitol Hill Baptist Church, Washington, DC;
President, 9Marks

"For most of Baptist history, the idea that baptism is required for church membership and for participation in the Lord's Supper has been the majority view, enshrined in a number of Baptist confessions and statements of faith. But in the past generation, many have dropped the requirement of baptism for participation in the Lord's Supper (moving to open Communion), and fewer, but some, have taken the next step and dropped the requirement of baptism for church membership (a move to open membership). I think the impetus for these changes has been largely cultural, with little consideration for the theological and ecclesiological reasons that led earlier Baptists to their views. That is why I am glad to commend Bobby Jamieson's work, *Going Public: Why Baptism Is Required for Church Membership*. I know of no other work that so thoroughly considers the ecclesiological, theological, and biblical issues that connect baptism to church membership and participation in the Lord's Supper and does so in a clear, readable, and irenic manner. It is not that I agree with all the answers he gives; we differ on a number of points. But he is raising the right questions, and they are questions few others are raising. I hope it receives a wide readership and sparks a lot of constructive discussions."

John Hammett
Professor of Systematic Theology and associate dean of Theological Studies,
Southeastern Baptist Theological Seminary

"Since the era of the Reformation, baptism has been an issue of contention among believers, and not only between credobaptists and paedobaptists. Among baptistic believers, especially in the seventeenth and nineteenth centuries, there has been significant disagreement about the relationship between baptism and the Lord's Supper and between baptism and membership in the local church. It is not surprising that over the past century Baptists have often skirted these issues so as to avoid controversy. But refusing to touch the issue for fear of being controversial or even too narrow is not helpful, as this new essay rightly points out. Jamieson helpfully navigates us through the issues related to this controversy, and while not all will agree with his conclusions, he cannot be faulted for lacking thorough biblical and historical reflection."

Michael A. G. Haykin
Professor of Church History and Biblical Spirituality
and Director of The Andrew Fuller Center for Baptist Studies at
The Southern Baptist Theological Seminary

"Ecclesiology is in many ways the chief contribution and distinctive of the Baptists. Sadly, you would not learn that by observing many Baptist congregations. Baptist ecclesiology has been eclipsed by pragmatism and undermined by neglect. *Going Public* is a theological antidote to that situation. Jamieson, one of the brightest young Baptist scholars today, has written a historically informed, biblically faithful, and theologically rich account of the doctrines of baptism and church membership."

Albert Mohler
President,
The Southern Baptist Theological Seminary

"Many books skim the surface of ecclesiology without diving into the depths of the doctrine of the church. With the skills of a master diver, Bobby Jamieson brings a unique perceptiveness combined with grace and courtesy while exploring practical matters every faithful pastor will face. This book will challenge and sharpen your understanding of baptism. If you take baptism and its relationship to church membership and the Lord's Supper seriously, you must read this book."

Thomas White
President and Professor of Systematic Theology,
Cedarville University

GOING
PUBLIC

GOING PUBLIC

Why Baptism Is Required
for Church Membership

BOBBY JAMIESON

ACADEMIC

NASHVILLE, TENNESSEE

Going Public: Why Baptism Is Required for Church Membership

Copyright © 2015 by Bobby Jamieson

B&H Publishing Group
Nashville, Tennessee

All rights reserved

ISBN: 978-1-4336-8620-7

Dewey Decimal Classification: 343.16
Subject Heading: BAPTISM \ LORD'S SUPPER \ CHURCH MEMBERSHIP

Printed in the United States of America
5 6 7 8 9 10 11 12 • 22 21 20 19 18

For Mark and Jonathan,
for putting me up to it.

CONTENTS

ACKNOWLEDGMENTS

I loved writing this book, and I hope that comes through in what's written. But what the reader likely can't see is the wealth of support I received in writing it.

First and foremost, I had the privilege of writing this book as part of my work for 9Marks. So I'm grateful to Ryan Townsend for leading 9Marks to produce not just bite-sized content to go, but also full Thanksgiving dinners. I hope this book is a worthy entrée! I'm also thankful for Mark Dever and Jonathan Leeman's commission to write the book, and for the freedom the 9Marks directors gave me to devote so much time to it. Thanks, also, to the whole 9Marks team for working hard together to build healthy churches, and to the donors who enable this work to happen.

The folks at B&H have been a pleasure to work with. Special thanks go to Chris Cowan and Chris Thompson, who have promptly and cheerfully guided the manuscript to publication.

Jon Pentecost, Austin Suter, Chris Bruno, and John Hammett all read the entire manuscript and provided critical, insightful feedback. Mike Carnicella, Justin Dillehay, Sam Emadi, Philip Van Steenburgh, and Will Pareja also read and commented on parts. Thank you, brothers, for your generous investment in this book and its author.

Thanks, finally, to my wife, Kristin, and our daughters, Rose and Lucy, for filling our home to overflowing with love.

Soli Deo gloria.

INTRODUCTION

This book is not exactly what you think it is. The subtitle, *Why Baptism Is Required for Church Membership*, is accurate, but it conceals much. It names the destination but says little about the journey.

This whole book aims toward the conclusion that churches should require prospective members to be baptized—which is to say, baptized as believers—in order to join. Among Christians who agree that only believers should be baptized, this issue is hotly disputed, and it remains an open question for many. Hence this book. But in order to answer this one question, I had to dig deeper than I anticipated at the outset. I had to burrow through sand and clay, so to speak, in order to find bedrock on which to build a convincing argument.

That's because this book is an exercise in rebuilding among the ruins of contemporary evangelical—and even Baptist—ecclesiology. By God's grace more and more evangelicals seem to be recovering more and more ecclesiology. But to say that our ecclesiological house is in order would be a bit too generous. Evangelical ecclesiology tends to be consumed by the question of "what works." Pragmatism has not only moved to the center of our churchly solar system, but like an aging star it has ballooned and swallowed everything in its orbit. So we tend to neglect ecclesiology as a theological subject altogether or at best sketch a bare outline of what a church birthed by the gospel and grounded on the final authority of Scripture should look like.

Our neglect of ecclesiology walks in lockstep with the individualistic and anti-institutional biases of the late modern West. The result is that in both theology and practice we have almost completely disconnected the ordinances of

1

baptism and the Lord's Supper from the local church. Baptism is a personal profession of faith—so what does it have to do with the church or church membership? And the Lord's Supper is a memorial and proclamation of the death of Christ—so shouldn't any gathering of believers be able to celebrate it?

I'd argue that a general inability to articulate what distinguishes any gathering of believers from a local church is at the root of the confusion surrounding the relationship between baptism and church membership. We can't very well articulate what makes a church a church, so we struggle to see why anyone who appears to be a Christian should ever be excluded from one. But as I'll argue throughout the book, baptism and the Lord's Supper are themselves the hinge between "Christians" and "church." Together baptism and the Lord's Supper mark off a church as a unified, visible, local body of believers. To put it more technically, they give a church institutional form and order.[1]

The thesis of this book, then, is that baptism and the Lord's Supper are effective signs of church membership: they create the social, ecclesial reality to which they point. Precisely because of their complementary church-constituting roles, baptism must precede the Lord's Supper and the status of church membership which grants access to the Lord's Supper. Therefore, what this book offers is not merely an answer to the question of whether baptism should be required for membership. Instead it offers an integrated account of how baptism and the Lord's Supper transform a scattered group of Christians into a gathered local church. This book traces the trajectory of a church's birth, how gospel people form a gospel polity. In that sense it offers much more than an answer to the question implied in the subtitle. Instead, it lays theological foundations for understanding exactly what the local church is from the ground up.

Even with all this journeying, the book's primary destination is still the conclusion that baptism is in fact required for membership in a local church. This means the book has a polemical purpose. A hundred years ago, B. B. Warfield was professor of didactic and polemical theology at Princeton. Today that first adjective is suspect, and the second has morphed into a rebuke. I wouldn't need to argue my case in quite the way I have if there weren't Christians arguing that baptism *isn't* required for membership; as it is, I'm trying to prove one position and disprove another. So this book is an argument from front to back.

---

[1] This language is borrowed from Oliver O'Donovan, *The Desire of the Nations: Rediscovering the Roots of Political Theology* (Cambridge: Cambridge University Press, 1996), 172. See chap. 7.

But it is an argument among brothers. I do not doubt for a moment the integrity or godliness of those with whom I disagree. Two of my primary interlocutors, John Bunyan and John Piper, have profoundly influenced my life and theology. So I would simply ask readers to extend to me the same kindness I try to show my dialogue partners throughout: a patient hearing prompted by love that weathers disagreement.

Even though this book has a polemical purpose, it's primarily positive. Most of the book is not taken up with addressing objections or critiquing others' views. Instead, as I said, I am seeking to rebuild an ecclesial understanding of the ordinances. Fundamentally, this book is a constructive theological account of how baptism and the Lord's Supper structure the church. Scripture teaches that baptism is the front door of the church, and the Lord's Supper is the family meal.

That this excludes from membership Christians who consider themselves baptized but aren't is deeply saddening. Believe me, I do not relish the thought of refusing to accept godly, fruitful, paedobaptist Christians into church membership. But it is far worse to disregard a command of Christ, confirm a Christian's disobedience to Christ, and erase the visible sign of our union with Christ. To remove baptism from church membership is to dig up and discard one of the foundations of the local church. Removing baptism from membership erases the line Jesus himself has drawn between the church and the world. In the short run it appears compassionate, but in the long run it weakens the church. Baptism is how Christians go public with their faith. To allow Christians not to profess faith in the form Christ appointed is to allow them to whisper what God wants shouted from the rooftops. Moreover, this exclusive implication is only a lamentable side effect of discerning how the Bible binds together baptism and membership and practicing accordingly. Yes, a door can keep people out, but its first purpose is to show you where to go in.

PART 1

Getting
Our Bearings

Chapter 1

Setting the Stage

Why would anyone write a whole book arguing that baptism is necessary for church membership? Is this even a debate worth having?

Not all debates are. Sometimes it's better just to walk away: "Leave the presence of a fool, for there you do not meet words of knowledge" (Prov 14:7). Sometimes, though, the gospel itself is at stake, which calls for public dispute: "But when Cephas came to Antioch, I opposed him to his face, because he stood condemned" (Gal 2:11).

This book is about an issue that falls somewhere between "just walk away" and "the gospel is at stake." It's not the Trinity, but it's not the color of your church's carpet. It lives somewhere in that vast, neglected real estate between "essential to salvation" and "not worth bothering about." You're reading this book, so presumably you don't think the question is a total waste of time, but it still helps to take a good look at what's at stake before we dive in. So in this chapter I'll give a few reasons this issue is worth arguing about.

That's one among a handful of stage-setting enterprises which will occupy our attention in this chapter. First, I'll clarify what this book is and isn't about. Second, as advertised, I'll give an account of why this is a debate worth having and why I'm entering it. Third, I'll lay out various positions in the debate, clarify some key terms, and describe the position I'll be taking. Fourth, I'm going to discuss two theological issues I think are crucial for getting this issue right and that haven't received the attention they deserve. Fifth, I'll comment on the shape the whole book takes in light of its effort to rebuild ecclesiological foundations. Finally, I'll sketch where we're heading in the rest of the book.

A One-Issue Book

What is this book about? In one sentence: in this book I argue that according to Scripture baptism is required for church membership and for participation in the Lord's Supper, membership's recurring effective sign. That's all, folks.

So I'm not going to argue for believer's baptism over against paedobaptism. Plenty of others have spoken well to that issue.[1] So in this book I will largely assume, rather than seek to prove, that the baptism of a professing believer in Jesus Christ is the only true baptism. I assume virtually everyone who will read this book is a credobaptist, someone who believes that only professing believers in Jesus should be baptized. Why? Because the church throughout history has held with near-perfect unanimity that baptism is a necessary prerequisite to the Lord's Supper and church membership. The only people who have departed from this consensus are a smallish slice of credobaptists.

The reason for this is not far to seek. Everyone acknowledges that we credobaptists have been baptized. Apart from Quakers no one denies that what we call baptism is baptism. But we, on the other hand, think a huge number of Christians simply haven't been baptized because sprinkling an infant is not what Jesus and the apostles meant by "baptism." There's asymmetry here. Plenty of baptists could join a Presbyterian church, but if baptism is a prerequisite for membership, then those same Presbyterians couldn't join a baptist church. As it happens, they sometimes want to; hence the problem. And the way some credobaptists have sought to solve that problem is to allow those who have been "baptized"[2] as infants to join their churches, a position I'll refer to as "open membership."

---

[1] An excellent, in-depth treatment of the issue is Stephen Wellum's essay "Baptism and the Relationship Between the Covenants," in *Believer's Baptism: Sign of the New Covenant in Christ*, ed. Thomas R. Schreiner and Shawn D. Wright (Nashville: B&H, 2007), 97–161. Bruce Ware also offers a helpful argument in *Baptism: Three Views*, ed. David F. Wright (Downers Grove, IL: InterVarsity Press, 2009).

[2] I'm putting "baptized" in quotes here and will often do so with reference to infant "baptism," since I believe infant baptism is not baptism at all. I'm not doing this to be a stick in the mud. Throughout the history of the baptism and membership debate, open membership advocates have sometimes used phrases like "haven't been baptized in the proper mode" or "haven't been baptized as we understand the ordinance" to avoid referring to

In other words, this is a distinctly baptistic burden. Paedobaptist brothers and sisters, you're welcome to stick around; just know that I'm not really talking to you. One more note on the audience of this book: this debate is not limited to those who call themselves "Baptists." If you believe that only believers should be baptized, then this issue is relevant to you, whatever your church is called and whichever other churches you do or don't formally associate with.[3]

Back to my theme of what this book isn't. This book will not attempt to comprehensively define what constitutes a valid baptism. Neither will I try to say all there is to say about baptism, the Lord's Supper, and church membership. Finally, I'm not going to attempt to provide a complete pastoral how-to manual on these three things, though I'll sketch a few practical guidelines in the last chapter.

To reiterate, I'm trying to do only one thing in this book: argue that baptism is necessary for church membership and the Lord's Supper. Along the way I aim to rebuild a coherent, biblical understanding of the role both ordinances play in the formation of the church. And wherever possible I'll point to resources on subjects I don't address in-depth. But I hope the book's laser focus on one issue renders it the more valuable to those pastors, elder boards, seminary students, and others for whom this issue is a live one.

A Debate Worth Having

Why then is this a debate worth having? Five reasons. First, even if this doesn't seem like a live issue for you or your church, there's a sense in which it always will be. Every church has to have a stance on this issue. The switch is either on or off: you'll either admit unbaptized persons into membership or you won't. And if you're a pastor who has either adopted or inherited the stance of requiring baptism for membership, you don't need me to tell you

---

persons they would admit to membership as "unbaptized." Sometimes this preserves a live distinction, in that some open membership advocates would admit those "baptized" as infants to membership but not those who have not been "baptized" in any sense at all. But whatever the nuances, I think this point involves more than mere semantics.

[3] Throughout the book I use the terms *credobaptists* and *baptists* (note the lowercase b) interchangeably to refer to Christians and churches who hold that believer's baptism is the only true baptism. This is for convenience, not to co-opt anyone to a particular denominational cause. Sometimes I'll use *Baptists* with a capital B when the believers in view self-consciously identify as such.

about the friction that can cause. So this is a debate worth having because there's no way to escape it.

Second, this is a debate worth having because of the cost of holding the position I argue. If you're going to have baptism as a prerequisite for church membership, you better have some good reasons for it. Excluding people from your church whom you're confident are Christians is no small matter, and it tends to generate no small pushback. If you hold this position, you better get used to being called divisive—or worse—whether by a church member's Methodist aunt Molly or by fellow pastors who agree with you on virtually everything but this. With that in mind, if you're inclined to see baptism as necessary for church membership but balk at the political price tag, I hope this book's biblical and theological arguments will stiffen your spine.

A third reason this is a debate worth having is that the issue lies at a crucial juncture between our ecclesiology and the prevailing winds of culture. As we'll discuss in the next chapter, for many reasons open membership feels instinctively right to us today. It seems wrong at a gut level to have to exclude R. C. Sproul or Kevin DeYoung from your church simply because he hasn't been baptized as you understand the ordinance. And yet this instinct departs from a nearly universal consensus of the entire church throughout history. Therefore I'd suggest that if your instinct says "open membership," that should open up a conversation rather than shutting it down.

Fourth, if holding to the historic position usually brings a certain social cost, adopting open membership creates its own set of problems, both practical and theological. On the practical side most churches who adopt open membership put some type of restriction on how unbaptized members may serve. But what restrictions do you set up and on what grounds? If your church is congregational, can unbaptized members vote? On every issue or only on some? Can they serve as elders? Why or why not? And if you allow them to serve as elders, how do you handle the division this introduces into your eldership?[4] Closed membership carries an up-front social cost, but open membership comes with a price tag of its own, of the "bill me later" variety.

On the theological side, how do you escape the conclusion that you deny in practice what you claim to believe about baptism? How do you escape the conclusion that your church is effectively making baptism an option rather

---

[4] I'll circle back to questions like these in chap. 10, especially point four.

than a command? Frankly, I don't think you can escape those conclusions, as I'll argue in chapter 10. But for now it's enough to recognize that for whatever problems it seems to solve, open membership creates problems of its own. And those problems should raise the question of whether the position is biblical in the first place.

Fifth and finally, the question of whether baptism is a prerequisite for church membership is a debate worth having because church polity matters. How your church is structured, governed, and constituted is important to the Lord of the church: he's said plenty about it in his Word.[5] Polity isn't the gospel, but it protects and preserves the gospel. Polity isn't the diamond, but it is one of the prongs which hold the diamond in place for all to see. Therefore, what your church says about baptism, by what you teach and by whom you admit to membership, is inescapably important.

This is also a debate we Baptists have been having among ourselves for nearly 350 years. As such you could be justified in asking what more could possibly be said about it. While much ground has been pretty well covered, I think a couple issues could use fresh attention. I'll introduce them below, and most of the book is taken up with exploring and unpacking them. Because the history of the debate is not critical for understanding the main issues involved, I'm not going to summarize the past four centuries of arguments. Instead I'll simply draw on some of the strongest arguments on both sides as I make and defend my case. In fact, my constructive theological work throughout the book simply waters seeds that are already found in the best historic defenses of baptism as a requirement for membership.

But this isn't just a historic debate; it's also an issue that's receiving renewed attention today. For example, John Piper made waves when he advocated the open membership position at Bethlehem Baptist Church in 2005.[6] Because Piper argued his case with his usual verve, he'll be a primary dialogue partner. Piper is a hero in the faith to me and many others, so please don't confuse critique with condemnation. Anecdotally it also seems like this issue is receiving

---

[5] See my article, "Why New Testament Polity Is Prescriptive," *9Marks Journal* 10, no. 4 (2013), available at http://www.9marks.org/journal/why-new-testament-polity-prescriptive.

[6] Ultimately, the elders of Bethlehem Baptist Church decided to withdraw their recommendation that the church revise its constitution to allow those who had been "baptized" as infants to join the church. Thus, the church continued to practice "closed" membership.

renewed attention among a variety of baptistic evangelicals in at least the US and the UK. So this is a debate that is clearly already taking place, and I think it's a debate worth having.

Granting this is a debate worth having, why have I personally chosen to enter it—and by writing a whole book at that? First let me say why I'm not writing. I'm not writing, as far as I can discern, because I love controversy and can't get enough of it. I'm not writing because I want to score points for my "team," whoever that may be. In fact, I'm entering this debate precisely because I'm on the same team as those who disagree with me on this issue. And if we're on the same team, we should be able to have frank conversations about how the game should be played. I'm certainly not writing because I think baptists are this lost world's great and only hope. And I'm not writing because I think paedobaptists are best kept out of sight and out of mind—far from it. Like so many baptists, many of my greatest theological influences—as well as many friends and partners in ministry—are committed paedobaptists. And I don't love them any less for it.

Why then am I writing? Because this is a pressing question for many pastors and churches, and I think there's a biblical way to answer it. And unless I'm badly mistaken, requiring baptism for membership is an increasingly unpopular stance, so it could use a fresh defense.

My hope and prayer is that this fresh defense will serve pastors and their churches in tangible ways. I think getting this issue right actually results in more unity, not more division. Further, putting baptism, the Lord's Supper, and membership together correctly is a crucial step in building a biblical ecclesiology, and removing baptism from membership has significant, unhelpful effects. I'd submit that settling this issue biblically ultimately helps churches preserve the gospel from generation to generation.

OK, but then why write a whole book on this one little issue? Why not just a blog post or two? We'll return to this question below. For now I'll simply say that lots of arguments need making and lots of arguments need answering. Once upon a time evangelicals wrestled long and hard over the biblical grounds of church polity and practice. I think our increasing willingness to do so once again is a sign of health. By God's grace the center is increasingly secure, but the center isn't all there is. And if we make the center everything and everything else nothing, we set ourselves up to lose the center itself. This book is an attempt to shore up some border territories in an effort, ultimately, to make the capital city a little more secure.

Terms and Conditions

The next bit of stage-setting we need to do is lay out some key terms and concepts for thinking through this debate. Historically the debate has been conducted in terms of "open Communion" versus "closed Communion." That is, some have argued that unbaptized persons (or, more narrowly, those "baptized" in infancy) should be admitted to the Lord's Supper. And others have argued that only baptized persons (that is, those baptized as believers) should be welcomed to the Lord's Supper. However, these terms mask a couple of key issues.

The first issue these terms can obscure is that most historic Baptist writers assumed that the "terms of Communion"—that is, what is required in order to participate—are also the terms of membership. When John Bunyan, Robert Hall Jr., and others argued that unbaptized persons should be admitted to the Lord's Supper, they were *not* arguing that such believers should be admitted to Communion but still excluded from membership. Instead, they held that unbaptized persons should be welcomed into full membership, which included and was most visibly realized in participation in the Lord's Supper. Both sides in the debate assumed that, in principle, to be qualified for Communion is to be qualified for church membership.[7] So even though the debate has been defined in terms of open versus closed Communion, these terms were meant to include, not exclude, the idea of church membership.

However, some churches require baptism for membership but deliberately allow unbaptized persons to the Lord's Supper. For instance, Ray Van Neste has argued for what he calls "open Communion," and yet his church does not admit unbaptized persons to membership.[8] When such a church celebrates the Lord's Supper, they might fence the Table—that is, declare who is welcome to

---

[7] So, for example, John Dagg argued that whoever may be admitted to Communion once may be admitted to membership; no wedge may be driven between the two (John L. Dagg, *An Essay in Defense of Strict Communion* [Penfield, GA: Benj. Brantley, 1845], 45–46).

[8] See Ray Van Neste, "The Lord's Supper in the Context of the Local Church," in *The Lord's Supper: Remembering and Proclaiming Christ's Death Until He Comes* (Nashville: B&H, 2010), 379–86. This position is not without some precedent in Baptist history, especially in the past century. See Anthony R. Cross, *Baptism and the Baptists: Theology and Practice in Twentieth-Century Britain*, Studies in Baptist History and Thought 3 (Milton Keynes: Paternoster, 2000), 418–26.

participate—by saying something like, "If you have repented of your sins and trusted in Jesus Christ for salvation, you are welcome to partake of the elements with us," or, "If you are a member in good standing of an evangelical church, you are welcome to the table."[9] Yet if an individual who had not been baptized or who had been "baptized" as an infant applied for membership in the church, they would not be allowed to join until they had been baptized. This means some advocates of open Communion also hold to open membership, and some do not. Though it's a little clunky, I'll call the open Communion/closed membership view the "open-closed" position.

Another problem with the terms *open Communion* and *closed Communion* is that in Baptist circles at least, some have distinguished between "closed" Communion and "close" Communion.[10] In this context, closed Communion refers to the position that only the members of a local church may celebrate the Lord's Supper. No visitors, whether baptized or unbaptized, are invited to the Table. And, as only baptized Christians are members, baptism is a requirement for both membership and Communion.

Close Communion, on the other hand, also admits members of other evangelical churches who have been baptized as believers. On this view baptism is a prerequisite both for church membership and for "occasional" or "visiting" Communion as well. Thus, closed and close Communion differ only on whether the Table should be open to nonmembers who are also baptized members of other true churches. Neither view would allow unbaptized persons to participate in the Lord's Supper.

My main goal in this book is not to adjudicate between closed and close Communion. I hold to the latter, though certainly a case can be made for the former. I'll address the issue in chapter 6. My point here is simply that this distinction makes the terms *open Communion* and *closed Communion* that much more difficult to use.

Further, the terms of the debate today have generally shifted to membership. One reason for this is that speaking about membership makes clear that we're not simply discussing occasional Communion. Another reason is that, as many churches recover meaningful membership, the question of who can be

---

[9] Van Neste's church fences the Table along the latter lines. See Van Neste, "The Lord's Supper," 386.

[10] For a discussion of "closed," "close," and "open" Communion, see Gregg R. Allison, *Sojourners and Strangers: The Doctrine of the Church*, Foundations of Evangelical Theology (Wheaton, IL: Crossway, 2012), 400–406.

a member naturally follows. Given how the debate has shifted, and because of the ambiguities in the historic terms *open* and *closed* Communion, if I need shorthand, I'll use "closed membership" and "open membership." Though often enough I'll refer to my own position simply by spelling it out, in part because the adjective *closed* isn't particularly flattering or fair.

But what about requiring baptism for membership but not the Lord's Supper? The open-closed position seems like a winsome compromise and a welcome pressure-release valve. However, as I'll argue, baptism is the new covenant's initiating oath-sign, and the Lord's Supper is its renewing oath-sign. By definition the former must precede the latter. Further, the Lord's Supper and church membership are too closely linked to allow baptism to be a prerequisite for one but not the other. So in due course I will argue that the open-closed position doesn't hold water, so to speak. The logic has to sweep clear through one way or the other.[11]

Key Terms at a Glance	
Closed Membership / Open Membership	Whether baptism is or is not required for church membership
Close Communion / Open Communion	Whether baptism is or is not required for participation in the Lord's Supper
Close Communion / Closed Communion	Whether baptized members of other churches may participate in the Lord's Supper ("close"), or only the members of that local church ("closed")
Occasional or Visiting Communion	Participating in the Lord's Supper in one church when one is a member of another
The Open-Closed Position	Requiring baptism for membership but not the Lord's Supper

Two Key Issues

In the end the open membership position rests on one primary, powerful argument: that local churches should not exclude from membership anyone whom

---

[11] John Hammett writes, "Furthermore, I support strict communion because I am not willing to follow the logic of open communion to open membership" (John S. Hammett, *Biblical Foundations for Baptist Churches: A Contemporary Ecclesiology* [Grand Rapids: Kregel, 2005], 287). I return to this issue in chap. 6.

they regard as genuine brothers or sisters in Christ. There are other arguments which flow from and elaborate on this assertion, but that's it in a nutshell. On this view, to use John Piper's phrase, closed membership churches are guilty of "preemptively excommunicating" genuine brothers and sisters simply because they have not been baptized, and that not due to willful rebellion but to their interpretation of Scripture.

We'll explore open membership arguments in detail later. For now I've simply sketched this one in order to introduce two key issues to which we'll give special attention throughout the book. These are also two issues that, in my opinion, haven't yet received the attention they deserve in this debate.

The first issue is the question of whether baptism is the initiatory rite into the church and how that bears on its relationship to church membership. Does baptism have an ecclesial shape? That is, does it sustain any intrinsic theological relationship to the local church? Typically, open membership advocates either assert or assume that baptism possesses no particular relationship to the church. Instead, it is simply a personal matter of obedience to Jesus.[12] On the other hand, closed-membership advocates typically hold that baptism is the initiatory rite into the visible church and that this is a decisive reason unbaptized persons should not be admitted to membership.[13]

However, on both sides this crucial point tends to be more asserted than argued. Therefore, after sketching most of a theology of baptism in chapter 3, in chapters 4 and 5 I will investigate whether Scripture gives baptism an ecclesial shape, that is, whether baptism is intrinsically tied to church membership.[14]

---

[12] So, e.g., John Bunyan, *Differences in Judgment About Water-Baptism, No Bar to Communion*, in *The Miscellaneous Works of John Bunyan*, vol. 4, ed. T. L. Underwood (Oxford: Clarendon Press, 1989), 200–201; John Brown, *The House of God Opened and His Table Free for Baptists and Paedobaptists* (London, 1777; repr., ECCO Books), 2.

[13] A sampling: William Kiffin, *A Sober Discourse of Right to Church Communion* (London, 1681; repr., Paris, AR: Baptist Standard Bearer, 2006), 67; R. B. C. Howell, *The Terms of Communion at the Lord's Table* (Philadelphia: American Baptist Publication Society, 1846; repr., Paris, AR: Baptist Standard Bearer, 2006), 101; John S. Hammett, "Membership, Discipline, and the Nature of the Church," in *Those Who Must Give an Account: A Study of Church Membership and Church Discipline*, ed. John S. Hammett and Benjamin L. Merkle (Nashville: B&H, 2012), 19; Allison, *Sojourners and Strangers*, 349.

[14] When I speak of baptism's "ecclesial shape" throughout the book, I am referring to the fact that the ordinance itself has a churchly and even church-constituting dimension. By saying that baptism has an "ecclesial shape," I mean not merely that it is performed by the church or somehow takes place in the context of the church, though both points are true. Instead, I mean that baptism initiates an individual's relationship of belonging to a

I'll examine the issue from two different angles: first covenant, then kingdom. As will become clear, I think closed-membership baptists have been right to discern an ecclesial shape to baptism. In these chapters, then, I'm simply trying to tend seeds they've planted in order to more thickly describe the ecclesial shape of baptism.[15] This ecclesial shape of baptism is decisive for establishing that baptism is required for church membership.

A second, closely related issue is the theological relationship—or better, interrelationship—between baptism, the Lord's Supper, and church membership. I briefly broached this subject when I asked whether the requirements for the Lord's Supper can legitimately differ from those for church membership. But the question has many more sides. For example, what exactly is church membership? Where do we see it in the Bible? What more does church membership entail that distinguishes it from the two ordinances? Can baptism and the Lord's Supper ever be legitimately separated from church membership? Should a church baptize someone who *isn't* joining that local body? And, theologically speaking, does such a thing as church membership without baptism even exist?

The answers to these questions, and more like them, all depend on a theological account of the relationship between baptism, the Lord's Supper, and church membership. So, after considering baptism and the Lord's Supper in their own light in chapters 3 through 6, in chapter 7 I redescribe church membership in light of the church-forming role of the two ordinances. We'll see that baptism and the Lord's Supper are effective signs of church membership: they create the ecclesial reality to which they point. Baptism binds one to many, and the Lord's Supper makes many one.

---

particular church and enacts a church's affirmation of a believer's profession of faith in Christ. To say that baptism is church-shaped is to say that one cannot rightly understand or practice the ordinance without discerning its relationship to the local church.

[15] See, for instance, Joseph Kinghorn: "If, according to the inspired records, [baptism] was intended to be an open recognition of our faith in Christ, and an ostensible act of subjection to him, in the way which he prescribed; it was like an oath of allegiance on entering the service of our country; or like a matriculation on being admitted a member of a public body; an act which is necessary, because it is legally required" (*Baptism, A Term of Communion* [Norwich, 1816; repr., Paris, AR: Baptist Standard Bearer, 2006], 30–31). See also William Kiffin's citation and discussion of John Owen's assertion that baptism is "the solemn form of our initiation into Covenant with God" (*Sober Discourse*, 14; citing John Owen, *PNEUMATOLOGIA or A Discourse Concerning the Holy Spirit*, in *The Works of John Owen*, ed. William H Goold, vol. 3 [repr., Edinburgh: Banner of Truth Trust, 1965], 72).

So we'll see that not only does baptism have an ecclesial shape, but church membership has a baptismal (and eucharistic) shape. The first leads us to the second; from the ecclesial shape of baptism we discern the baptismal shape of membership. In some ways, then, these two issues are simply two sides of one coin: the relationship between the ordinances and the membership, and even existence, of a local church. I'm going to argue that this relationship has a discernible theological shape, and this shape makes baptism a requirement for church membership.

Rebuilding Foundations

I hope it's even clearer now why I've given a whole book to this subject. For one, simple proof texting won't settle the issue either way. Churches have no explicit biblical command to admit only baptized persons to membership; yet all Christians are commanded to be baptized, and the New Testament Epistles address all church members as having been baptized (e.g., Rom 6:1–4; Gal 3:27). So again, I think the way forward lies through a holistic theological account of the relationship between the ordinances and church membership.

On one hand I think the ecclesial shape of baptism and the baptismal shape of membership have simply been underexamined. We've been conditioned not to look for it, so we don't see it. And there's some truth in the common charge that baptists have said far more about what baptism isn't than what it actually is. But on the other hand I think our cultural lenses predispose us against discerning the links between the ordinances and the church that stare up at us from the pages of Scripture. If we think of the whole Christian life in individual terms, we'll think of the ordinances in individual terms. We'll see baptism as an intensely individual profession of faith and the Lord's Supper as a personal, almost private devotional experience of the cross. What we won't see is how these ordinances knit us to the church and knit the church together. From one angle, then, this book is an attempt to rebuild ecclesiological foundations that the acid rain of individualism has burned away.[16]

---

[16] One could also say that at present there's a dearth of institutional thinking, which weakens our ability to think well about the institutional dimensions of the church. For brief reflections on this dearth, see Hugh Heclo, "Thinking Institutionally," in *The Oxford Handbook of Political Institutions*, ed. R. A. W. Rhodes, Sarah A. Binder, and Bert A. Rockman (New York: Oxford University Press, 2008), 740–41.

Because I'm trying to rebuild foundations, the argument will take a little while to unfold. Chapters 3–8 proceed in a primarily constructive rather than polemical mode. I put all the pieces of my case on the table before defending the case and then cross-examining the opposition. So I ask for patience from readers who object to the position I'm arguing. I devote a whole chapter to answering objections but only after I've built the framework in which my answers will make sense. Because of this predominantly constructive approach, readers who aren't persuaded by aspects of my case—or even its central claim—should still profit from the biblical and theological exposition that forms the heart of the book. While my main goal is to establish that baptism is required for membership, the theological picture I paint also points in many other practical directions. I hope even readers who disagree with the final destination will be greatly enriched by the journey.

What's Ahead?

I've just introduced the big picture of the book, but I want to close the chapter with a more detailed road map, including a preview of my main arguments. In the next chapter we'll clear some ground for our ecclesiological building project by considering why open membership just feels right to this generation of evangelicals. To put it more technically, I'll question several plausibility structures for open membership.[17] In chapter 3 I'll sketch a concise theology of baptism, unpacking the rite's theological significance minus its ecclesial shape. We'll see that baptism is where faith goes public, which lays the foundation for a cohesive theology of baptism, the Lord's Supper, and church membership.

In chapter 4 we take our first look at the ecclesial shape of baptism and discover that it is the initiating oath-sign of the new covenant. God means for his new covenant people to be visible, and one enters that people through baptism. This means that when churches ask, "Who is a member of the new covenant?" in order to extend membership to them, a necessary part of the answer is asking, "Who has sworn the covenant oath?"—that is, "Who has been baptized?"

In chapter 5 we take a second, complementary look at the ecclesial shape of baptism, this time through the lens of the kingdom. When Jesus inaugurated his kingdom on earth, he gave the church the "keys of the kingdom": the

---

[17] The term *plausibility structure* is from Peter L. Berger, *The Sacred Canopy: Elements of a Sociological Theory of Religion* (New York: Doubleday, 1967).

authority to speak for heaven on earth, to representatively declare who belongs to him (Matt 16:18–19; 18:18). And the initial and initiating means by which the church does this is baptism. Baptism, then, is both the passport of the kingdom and a kingdom citizen's swearing-in ceremony. It's how a church publicly identifies someone as a Christian and unites that person to itself. Therefore, it's essential to—and normally *confers*—church membership.

In chapter 6 we consider the ecclesial shape of the Lord's Supper. We'll see that while baptism binds one to many, the Lord's Supper binds many into one (1 Cor 10:17). While baptism is the initiating oath-sign of the new covenant, the Lord's Supper is the renewing oath-sign of the new covenant. Which means the former must come before the latter.

As I mentioned above, one way to sum up the ecclesial shape of both baptism and the Lord's Supper is to say that they are effective signs of church membership: they create the reality to which they point. So chapter 7 theologically redescribes church membership in light of its two effective signs. One takeaway, drastic as it may sound, is that speaking of church membership without baptism is like speaking of marriage without vows: such a thing does not actually exist.

In chapter 8 I summarize the whole argument and draw out a few points we see most clearly when all the pieces of the puzzle are put together. In chapter 9 I respond to the seven strongest objections I've encountered to requiring baptism for membership. Then in chapter 10 I mount seven objections of my own to the open-membership position. Finally, in chapter 11 I provide a few practical sketches of how this theology of baptism, the Lord's Supper, and church membership should play out in the life of the church.

| Chapter 2 |

Clearing Ground

For many Christians today the stance that no genuine Christian should be excluded from church membership because they were "baptized" as an infant rather than as a believer seems almost self-evidently right. To argue against it seems narrow and judgmental. But why? That's our subject for this chapter.

In what follows I'm going to outline six reasons open membership can seem intuitively right and closed membership intuitively wrong. And I'm going to try to show why those factors shouldn't decide the question in advance. Before we make a biblical and theological case for why baptism is required for membership, this chapter clears the ground to make sure we build on a smooth, level plane.

Six Reasons Open Membership Just Feels Right

First, let me underscore that I'm not saying any of these six factors explains why a particular open membership advocate holds the position he does. Nor am I accusing anyone of letting emotion or instinct drive his theology, though I think that's a danger we all need to guard against in this debate. Instead, I'm simply offering a few reasons this position is so plausible today and registering a few critiques of these plausibility structures.

This chapter, then, is an exercise in critically analyzing aspects of the prevailing evangelical worldview, the broader culture which informs it, and the

21

unique pressures baptists feel because of both. It's an attempt to help the fish notice the temperature and currents of the water he lives in and therefore takes for granted.

The six plausibility structures for open membership I'd like to shake up are: (1) today's culture of tolerance; (2) a pendulum swing on church discipline and denominational divisions; (3) evangelicals' cooperative DNA; (4) evangelical essentialism; (5) advancing secularism and the need to stick together; and (6) no one likes being the odd man out. These six plausibility structures interlock in many ways, some of which I'll tease out as we go.

1. The Culture of Tolerance

It's no great revelation to say that our culture prizes tolerance—or perhaps I should say "tolerance." On the one hand, in America and the West today there is widespread concern for the rights of individuals, freedom from oppression, and equal treatment under the law. All of this is a blessing, a gift of God's common grace. On the other hand, tolerance itself has ironically become an intolerant, oppressive regime. As D. A. Carson has put it:

> Although a few things can be said in favor of the newer definition, the sad reality is that this new, contemporary tolerance is intrinsically intolerant. It is blind to its own shortcomings because it erroneously thinks it holds the moral high ground; it cannot be questioned because it has become part of the West's plausibility structure. Worse, this new tolerance is socially dangerous and is certainly intellectually debilitating.[1]

When tolerance becomes an absolute, it becomes a sin to exclude anyone from anything for any reason. Of course, Christians stand against this totalitarian tolerance in myriad ways, since we serve a God who both judges and saves and indeed saves through judgment. Yet it would be foolish to assume that the broader culture of tolerance hasn't tweaked our moral compass.[2]

---

[1] D. A. Carson, *The Intolerance of Tolerance* (Grand Rapids: Eerdmans, 2012), 2.

[2] For a penetrating account of how contemporary culture has distorted Christians' concepts of love—a complementary angle on what I'm describing here—see chap. 1 of Jonathan Leeman, *The Church and the Surprising Offense of God's Love: Reintroducing the Doctrines of Church Membership and Discipline* (Wheaton, IL: Crossway, 2010). For instance: "The one boundary most people agree upon these days is the boundary keeping boundary makers out!" (41).

What does this have to do with requiring baptism for membership? Our culture regards virtually any act of exclusion as unjust. Therefore, unless we deliberately exercise the moral muscles our culture inclines us to neglect, excluding someone from a church over something as seemingly trivial as baptism will appear not only intolerant but petty.

Further, the regime of tolerance has weakened the concept of tolerance itself to the point where tolerance cannot coexist with any degree of disapproval.[3] For instance, if you disapprove of homosexuality on moral grounds, you are intolerant—full stop. Transplanted into our ecclesiological debate, this gutted tolerance would cast closed membership as oppression rather than as a fair consequence of principled disagreement. Previous generations of Christians could tolerate one another's views by, as was commonly said, shaking hands often over low fences. But modern tolerance won't let up until the fences come down. Nothing less than full acceptance and approval will do.

So one reason requiring baptism for membership seems intuitively intolerant is that many of us have imbibed a redefined notion of tolerance. Just as we can't allow our culture's charge of intolerance to determine our sexual ethic, so we should not allow a similar judgment to prejudice us against requiring baptism for membership. If you want to argue on biblical grounds that requiring baptism for membership is divisive, so be it. I'll address those arguments in due time. For now it's enough to note that culturally inherited concepts of tolerance shouldn't preempt a biblical discussion of the qualifications for local church membership. If something smells intolerant, it's possible that says more about our sense of tolerance than about the thing itself.

2. A Pendulum Swing on Discipline and Denominational Divisions

A second factor contributing to open membership's intuitive appeal is a historic pendulum swing among Southern Baptists and other evangelicals regarding church discipline and the related issue of denominational divisions. As Gregory Wills ably chronicles in his book *Democratic Religion*, church discipline was a defining feature of Southern Baptist churches throughout most of the nineteenth century. Departures from truth and holiness required correction, sometimes public correction. And unrepentant or scandalous sin resulted

---

[3] For an illuminating discussion of the recent transformation of "tolerance" into something unlike its former self, see Carson, *The Intolerance of Tolerance*, chaps. 2–3.

in excommunication—exclusion from the church. As Wills documents, Baptist churches in pre-Civil War Georgia excommunicated nearly 2 percent of their membership every year, yet they grew at over twice the rate of the population. However, after the Civil War, church discipline declined until it virtually disappeared from Southern Baptist life in the late-nineteenth century.[4]

In what sense is this decline a pendulum swing? I would submit that over the course of the period Wills chronicles, Baptists morphed from too strict to too lax, too exclusive to too inclusive. This is discernible on two related fronts, the first of which is moral. Early Southern Baptists, along with Presbyterians and Methodists, characteristically excommunicated members for dancing, which was viewed as a "vain amusement." Yet as dancing grew increasingly popular, especially among young people, churches grew ever more hesitant to excommunicate over it. Add to the mix a growing preoccupation with efficiency and progress, and the messy, exclusive practice of church discipline was quietly discarded.[5] And over the past hundred years church discipline continued to vanish to the point where, until recently, finding a church that practiced it was like stepping into Jurassic Park. If disciplining for dancing may well have been too strict, ditching discipline altogether is the definition of too lax.

This laxity in church discipline, which characterizes not just Southern Baptists but a majority of evangelical churches today, is an important factor in why open membership just feels right. If we're not in the habit of excluding anyone from the church, why would we exclude someone over baptism? If an adulterer can stay in, why would we keep a paedobaptist out?

The other front on which Southern Baptists have perhaps swung from too exclusive to too inclusive is the question of denominational divisions. Earlier Southern Baptists consistently excommunicated members who sought to join Presbyterian or Methodist churches, since "to leave a Baptist church was to leave the faith." These Baptists considered that to allow a member to join one of these bodies was to "endorse the errors of other denominations."[6] Yet by the 1920s, following the earlier example of their Northern counterparts, most Southern Baptists simply dropped someone from the membership rolls when they joined another denomination, rather than excommunicating them.[7]

---

[4] Gregory A. Wills, *Democratic Religion: Freedom, Authority and Church Discipline in the Baptist South 1785–1900* (New York: Oxford University Press, 1997), 9, 22.

[5] Ibid., 119–38.

[6] Ibid., 95.

[7] Ibid., 95–96.

Today it's easier to die than to get your name taken off a Southern Baptist church's membership roll. Among other things this means today's Southern Baptist churches do not characteristically take a great interest in what type of church, if any, a member joins if he or she moves away.

While the relation may be a distant one for some, contemporary American credobaptists are all in some sense descendants of earlier baptists, whether Northern or Southern.[8] With that in mind, I'd suggest that current attitudes about church unity and fellowship pick up this same trajectory and take it further. Where earlier baptists viewed ecclesiastical distinctives as worth excommunicating over, contemporary credobaptists are reluctant to make them a term of membership in the first place. After generations of interdenominational warfare, contemporary credobaptists are wary of erecting any boundaries between churches. In short, a similar transition has taken place with denominational divides and discipline. That these two issues have swung in the same direction over roughly the same time should at least make us stop and think.

Both the old exclusivity and the new inclusivity have their problems. The earlier Baptist stance falters in that it has no category for a genuine though erring brother. To excommunicate someone over issues of baptism and polity is to imply that Presbyterian or Methodist views on these subjects are equivalent to heresy—that they're incompatible with a Christian profession.[9] And nineteenth-century baptists characteristically claimed that, because of their faulty doctrine of baptism, Presbyterian and Methodist "churches" were not true churches.[10] Contemporary baptists are right to reject reasoning that implies Presbyterians aren't Christians and their congregations aren't churches.

However, I would also suggest that the pendulum has swung too far. If previous baptists refused to recognize a Presbyterian body as a true church, some contemporary baptists seem to feel that it's wrong for us to have separate churches at all. If older baptists were too quick to anathematize Presbyterians, some baptists today are too quick to throw our own distinctives overboard.

---

[8] For a detailed discussion of British Baptists' relations to other denominations throughout the twentieth century, see Anthony R. Cross, *Baptism and the Baptists: Theology and Practice in Twentieth-Century Britain*, Studies in Baptist History and Thought 3 (Milton Keynes: Paternoster, 2000), chaps. 3–8.

[9] How this differs from refusing membership to unbaptized persons in the first place will be treated later in the book, particularly chap. 9.

[10] Witness the common older practice of referring to Presbyterian and Methodist congregations as "ecclesiastical societies" or some other circumlocution to avoid calling them "churches."

Consider a common response to the biannual Together for the Gospel conference, whose leaders include Baptist, Presbyterian, and nondenominational ministers. One of the goals of the conference is to showcase the unity such brothers can enjoy in the gospel. Yet many have argued that such unity remains a sham as long as those men cannot sit together at the Lord's Table. In other words, partial unity is no unity at all. Yet Ligon Duncan, the Presbyterian of the bunch, is happy to have fellowship with baptists who would not admit him to the Lord's Supper:

> I appreciate the conviction of a Baptist who . . . would argue strenuously that people who have not been baptized as believing adults are not baptized and therefore shouldn't be welcomed into church membership and communion because, in our day-and-age, that sounds mean to a lot of people. We're about inclusion. It's the Baptist who won't let me join his church who is the Baptist with whom I want to fellowship.[11]

In response to this specific example, as well as to the broader trajectory, I'd simply suggest that unity must be grounded in truth. Unity among Christians is a good and a duty, but that duty comes with conditions. We're not to unite with false brothers (1 Cor 5:11). We're to have nothing to do with those who preach a different gospel (Rom 16:17; 2 John 10–11). So unity is not a blanket command, a categorical imperative. Instead, a necessary condition for it is truth.

Those who say Together for the Gospel-type unity is a sham are simply begging the question. Instead, we first need to ask: given convictional disagreement about issues that bear on the constitution of a church, how much unity is possible? If unity isn't grounded in truth, it comes at the expense of truth. And a unity that sacrifices truth is no Christian unity.

Southern Baptists aren't the only ones who have swung from too strict to too lax, too exclusive to arguably too inclusive. If we've lost the habit of excluding unrepentant sinners from membership, making baptism a term of membership will seem triply odd. And if our Baptist forebears perhaps built the denominational walls too high, we're reluctant to build them at all, even when the building blocks are biblical convictions about matters of inescapable importance to local churches.

---

[11] "The Priority of Distinctives, the Primacy of the Gospel," *Towers: A News Service of the Southern Baptist Theological Seminary* (April 2012), 15, available at http://issuu.com /sbts/docs/towers_2012_april/15.

For many a certain practical stance on church unity is simply taken as a given, in need of no justification. Yet just as many churches are coming to rightly recover the practice of church discipline, so we should also give fresh attention to church distinctives we may have too quickly tossed overboard.

3. Evangelicals' Cooperative DNA

A third reason open membership seems intuitively right is that interdenominational cooperation is wired into evangelicals' DNA. Insofar as one can speak of evangelicalism as a movement, that movement's most recent expression has been decisively shaped by the post-World War II emergence of what was then called the "new evangelicalism."[12] These "new evangelicals" built a cooperative ethos into the ground floor of their movement in reaction to the perceived hyper-separatism of the fundamentalism from which they emerged. As such, they emphasized the evangelical essentials they held in common rather than the ecclesiastical distinctives which divided them. This was given concrete shape in the raft of parachurch institutions that sprang into being after the war and defined the landscape of evangelicalism for decades: Fuller Seminary, the NAE, Youth for Christ, Campus Crusade for Christ (now Cru), InterVarsity Christian Fellowship, and so on.[13] And although plenty has changed in seventy years of evangelical history, the basic trajectory of cooperation, common ground, and parachurch activism still holds.

An evangelicalism that majors on "core doctrines" and operates extensively through parachurch organizations has little patience for church distinctives that

---

[12] If the last point was focused on Southern Baptists with secondary reference to broader evangelicalism, this point reverses the order. To glance at just one non-American context, the way these issues have developed in the UK is, of course, rather different. But as an amateur observer, it seems to me a somewhat similar ethos has developed, though for different reasons. This is confirmed by Stanley Fowler, who writes that British Baptists' increasing practice of open membership throughout the twentieth century "seems to have stronger roots in the sociology of British ecclesiastical life than in the theology of Baptist sacramentalism." For support, Fowler points to British Baptists' historically close ties to (paedobaptist) nonconformists, their minority status over against the established church, and the ecumenical commitments of key leaders in the Baptist Union of Great Britain. See Stanley K. Fowler, *More than a Symbol: The British Baptist Recovery of Baptismal Sacramentalism*, Studies in Baptist History and Thought 2 (Carlisle: Paternoster, 2002), 105.

[13] For an engaging history of the emergence of the "new evangelicalism" with a focus on its flagship school, see George M. Marsden, *Reforming Fundamentalism: Fuller Seminary and the New Evangelicalism* (paperback ed.; Grand Rapids: Eerdmans, 1995).

divide. However unintentionally, Christians reared in this context can come to view any sources of division as counterproductive distractions from the real mission. As such, open membership fits right into the contemporary evangelical ethos. To put it negatively, dividing over "nonessentials" has become a cardinal sin of evangelicalism. Shutting the door of the church in the face of paedobaptists who agree with us about virtually every other doctrine? Isn't that the kind of divisiveness we moved out of our fundamentalist parents' house to escape?

One pitfall of this type of thinking is that it defines Christian identity in terms of some nebulous "movement" rather than in terms of the local church. And there's no chapter and verse for "evangelicalism," but there are plenty for the local church. The local church is where we fulfill the biblical "one another." It's the primary place where we prove our love to Christ by loving his people (1 John 4:19–21). It's where we submit to and imitate godly elders (1 Thess 5:12; Heb 13:7, 17). It's the body—I'd argue the *only* body—that has the authority to declare to the world who does and does not belong to the kingdom of Christ (Matt 16:18–19; 18:17–20).[14] It's where we celebrate the ordinances of baptism and the Lord's Supper. The local church is ground zero for Christian discipleship and the Great Commission. If biblical priorities for local churches conflict with what will advance a "movement," churches should adjust the movement rather than vice versa.

Of course, this ties in with our previous discussion of a pendulum swing on the issue of denominational divisions. The shift from fundamentalist separation to evangelical cooperation is itself a pendulum swing that mirrors the Southern Baptist trajectory on denominational divides. And too few evangelicals have given serious thought to whether this pendulum swing may in fact be an overcorrection.[15]

4. Evangelical Essentialism

A fourth plausibility structure of open membership is the evangelical essentialism our cooperative DNA naturally nurtures. By evangelical essentialism I

---

[14] For more on this, see chap. 5.

[15] Two provocative works which do just this, from somewhat different vantage points, are Iain H. Murray, *Evangelicalism Divided: A Record of Crucial Change in the Years 1950 to 2000* (Edinburgh: Banner of Truth, 2000); and Roland McCune, *Promise Unfulfilled: The Failed Strategy of Modern Evangelicalism* (Greenville, SC: Ambassador International, 2004). Regarding the latter, I'm more sympathetic to the diagnosis than the prescription.

mean the impulse to boil our doctrinal commitments down to a bare minimum that is "essential to salvation" and pay little attention to—much less maintain divisions over—anything else. Sometimes the category "essential doctrines" covers a slightly broader range of beliefs seen as necessary to preserve the gospel itself. All told, the inspiration and inerrancy of Scripture, the deity of Christ, the Trinity, substitutionary atonement, justification by faith alone, and the exclusivity and second coming of Christ tend to make the cut. But many of us consign everything else to a dusty old attic shelf marked "nonessential."

Why are we essentialists? First, because cooperation tends to exert pressure to downplay differences. It takes rare humility and grace to partner closely yet differ strongly. One crucial test of a partnership is how you handle differences, and papering over them is no mark of a thriving relationship. In any case, our cooperative instinct as evangelicals can lead us to think, "If good men disagree about a doctrine, how important could it be? Certainly not important enough to divide over." Yet if disagreement among professed evangelicals rules out putting a doctrine to any practical use, we'll soon be left with no doctrines we can actually use.

Another reason we're essentialists is that to one degree or another, all of us have imbibed from our culture a deeply pragmatic mind-set. Modern Americans, and many of our neighbors throughout the postindustrial West, prize efficiency. We're all about doing what works. If a doctrinal commitment doesn't seem to have an immediate practical payoff, we discard it, like we simply delete an e-mail containing no apparent "action item."

A final reason we're essentialists is that we overreact to those who endlessly obsess over issues that matter little. We see a guy with eight feet of eschatology charts on his office wall and say, "No thanks. I'm all about the gospel." Of course, balance is important. If you get the flu, don't act like you're having a heart attack. Yet if you went to your doctor with flu symptoms, what you wouldn't want to hear is, "I don't get bogged down in secondary issues. I've decided to only treat heart attacks." Balance means putting secondary doctrines in their proper place, not giving them no place at all.

Evangelical essentialism views open membership as a given since it sees baptism as one among a laundry list of "nonessential" doctrines it would be wrong to divide over. To an essentialist, requiring baptism for membership in a church is nothing less than elevating baptism above the gospel. If you agree about the gospel but let baptism get in the way of church fellowship, then by default you've got your priorities out of whack.

The basic problem with this kind of essentialism is that the gospel isn't the only thing God tells us in his Word. The gospel is Scripture's center, goal, heartbeat, and more. Yet the gospel is not all that God has to say. So-called "secondary issues" matter in their own right because they matter to God. Therefore, seeking to faithfully obey God's commands about secondary issues poses no inherent threat to primary issues. It's no threat to your health that you not only eat right and exercise but also floss before bed.

Further, baptism is not unrelated to the gospel. Instead, as we'll see, baptism is a picture of the gospel, and baptism plays a role in confirming the gospel to the Christian, the church, and the world. To say we need to sacrifice baptism for the sake of the gospel is like saying I need to neglect my children in order to love my wife. So-called secondary issues are often important not just in their own right but also in the supporting role they play in preserving and propagating the gospel itself.

5. Advancing Secularism and the Need to Stick Together

Another reason open membership is particularly appealing today is that secularism continues its militant advance, pushing evangelical Christians farther into the margins of society. In a culture where Christians are increasingly viewed as enemies of the common good, baptism seems like an awfully small fish to be frying. Shouldn't we be looking for any possible way to maintain a unified front? Shouldn't we value working together more than squabbling over who's right on baptism?

For some churches this issue can touch on their survival. In the UK paedobaptist and Baptist congregations in the same town have occasionally merged because on their own neither of them could afford to pay a pastor. Similarly, if a Baptist church could only support a full-time gospel ministry by accepting paedobaptist members, wouldn't it serve the gospel to simply flex on baptism? Isn't that a lesser evil than allowing a church to fail because of stubborn insistence on principle?

Of course, this simply begs the question. Baptism either is or is not required for church membership. If it isn't, we shouldn't require it for membership whether we're beleaguered by secularism or nestled in what remains of the Bible belt. And if it is, then we should trust that God is able to build a church according to the blueprint he himself has written. "Flexing" a principle for the sake of results assumes it's finally within our power to grow a church. Yet if you can simply flip a switch that results in church growth, that "growth" is never the kind that matters. Instead, the growth and strength of a church depend on God's sovereign blessing from first to last. We shouldn't be afraid to obey a biblical principle that seems to limit our churches' size. And we shouldn't think that discarding a biblical principle will result in the kind of growth God is looking for.

Certainly we should strive for a common front as secularism closes in around us. Yet we shouldn't idolize unity. If unity demands we sacrifice a biblical conviction, it's our concept of unity that needs paring down, not our convictions.

6. No One Likes Being the Odd Man Out

The final plausibility structure for open membership I want to shake up is that no one likes being the odd man out. What I mean is, this issue puts baptists in a unique and rather unenviable position. To many of our paedobaptist brothers, our traditional stance on this issue seems unaccountably exclusive. Within the mainstream Protestant tradition, we're the only ones with the gall to go around excluding everyone else from our churches just because we think they're unbaptized. Baptists draw a tighter line around church fellowship than anyone else. And what gives us the right to do that? So the story goes.

So we baptists are the odd man out, and no one likes to be that guy. It's one thing to be called intolerant for being a Christian; that's a burden we can all bear together. But to be called intolerant over baptism begins to make open membership look pretty appealing.

I'll deal with this issue more fully in chapter 9 when I answer arguments against requiring baptism for membership. For now I'll simply make two observations. The first is that if credobaptism is true, then those "baptized" as infants haven't been baptized. Infant baptism, therefore, is not a somewhat defective version of baptism, like a broken arm is still an arm. Instead, infant baptism is simply not baptism. Again, this means we baptists think a large portion of the Christian world is unbaptized, whereas no one disputes that we're baptized. The asymmetry here is simply a necessary consequence of our differing views on baptism. To put it bluntly, this shouldn't surprise us.

Second, paedobaptists who level this charge are guilty of precisely the same exclusivism they decry. Virtually all paedobaptist churches require baptism before membership; they simply understand infant "baptism" to be legitimate baptism. So we could turn the tables. Paedobaptist readers, assuming you've

gamely stuck around after I showed you the door, consider the plight of the
evangelical Quaker or member of the Salvation Army who wants to join your
church. He believes the same gospel you do. He lives a godly life. You're convinced he's a genuine believer. He understands himself to have been baptized,
by the Spirit, upon conversion, rendering an act of water baptism unneces-
sary. What could possibly justify excluding him from your church? Why on
earth would you slam the door in his face over a second-order disagreement?
He is not willfully disregarding the Lord's command—far from it. Based on
his interpretation of Scripture, he is absolutely convinced he has been faithful
to Jesus' teaching. So why do you insist on making baptism a term of church
membership when it is clearly not essential to salvation?[16]

I would argue that we closed-membership baptists are doing nothing different from what virtually every paedobaptist communion does with someone
who believes themselves baptized but whom the church is convinced actually
isn't. The results look different, but the principle is the same. So the charge of
divisiveness may sting, but it doesn't stick.

Time to Start Building

I've spent so much time clearing ground because this debate tends to generate more than its share of emotional heat. Tempers don't usually flare over,
say, the authorship of Hebrews, but they frequently do over whether baptism
should be required for church membership. So in this chapter I've attempted
to unplug some of the sources of that heat, as well as clear the way for my arguments to follow, by calling open membership's instinctive appeal into question.

This chapter does not substitute for engaging open membership arguments; all of chapter 9 is devoted to that task. Instead, I've sought to address
intuitive reflexes more than reasoned arguments. If a position just feels wrong,
it's easy to tune out arguments in its favor. So, before setting out what I think
are compelling arguments in favor of requiring baptism for membership,
I've tried to make sure we don't reject it for the wrong reasons. Now that the
ground is clear, it's time to start building. First, we pour the foundation (most
of) a theology of baptism.

---

[16] Countless Baptists have made this argument. For a well-spoken representative, see
Abraham Booth, *An Apology for the Baptists* (London, 1778), in *A Defense of the Baptists*
(Paris, AR: The Baptist Standard Bearer, 2006), 10–11, 15.

PART 2

Building a Case

Chapter 3

Where Faith Goes Public: (Most of) a Theology of Baptism

Becoming a Christian is not a private act. Personal, yes, but never private.

Of course, some of our most cherished evangelistic methods argue otherwise. "Just bow your head," the preacher says. "Close your eyes. Tune out everything and everyone around you. This moment is between you and God alone. If you're ready to accept Jesus as your Savior, then in the quiet of your own heart, pray these words after me." So you do. "If you just prayed to accept Jesus as your Savior, you're a Christian now. You will spend eternity with Jesus in heaven." What then? Maybe you're encouraged to speak with someone up front after the meeting. Maybe you're invited to church on Sunday. Maybe you just disappear.

If this is ringing a bell, you could be excused for thinking that becoming a Christian is merely an invisible transaction between your invisible soul and an invisible God. But what does Jesus say? "So everyone who acknowledges me before men, I also will acknowledge before my Father who is in heaven, but whoever denies me before men, I also will deny before my Father who is in heaven" (Matt 10:32–33). That doesn't sound very private.

Jesus is saying there are no secret Christians. To be a Christian is to be a public witness to Christ. Of course, our witness to Christ is ultimately a matter of lifelong faithfulness to his word: "If we endure, we will also reign with him; if we deny him, he also will deny us" (2 Tim 2:12). And some Christians will bear witness in higher-stakes settings: "And you will be dragged before governors and kings for my sake, to bear witness before them and the Gentiles" (Matt 10:18). But if all Christians are public witnesses to Christ, how does that life of witness begin? Is it when we start evangelizing our friends and family? When we walk an aisle to the front of the church? Not according to the New Testament. In the New Testament, baptism is where faith goes public.

Baptism: Where Faith Goes Public

As a foundation on which to establish baptism's relationship to church membership, this chapter is going to sketch most of a theology of baptism, leaving baptism's ecclesial shape for the next two chapters. We can't discern whether baptism is required for church membership until we know what baptism is.

First, we're going to see that according to the New Testament, baptism is where faith goes public. Second, we'll consider what this means for how we speak about baptism and becoming a Christian. Third, we'll see how baptism stands for the whole conversion process in a number of key New Testament passages since it's where faith becomes visible. Fourth, we'll briefly examine several of the most prominent facets of baptism's theological significance. Fifth and finally, we'll look at two practical implications of this theological sketch: the obligation of baptism, and the theological status of infant baptism.

Faith Going Public at Pentecost

What if instead of hearing the gospel at a modern evangelistic rally, you heard it from the apostle Peter at Pentecost?

Just a few weeks prior, the bold, enigmatic prophet Jesus was executed by the Roman government. Seems like he picked the wrong time of year to provoke the Jewish leaders, who ran to the Romans to do their dirty work. But three days later this Jesus rose from the grave and appeared to his followers—so they say. Now, just a few weeks later, his followers are together at the feast of Pentecost, and the strangest thing happens: fire from the sky comes down onto each of them, and they start preaching about Jesus in languages they can't possibly have learned the old-fashioned way.

"Sounds like they've been cracking open the old wineskins a little earlier than normal," your friend James murmurs. Then Peter, their leader, stands up and starts shouting out over everyone. He says these people aren't drunk but are filled with the Holy Spirit, just like the prophet Joel said would happen (Acts 2:14–21). Peter says this all has to do with Jesus: "This Jesus, delivered up according to the definite plan and foreknowledge of God, you crucified and killed by the hands of lawless men. God raised him up, loosing the pangs of death, because it was impossible for him to be held by it" (vv. 23–24). Peter explains that King David himself foresaw that Jesus would be raised from the dead (vv. 25–31). And he claims this prophecy and the spectacle of fire and languages are proof that Jesus is the long-awaited Messiah (vv. 32–35), driving the point home: "Let all the house of Israel therefore know for certain that God has made him both Lord and Christ, this Jesus whom you crucified" (v. 36).

At first you're feeling about as skeptical as your friend James. But as Peter explains the Scriptures, the words start to stick. You think back to when Jesus was on trial, and you shouted out for him to be crucified like everybody else did, just to end the trouble. Conviction of your sin starts as a trickle and grows to a flood. By the time Peter finishes his impromptu sermon, you call out to him and his friends, "Brothers, what shall I do?"

Peter responds, "Repent and be baptized every one of you in the name of Jesus Christ for the forgiveness of your sins, and you will receive the gift of the Holy Spirit. For the promise is for you and for your children and for all who are far off, everyone whom the Lord our God calls to himself" (vv. 38–39). Peter is urging you to believe in Jesus and get baptized *now*. He's urging you to step out of the crowd, leave your friend James behind, and publicly align yourself with Jesus and his followers. Peter continues, exhorting the crowd, "Save yourselves from this crooked generation" (v. 40). Even as he does, you believe what he's saying, turn your back on your former life, and get baptized by one of the disciples, along with 3,000 other people (v. 41).

Think about what baptism means in this setting. You're in a crowd of Jewish people, some of whom called for Jesus' execution just a few weeks ago. Jesus' disciples are causing a public spectacle. And they're calling others to join them by believing in Jesus and getting dunked in water right in front of everyone. To turn to Jesus in faith and baptism is to identify yourself with him and his followers and to distance yourself from those who reject him.[1] You're being

---

[1] G. R. Beasley-Murray, *Baptism in the New Testament* (repr., Grand Rapids: Eerdmans, 1973), 98.

called to a public decision to follow Christ, and that decision is sealed publicly in baptism. Baptism is how you go public with your newfound faith in Christ.[2]

Baptism and Becoming a Christian

This pattern set by Pentecost is confirmed explicitly and implicitly throughout the New Testament. Explicitly, in the rest of Acts, we read over and over again of people accepting the gospel and being immediately baptized. As the Ethiopian eunuch put it immediately after hearing the gospel from Philip, "See, here is water! What prevents me from being baptized?" (Acts 8:36; cf. 10:48; 16:15, 33; 19:5). Implicitly, throughout Paul's Epistles, he assumes that all the Christians he writes to have been baptized: "Do you not know that all of us who have been baptized into Christ Jesus were baptized into his death?" (Rom 6:3; cf. 1 Cor 12:12–13; Gal 3:26–27; Col 2:11–12).

In the New Testament all Christians were baptized, and all the evidence we have points to people being baptized as soon as they embraced the gospel. After trusting Christ, baptism is the first thing a believer does. It's how faith shows itself before God, the church, and the world. Baptism is where faith goes public. As Robert Stein argues: "In the New Testament, conversion involves five integrally related components or aspects, all of which took place at the same time, usually on the same day. These five components are repentance, faith, and confession by the individual, regeneration, or the giving of the Holy Spirit by God, and baptism by representatives of the Christian community."[3]

Given how these components of conversion were invariably linked, Stein suggests that a first-century Christian could have naturally referred to

---

[2] The context of Acts 2:38ff., the first instance of Christian baptism, seems to imply that public witness is an intrinsic component of baptism. That said, believers in more hostile contexts typically experience this more vividly than we in the more Christianized West. Will Willimon tells the story of a friend who visited Soviet Georgia: "A Georgian Baptist was showing him his church. 'To be a Christian here, to be baptized, is to be motherless,' said the man. 'When one comes up out of the water, one has lost country, parents, all.'" William H. Willimon, *Peculiar Speech: Preaching to the Baptized* (Grand Rapids: Eerdmans, 1992), 114; cited in Anthony R. Cross, *Recovering the Evangelical Sacrament: Baptisma Semper Reformandum* (Eugene, OR: Pickwick, 2013), 39n163.

[3] For a clear, helpful treatment of this idea based on Acts, see Robert H. Stein, "Baptism and Becoming a Christian in the New Testament," in *Southern Baptist Journal of Theology* 2, no. 1 (1998): 6.

their conversion by mentioning any one of them. To mention any is to imply the rest.[4]

Therefore, according to the New Testament, baptism is part of how someone becomes a Christian. We baptists, on the other hand, are used to talking about baptism as something you do *after* you become a Christian. We don't baptize babies; instead, we only baptize people who already profess to believe. There's a sense in which this is right: only those who profess faith in Jesus Christ should be baptized. And, at a more precise theological level, it is surely correct to view regeneration—the act of God the Holy Spirit whereby a sinner is given a new nature and comes to believe in Christ—as taking place at a specific moment in time.[5] Regeneration remains punctiliar however long it took for someone to come to faith and however uncertain they may be about when exactly they first believed.

Further, it is crucial to affirm that in exceptional circumstances a person can come to faith in Christ, not be baptized, and be eternally saved. Consider the thief on the cross, to whom Jesus said, "Truly, I say to you, today you will be with me in Paradise" (Luke 23:39–43).[6] Baptism itself doesn't save anybody, since the thief on the cross went to heaven without it and Simon the magician went to hell with it (cf. Acts 8:14–24).

And yet the apostle Peter can come along and say something most contemporary evangelicals would never dream of saying: "Baptism, which corresponds to this, now saves you, not as a removal of dirt from the body but as an appeal to God for a good conscience, through the resurrection of Jesus Christ" (1 Pet 3:21). To be sure, Peter qualifies the assertion that baptism saves in two crucial ways. One, it's not the external washing but the internal appeal to God which mediates salvation. Two, the power which saves in baptism is the resurrection of Jesus. Yet somehow, consistent with these two qualifications, Peter can still use "baptism" as the subject of the verb "save." The takeaway?

---

[4] Ibid., 12–13.

[5] See John Murray, *Redemption Accomplished and Applied* (Grand Rapids: Eerdmans, 1955), 100–106. Murray writes that regeneration "immediately registers itself in the conscious activity of the person concerned in the exercises of faith and repentance and new obedience" (ibid., 105).

[6] After commenting on the thief on the cross along these lines, Stein helpfully adds, "If the Philippian jailer had died of a heart attack before reaching the waters of baptism on that eventful night, he would have been a second example. If one has faith but no access to baptism, one has Christ! On the other hand, if one has baptism but has no faith, one has nothing (1 Cor. 10:1–5)!" ("Baptism and Becoming a Christian," 14–15).

Whatever else he may be doing, in this passage Peter speaks of baptism as part of becoming a Christian. And he's not the only one who does this. Consider the following passages from Paul:

> Do you not know that all of us who have been baptized into Christ Jesus were baptized into his death? We were buried therefore with him by baptism into death, in order that, just as Christ was raised from the dead by the glory of the Father, we too might walk in newness of life. (Rom 6:3–4)

> But now that faith has come, we are no longer under a guardian, for in Christ Jesus you are all sons of God, through faith. For as many of you as were baptized into Christ have put on Christ. (Gal 3:25–27)

> In him also you were circumcised with a circumcision made without hands, by putting off the body of the flesh, by the circumcision of Christ, having been buried with him in baptism, in which you were also raised with him through faith in the powerful working of God, who raised him from the dead. (Col 2:11–12)

Paul says that we were baptized into Christ's death, buried with him in baptism, we put on Christ in baptism, and we were raised with Christ in baptism. On the face of it, all of these statements about baptism refer not to something that happened *after* we became Christians but speak of precisely what happened to us *when* we became Christians.

As I said, when we seek to give an account of Scripture's teaching as a whole, we certainly need to take account of the exceptional cases in which someone can be saved but never baptized. And, as a matter of systematic-theological description, it is appropriate to identify regeneration as a discrete moment which should precede baptism. When we zoom all the way in like this, we can speak of "becoming a Christian" before being baptized. Yet for all these necessary refinements we need to make sure we can still speak like the Bible speaks. And the New Testament tends to keep the lens pulled back. As a result, it can look at the process of conversion as a unified whole, baptism included.

According to the New Testament, baptism is where faith goes public, which means it's an integral part of becoming a Christian. In order to align our vocabulary with the New Testament, we shouldn't think of becoming a Christian as merely an invisible, private transaction that is attested after the fact by the visible act of baptism. Instead, becoming a Christian in a comprehensive, biblical sense involves the public act of baptism.[7]

Faith, Baptism, and a Fifty-Cent Word

One of the reasons the New Testament authors can speak of baptism as part of how one becomes a Christian is that when they do so, they always assume the presence of faith.[8] If baptism is where faith goes public, then baptism is where you can *see* faith: "Look, that person believes in Jesus; he just nailed his colors to the mast in baptism."

Baptism renders faith visible; it gives the believer, the church, and the world something to look at.[9] When you trust in Christ, you make that decision visible in baptism. This helps explain why the New Testament authors often speak of baptism in ways that could be taken to indicate that the blessings of salvation come through baptism itself. When they wanted to refer to conversion as a unified whole, the New Testament authors often deployed baptism as shorthand for the whole thing. Lars Hartman writes: "We should . . . beware of isolating the different elements of initiation [i.e., conversion] from each other. They form a unity, and baptism is the gathering, visible, effective sign around which the others can be grouped."[10] Baptism is where conversion comes to a head. Baptism is where you can *see* salvation enacted.

Therefore, if you're looking for a visible hook to hang your hat on when you speak about conversion, baptism is the natural choice. And this seems to be exactly what is going on in passages like Romans 6:1–4; Galatians 3:26–27;

---

[7] Reformed theologian Michael Allen writes, "Christian baptism initiates the Christian life in a public sense. . . . In baptism, one is no longer identified with Adam—sin, death, and devil—but with the new Adam and the people of God. . . . Baptism marks that new identity in public" (R. Michael Allen, *Justification and the Gospel: Understanding the Contexts and Controversies* [Grand Rapids: Baker, 2013], 67).

[8] See, for example, Beasley-Murray, who writes, "In the New Testament it is everywhere assumed that faith proceeds to baptism and that baptism is for faith" (*Baptism in the New Testament*, 272).

[9] Michael Green notes the "universal and quite unselfconscious link in the early church between the invisible encounter of man's faith with God's grace, and its outward expression in baptism" (Michael Green, *Evangelism in the Early Church* [repr., London: Highland Books, 1984], 183; cited in Cross, *Recovering the Evangelical Sacrament*, 47).

[10] Lars Hartman, *"Into the Name of the Lord Jesus": Baptism in the Early Church*, Studies of the New Testament and Its World (Edinburgh: T&T Clark, 1997), 145.

Colossians 2:11–12; and 1 Peter 3:21.[11] As Anthony Cross and others have argued, we should understand these passages as examples of synecdoche.[12] Synecdoche is a figure of speech in which a part stands for the whole or vice versa. "All hands on deck!" uses "hands" to stand for the sailors without whose hands the ship might sink. Or if you just bought a car you might say, "Check out my new wheels," without expecting someone to drop down and inspect the tires and rims. So, when New Testament authors speak of baptism as saving us, uniting us to Christ, burying us with Christ, and so on, we should understand these references to baptism as a synecdoche for the whole conversion experience.

Consider again Galatians 3:26–27. In verse 26 Paul tells the Galatians, "You are all sons of God, through faith." The adoption described here is the crowning blessing of our salvation (Gal 4:4–7), and we receive it through faith. Paul's central point in Galatians is that we are saved by faith alone, not by works of the law (Gal 2:15–16; 3:1–14), so this fits his broader argument perfectly. In the next verse Paul writes, "For as many of you as were baptized into Christ have put on Christ" (Gal 3:27). Is Paul saying we're made sons of God through faith but are only united to Christ in baptism? Is he parceling out the components of our salvation and assigning some to faith and some to baptism? Of course not; that would contradict his entire argument. Instead, he's using "baptism" and

---

[11] See, for example, Douglas J. Moo, *The Epistle to the Romans*, New International Commentary on the New Testament (Grand Rapids: Eerdmans, 1996), 366: "In vv. 3–4, then, we can assume that baptism stands for the whole conversion-initiation experience, presupposing faith and the gift of the Spirit." See also Tom Schreiner's comments on Rom 6:1–4 and Col 2:11–12: "Paul refers to baptism in Romans 6 and Colossians 2 because baptism recalls the conversion of the readers from the old life to the new. The grace of God secured their freedom from the power of sin at conversion, and the simplest and easiest way to recall the readers' conversion is to speak of their baptism" (Thomas R. Schreiner, "Baptism in the Epistles," in *Believer's Baptism: Sign of the New Covenant in Christ*, ed. Thomas R. Schreiner and Shawn D. Wright [Nashville: B&H, 2007], 75).

[12] Cross, *Recovering the Evangelical Sacrament*, 72–83. Cross views Matt 28:19; 1 Cor 12:13; Gal 3:27; Eph 4:5; Col 2:12; and 1 Pet 3:21 as examples of synecdoche. See also Robert Stein's explanation that in Luke and Acts, "'repentance' is an example of synecdoche in which 'repentance' refers to 'repentance-faith-baptism.' Similarly, 'faith' refers to 'faith-repentance-baptism' and 'baptism' refers to 'baptism-repentance-faith,' i.e., a baptism preceded by repentance and faith" (Robert H. Stein, "Baptism in Luke-Acts," in Schreiner and Wright, *Believer's Baptism*, 51–52). And Daniel A. Tappeiner's comment about baptism as a "spiritual metonymy" is a slightly looser way of referring to the same phenomenon ("Hermeneutics, the Analogy of Faith and New Testament Sacramental Realism," in *Evangelical Quarterly* 49 [1977]: 50).

"faith" interchangeably, though not as if you could choose to be saved through either faith *or* baptism. The clearest way to understand Paul's interchangeable references to baptism and faith is that baptism is a synecdoche. It stands for the whole event in which a person came to faith and publicly professed faith.[13]

What's the point of throwing a fifty-cent word like synecdoche into the mix? First, understanding the New Testament use of baptism as synecdoche gives us at least a partial answer to the question posed most acutely by 1 Peter 3:21: how can the text say that baptism saves us? If baptism is where faith goes public and is used as shorthand for the whole conversion process, then this tension is substantially resolved.

Second, understanding baptism as synecdoche reinforces just how tightly the New Testament ties baptism to conversion. As I said, this can seem strange to us baptists because our normal speed is to think of baptism as coming after conversion rather than being an aspect of conversion. For a variety of reasons, people sometimes get baptized months or even years after becoming a Christian. But it's important to note that this common experience differs from what we see in the New Testament. When the New Testament talks about baptism, it's talking about conversion.

I should point out that even among baptists who recognize that baptism can be shorthand for conversion in the New Testament, the precise theological and spiritual significance of baptism is disputed. The lines generally fall between those who describe baptism as having some kind of "sacramental" significance and those who see it as purely "symbolic."[14] This is a debate I will not

---

[13] F. F. Bruce identifies Gal 3:26–27 as synecdoche, though without using the term, when he writes, "If it is remembered that repentance and faith, with baptism in water and the reception of the Spirit, followed by first communion, constituted one complex experience of Christian initiation, then what is true of the experience as a whole can in practice be predicated of any element of it" (F. F. Bruce, *The Epistle of Paul to the Galatians: A Commentary on the Greek Text*, New International Greek Testament Commentary [Grand Rapids: Eerdmans, 1982], 186).

[14] For an overview of the history of "sacramental" and "symbolic" baptist understandings of baptism, see Stanley K. Fowler, *More than a Symbol: The British Baptist Recovery of Baptismal Sacramentalism*, Studies in Baptist History and Thought 2 (Carlisle: Paternoster, 2002). Although the debate is often presented as a black-and-white opposition between sacramental and symbolic understandings, there is in fact a spectrum of views. For an assessment of various sacramental proposals, see Brandon C. Jones, *Waters of Promise: Finding Meaning in Believer Baptism* (Eugene, OR: Pickwick, 2012). Further, there is much exegetical common ground between proponents of a sacramental view (such as Beasely-Murray, Cross, and Fowler) and proponents of a symbolic view (such as Stein and

address head-on since I don't think it's decisive for my argument that baptism is required for church membership.[15] Instead, in the following section I will canvass some of the main contours of the meaning of baptism in a way people on either side of that fence can affirm.

Circling the Diamond of Baptism

Our next task is to set the diamond of baptism in the light and circle it in order to glimpse some of its most prominent theological facets. I'm leaving baptism's ecclesial shape to the next two chapters—hence this chapter's subtitle. But this chapter's broad theology of baptism, including the six facets we're about to survey, form the foundation of baptism's ecclesial significance.

Without further ado, we'll consider baptism as (1) a public profession of faith and repentance; and a sign of (2) forgiveness and cleansing; (3) the believer's union with Christ in his death, burial, and resurrection; (4) the believer's new life in Christ; (5) the gift of the Holy Spirit; and (6) the new creation that has dawned in Christ.

1. A Public Profession of Faith and Repentance

We've already established that baptism is where faith goes public, but the point is worth elaborating. As we see at Pentecost, the gospel comes with imperatives to believe and be baptized. In order to respond to the gospel, we are commanded to turn to Jesus both inwardly and outwardly, and the outward declares the inward. As G. R. Beasley-Murray writes, "Baptism is an overt, public act that expresses inward decision and intent; since it is performed in

---

Schreiner), including the crucial issue of synecdoche. This suggests the boundary between the two positions is somewhat more porous than the binary terminology would indicate.

[15] Fowler suggests, "If conversion is consciously completed apart from baptism, and baptism is reduced to sheer obedience and pure symbolism, then the narrow [i.e., closed membership] Baptist practice is indeed mystifying, especially in its close communion form" (*More than a Symbol*, 57). In response, I'd certainly agree that the theological significance of baptism is critical to understanding its relationship to church membership—hence this chapter and the next two. However, I'm not sure the binary lens of sacramental versus symbolic is the most illuminating angle on the question. Further, as I hope to demonstrate in the following chapters, I think the question of baptism's relationship to church membership is better answered by discerning the ecclesial shape of baptism through the lenses of covenant and kingdom.

the open, and not in secret, it becomes by its nature a confession of a faith and allegiance embraced."[16]

Recall Peter's words from Pentecost: "Repent and be baptized every one of you in the name of Jesus Christ for the forgiveness of your sins" (Acts 2:38). Peter tells the crowd to repent—to acknowledge their guilt, turn from their sin, and cast themselves on God's mercy. Repentance propels one to baptism. Therefore, baptism is a public profession of repentance every bit as much as a public profession of faith.

We see from the apostles' preaching throughout the New Testament that faith and repentance are two sides of the same coin: repentance is turning *from* sin, and faith is turning *to* Christ as Lord and Savior.[17] As such, baptism is the visible embodiment of a person's decisive turn from sin to Christ. It is a symbolic way to say before God, the church, and the world, "I renounce my former way of life, repent of my sins, and trust in Christ alone for salvation."[18]

2. A Sign of Forgiveness and Cleansing

Second, baptism is a sign of forgiveness of sin and cleansing from sin. In Acts 22:16 the apostle Paul recounts how Ananias told him, "And now why do you wait? Rise and be baptized and wash away your sins, calling on his name." And, as we've just considered, at Pentecost Peter tells the crowd to be baptized "for the forgiveness of your sins" (Acts 2:38). Baptism is a sign of forgiveness and cleansing.

Since baptism is an immersion in water, the symbolism of cleansing could hardly be plainer.[19] The primary background to this imagery is the Old

---

[16] Beasley-Murray, *Baptism in the New Testament*, 101. As we'll see later, even if baptism is performed in private (as in, e.g., Acts 16:33), this public aspect still holds, since the act is performed by, and therefore in the presence of, another Christian.

[17] See Acts 3:19; 10:43; 13:38; 16:31; 17:30; 19:4; 20:21; cf. 1 Thess 1:9–10.

[18] Certainly not all baptisms are as "public" as those performed at Pentecost. The Philippian jailer was baptized in the middle of the night, and the Ethiopian eunuch was baptized in the middle of the desert! I'll discuss the public aspects of baptism in more detail later. For now I'll simply reiterate that since baptism is performed by someone else—John Smyth's self-baptism notwithstanding—there is always at least *one* witness to the act. And that witness, significantly, is a fellow Christian and a representative of the body of Christ.

[19] For a brief discussion of immersion as the mode of baptism in the New Testament, see Gregg R. Allison, *Sojourners and Strangers: The Doctrine of the Church*, Foundations of Evangelical Theology (Wheaton, IL: Crossway, 2012), 352–53. For a thorough lexical

Testament's water purification rites, which symbolized forgiveness and cleansing from sin as well.[20] Seen in this light, baptism pictures the fulfillment of God's promise to decisively forgive his people's sin and cleanse them from all defilement, a promise fulfilled in the saving, new covenant-inaugurating work of the Lord Jesus Christ (Jer 31:34; Ezek 36:25; Heb 9:13–14; 10:19–22).

3. A Sign of Union with Christ in His Death, Burial, and Resurrection

A third facet of baptism's meaning is really the key to all the others: baptism is a sign of the believer's union with Christ in his death, burial, and resurrection.[21] This theme dominates the three passages from Paul we've already mentioned (Rom 6:1–4; Gal 3:25–27; Col 2:11–12). Consider again some of the key phrases:

- "All of us who have been baptized into Christ Jesus were baptized into his death" (Rom 6:3).
- "We were buried therefore with him by baptism into death" (Rom 6:4).
- "For as many of you as were baptized into Christ have put on Christ" (Gal 3:27).
- "Having been buried with him in baptism, in which you were also raised with him through faith in the powerful working of God" (Col 2:11–12).

---

survey which further supports these conclusions, see Eckhard J. Schnabel, "The Language of Baptism: The Meaning of βαπτίζω in the New Testament," in *Understanding the Times: New Testament Studies in the 21st Century*, ed. Andreas J. Köstenberger and Robert W. Yarbrough (Wheaton, IL: Crossway, 2011), 217–46.

[20] Cf. Exod 30:17–21; Leviticus 15; Num 19:18; Ps 51:7; Isa 1:16; Zech 13:1. Citing these passages and drawing particular attention to Num 19:18, John Fesko concludes, "In other words, ideally, the ritual cleansing of a person was supposed to reflect both his confession and the divine forgiveness of sin." In J. V. Fesko, *Word, Water and Spirit: A Reformed Perspective on Baptism* (Grand Rapids: Reformation Heritage Books, 2010), 202.

[21] As Stephen Wellum writes, "The most fundamental *meaning* of baptism is that it signifies a believer's union with Christ, by grace through faith, and all the benefits that are entailed in that union." In Peter J. Gentry and Stephen J. Wellum, *Kingdom Through Covenant: A Biblical-Theological Understanding of the Covenants* (Wheaton, IL: Crossway, 2012), 697.

Consider also 1 Corinthians 12:13: "For in one Spirit we were all baptized into one body—Jews or Greeks, slaves or free—and all were made to drink of one Spirit."[22]

All of these phrases describe our union with Christ, a union signified by baptism. Constantine Campbell writes that in Paul's theology, union with Christ is "the essential ingredient that binds all other elements together; it is the webbing that connects the ideas of Paul's . . . theological framework. It is for this reason that we can say that every blessing we receive from God is through our union with Christ."[23] Campbell describes our union with Christ in terms of *participation* with Christ in the saving events of the gospel narrative, *identification* with Christ since we are "in" him and subject to his lordship, and *incorporation* into his body, the church.[24] All of these realities are depicted in baptism.

The physical movements of baptism provide a vivid picture of our being joined to Christ's death, burial, and resurrection. We are "buried with Christ" as we are plunged under the water, and our rising from the watery grave images our union with Christ's resurrection.[25] The sign vividly corresponds to the signified.

4. A Sign of New Life in Christ

One aspect of our union with Christ is that we share, here and now, in his resurrection life. To be sure, the end-time bodily resurrection has not yet happened

---

[22] There is much debate about exactly what "baptism" this verse refers to. I think Anthony Cross is on track in identifying Spirit baptism (i.e., conversion) as the primary referent, with a clear secondary reference to water baptism via synecdoche: "It is hardly conceivable that when they first heard Paul's letter read to them the Corinthians would *not* have called to mind their water-baptism with the Spirit-baptism which is the primary referent of 12.13. This point receives support from the way that Spirit- and water-baptism were equated by the early Christian writers before initiation began to be broken up into clearly separate and distinctive rites and theologies" (Anthony R. Cross, "Spirit- and Water-Baptism in 1 Corinthians 12.13," in *Dimensions of Baptism: Biblical and Theological Studies*, ed. Stanley E. Porter and Anthony R. Cross [Edinburgh: T&T Clark, 2003], 142).

[23] Constantine R. Campbell, *Paul and Union with Christ: An Exegetical and Theological Study* (Grand Rapids: Zondervan, 2012), 442.

[24] Ibid., 413.

[25] The symbolism of rising with Christ in baptism seems to be implicit in Rom 6:4 and explicit in Col 2:12. Romans 6:9–10 also unpacks the implicit element of resurrection in the baptismal symbolism of vv. 1–4, as discussed below. On Col 2:12, see Beasley-Murray, *Baptism in the New Testament*, 155–56.

(2 Tim 2:18). Yet there is a real sense in which we have already been raised with Christ (Rom 6:13; Eph 2:5–6). Baptism signifies this: "having been buried with him in baptism, in which you were also raised with him through faith in the powerful working of God" (Col 2:11–12).

At present our union with Jesus' resurrection is manifested in the new life we enjoy by the gift of the Spirit. The Spirit gives us a new nature, a new self. This new self fulfills the prophetic hope that the people of Israel would obtain a circumcised heart, a heart totally devoted to all God's ways (Deut 30:6; cf. Deut 4:4; 10:16; Jer 4:4). Now, in Christ and through the Spirit, God has at last circumcised his people's hearts. This is why Paul says that we were "circumcised with a circumcision made without hands" (Col 2:11) and then explains this by pointing to Christ's death and our union with his death and resurrection in baptism. As we've already seen with cleansing and forgiveness, baptism doesn't signify merely the fact of our union with Christ; it also pictures that union's glorious consequences.

5. A Sign of the Gift of the Holy Spirit

A fifth facet of baptism's meaning is that it is a sign of the gift of the Holy Spirit. When John the Baptist describes Jesus' future ministry of bestowing the Spirit, he describes this as a baptism (Mark 1:8). Certainly this refers to Jesus' gift of the Spirit at Pentecost and subsequent gift of the Spirit to each individual believer. Yet John's choice of metaphor suggests some kind of link, if only a symbolic one, between water baptism and Spirit baptism.

In this light recall 1 Corinthians 12:13: we are "baptized" in the Spirit at conversion. If this passage does indeed have a secondary reference to water baptism,[26] then it's difficult not to see the parallel with Spirit baptism as informing the symbolism of baptism itself. Remember Peter tells the crowd at Pentecost to repent and be baptized with the result that "you will receive the gift of the Holy Spirit" (Acts 2:38). Repentance, baptism, and receiving the Spirit are all components of the same unified conversion event.

Taking all this together, and given what we've already seen about baptism picturing the fulfillment of Old Testament anticipations of inward cleansing

---

[26] As Schreiner rightly insists, "Once again we should not separate Spirit baptism from water baptism as if Paul were attempting to segregate the one from the other" ("Baptism in the Epistles," in Schreiner and Wright, *Believer's Baptism*, 72).

and new life, baptism should also be seen as a sign of the gift of the Holy Spirit. Our immersion in water points to our "immersion" in the Spirit, in whom we now live.

6. A Sign of the Dawning New Creation in Christ

Finally, baptism is a sign of the dawning new creation in Christ. Cleansing from sin, resurrection life, the circumcision of the heart, and the gift of the Holy Spirit are all features of the glorious new creation God promised in the Old Testament and inaugurated through the work of Christ.[27] In baptism we are symbolically plunged into the events which brought God's future kingdom crashing into the present.

Just as baptism looks back to Jesus' death and resurrection, it also looks forward to our own resurrection and the new creation: "For if we have been united with him in a death like his, we shall certainly be united with him in a resurrection like his" (Rom 6:5, cf. 6:8–10).[28] Baptism witnesses that, by being united to Christ, we have already entered the new age. Death and judgment are past. Life is ours: a foretaste now, fullness to come.

Two Takeaways

This chapter has attempted a reasonably thick answer to the question, What is baptism? Baptism is where faith goes public. More specifically, baptism is a public profession of faith and repentance which signifies cleansing, forgiveness, union with Christ, new life in Christ, the gift of the Holy Spirit, and the new creation.

Two points arise from this theological survey of baptism which bear on the book's central thesis. The first is that all who profess faith in Christ are under obligation to be baptized. Except for Quakers and the Salvation Army, no one disputes this; yet it's still worth stating explicitly. Jesus commands his disciples, "Go therefore and make disciples of all nations, baptizing them in the name of the Father and of the Son and of the Holy Spirit, teaching them to observe all that I have commanded you" (Matt 28:19–20). In bringing the gospel to

---

[27] See, e.g., Deut 30:6; Jer 32:37–41; Ezek 36:33–36; 37:11–14; Joel 2:28–32.

[28] For fuller discussion of this theme, see Beasley-Murray, *Baptism in the New Testament*, 290–96.

the nations, the church is commanded to baptize all who respond in faith and repentance. And, as we've seen in Acts 2:38, all those who believe the gospel are commanded to be baptized. Therefore, someone who claims to follow Jesus but hasn't been baptized has not yet obeyed the first item on the list marked "All that I Have Commanded You." I don't think this point alone decides the baptism and membership question, but it's certainly a factor.

Second, the theology of baptism sketched in this chapter determines how we think about infant baptism. I don't mean that this chapter decisively refutes infant baptism, though I'd argue it does create insuperable difficulties for that doctrine.[29] Remember that every New Testament reference to baptism assumes faith. Baptism is where faith goes public, and each facet of baptism's meaning assumes the one being baptized believes in Christ. Take away faith and what's left? Not baptism. If baptism is what this chapter says it is, then infant "baptism" is not baptism.

This might seem an obvious point, but open membership advocates tend to obscure it in at least two ways.[30] First, some argue that membership should be opened to include those "baptized" in infancy, not those who have never been "baptized" at all. Further refining this position, John Piper has argued for opening membership only to those baptized as infants who hold to a Reformed, covenantal rationale for infant baptism.[31] Piper does not argue that, as an across-the-board theological principle, baptism simply is not required for church membership.[32] Instead, Piper implies that a church should allow an

---

[29] For a thorough biblical-theological critique of infant baptism, see Stephen J. Wellum, "Baptism and the Relationship Between the Covenants" in Schreiner and Wright, *Believer's Baptism*. Also useful are Paul K. Jewett, *Infant Baptism and the Covenant of Grace* (Grand Rapids: Eerdmans, 1978); and Fred A. Malone, *The Baptism of Disciples Alone: A Covenantal Argument for Credobaptism Versus Paedobaptism* (Cape Coral, FL: Founders Press, 2003).

[30] I say "at least" because in addition to the issues I discuss below, some open-membership baptists have deliberately moved toward granting infant baptism some kind of theological validity. For instance, a 2005 report accepted by the Baptist Union of Great Britain encouraged congregations to consider whether "they might recognize a place for the baptism of infants within the whole journey that marks the beginning of the Christian life." See discussion in Stephen R. Holmes, *Baptist Theology* (London: T&T Clark, 2012), 93.

[31] In John Piper with Alex Chediak and Tom Steller, "Baptism and Church Membership at Bethlehem Baptist Church: Eight Recommendations for Constitutional Revision," 14, available at http://cdn.desiringgod.org/pdf/baptism_and_membership.pdf.

[32] On the other hand, that's precisely what Bunyan argues in *Differences in Judgment About Water-Baptism, No Bar to Communion*, in *The Miscellaneous Works of John Bunyan*,

individual's conviction of the validity of their infant baptism to take precedence over the church's conviction that believer baptism is the only valid baptism.

Yet to allow paedobaptists to join a church on these terms is to grant infant baptism a status other than "not baptism." This grants infant baptism sufficient theological weight to qualify a person for membership who would not qualify if they had never been "baptized" at all. Thus, in these circumstances, infant baptism is allowed to stand in for a valid baptism. The church counts a person as baptized on the basis that the person considers him- or herself baptized. But a church can't have it both ways. If baptism isn't required for membership, then any professing believer should be admitted with no questions asked about baptism. Yet if baptism is required for membership, then when the church admits a paedobaptist to membership, it effectively declares infant "baptism" to be true baptism—whatever their statement of faith may say to the contrary. This is to unintentionally participate in a theological fiction. Therefore open membership sits uneasy with the theological claim that infant baptism is not baptism.

A second way open membership advocates tend to obscure the point that infant baptism is not baptism is their apparent reluctance to label paedobaptists "unbaptized." For example, Piper writes:

> Different convictions about the proper mode of baptizing believers (sprinkling, pouring, immersing), and different backgrounds with respect to the mode of baptism a person has experienced, are not weighty or central enough matters to exclude a person from membership in the local church if he meets all other relevant qualifications and is persuaded from Bible study and clear conscience that his baptism is valid.[33]

Notice how Piper frames the issue: "Different backgrounds with respect to the mode of baptism a person has experienced" are not "weighty or central enough matters to exclude a person from membership in the local church." Piper's use of "mode" here obscures the central question. Piper defined the term "mode" immediately prior as referring to whether baptism is administered *to believers*

---

vol. 4, ed. T. L. Underwood (Oxford: Clarendon Press, 1989); as does Robert Hall in *On Terms of Communion; with a Particular View to the Case of the Baptists and Paedobaptists* (1st American ed., from the 3rd English ed., Philadelphia, 1816; repr., London: Forgotten Books, 2012). Along with Bunyan's *Differences in Judgment*, Hall's work is the most popular and enduring apologetic for open membership.

[33] Piper, Chediak, and Steller, "Baptism and Church Membership," 13.

by means of sprinkling, pouring, or immersing. Yet the context of his whole proposal indicates that here he uses the phrase "mode of baptism" to specify infant baptism over against believer's baptism. When Piper speaks of "the mode of baptism a person has experienced," he's referring to those baptized in infancy as having experienced baptism, only in a different "mode" than what he would understand to be biblical. An apparent aversion to describing paedobaptists as unbaptized has backed Piper into saying that they *have been baptized*, which contradicts his own stated theological convictions. Why back into a contradiction instead of simply saying paedobaptists have not been baptized?[34]

I'll circle back to these issues in chapter 10. My point here is that if baptism is where faith goes public, and if it signifies the realities of salvation we experience by faith, then infant baptism simply is not baptism. Infant baptism's status as "not baptism" is an inescapable corollary of a biblical doctrine of baptism. And the account we give of baptism and church membership needs to be consistent with this.

A Seed Planted

In this chapter I've done my best to outline most of a theology of baptism. As we've seen, becoming a Christian is not a private act. Jesus calls us to a lifetime of public witness, and that witness begins in baptism where faith goes public. Because of this, the New Testament speaks of baptism as an integral part of what it normally means to become a Christian. As such, it often uses baptism as shorthand—specifically, synecdoche—for conversion.

After putting this framework in place, we saw that baptism, as a public profession of faith and repentance, is also a sign of forgiveness and cleansing, union with Christ, new life in Christ, the gift of the Holy Spirit, and the new creation. Finally we considered two implications of this theological survey. First, all who profess faith in Christ are obligated to be baptized. Second, infant baptism is not baptism and should not be counted as baptism.

---

[34] Piper isn't the only open membership advocate to equivocate on the theological status of infant baptism. John Brown, for instance, writes that churches can enjoy unity despite "different sentiments about the mode of Water-Baptism," using "mode," like Piper, to refer to disagreement over not just the means of baptism but its subjects. See John Brown, *The House of God Opened and His Table Free for Baptists and Paedobaptists . . .* (London, 1777; repr., Hampshire, UK: ECCO Books, 2010), 4.

Again, we can't determine whether baptism is required for church membership until we know what baptism is. So this chapter has laid a foundation that the rest of the book builds on. By establishing that baptism is where faith goes public, I've also planted a seed that I intend to nurture to full flower over the next several chapters. Understanding that baptism is where faith first becomes visible is the first step to discerning baptism's ecclesial shape, which is what enables us to rightly fit together baptism, the Lord's Supper, and church membership. To preview: in the next two chapters we'll discover that baptism isn't just where faith goes public; it's also a badge of belonging.

Headlines
Baptism is where faith goes public (Acts 2:38–41). It is Jesus' appointed means by which someone nails their colors to the mast as one of his followers.
In addition to serving as a public profession of repentance and faith in Christ, baptism signifies forgiveness and cleansing (Acts 2:38), union with Christ (Rom 6:1–4), new life in Christ (Col 2:11–12), the gift of the Holy Spirit (1 Cor 12:13), and the dawning new creation in Christ (Rom 6:5, 8–10).
All who claim to believe in Christ are obligated to be baptized (Matt 28:19).
Because baptism is where a believer's faith goes public, infant baptism simply isn't baptism, and churches should not treat it as baptism.

Chapter 4

The Initiating Oath-Sign of the New Covenant

The big questions the next four chapters seek to answer are: How does baptism relate to the church? Is baptism purely a matter of individual obedience, or is it intrinsically linked to a person's entrance into the church? Does baptism have an ecclesial shape?

This is a critical impasse in the debate over baptism and church membership. Many open-membership advocates would assert with John Bunyan that baptism is *not* the "initiating, and entring [*sic*] ordinance into church-communion."[1] On the other hand, William Buttfield speaks for many closed-membership Baptists when he writes, "For Baptism is not only a personal duty out of the church, but it is also the only way in which the word of God directs us *into* the church."[2] Yet on this issue both sides tend more to assert their position than to argue it.

That's why I'm spending the next two chapters directly engaging the question of baptism's ecclesial shape. This chapter and the next will examine baptism through the complementary lenses of the new covenant and the kingdom of

---

[1] John Bunyan, *A Confession of My Faith, and A Reason of My Practice*, in *The Miscellaneous Works of John Bunyan*, vol. 4, ed. T. L. Underwood (Oxford: Clarendon Press, 1989), 162. Throughout the book, when I quote Bunyan, I modernize his capitalization and occasionally punctuation.

[2] William Buttfield, *Free Communion an Innovation: or, an Answer to Mr. John Brown's Pamphlet . . .* (London, 1778; repr., Hampshire, UK: ECCO books), 14.

God in order to discern and describe its ecclesial shape—that is, its intrinsic connection to local church membership. As I hope to demonstrate, baptism does have an ecclesial shape, and that shape is decisive for how we relate baptism to church membership. After these two chapters we'll consider the ecclesial shape of the Lord's Supper and then flip the telescope around to examine the baptismal (and eucharistic) shape of the relation we call church membership.

Most everyone in this debate would agree that the church is the people of the new covenant (Heb 8:1–13). We credobaptists all tend to agree that the newness of the new covenant is crucial for discerning the proper subjects of baptism—that is, believers, not infants. Yet too few baptist treatments of baptism have attempted to positively describe the theological relationship between baptism and the new covenant.[3] If we become new covenant members by faith, what role, if any, does baptism play in our entrance into the covenant? And what form does this new covenant take here on earth? Is it purely an invisible reality? After all, the Spirit blows where he wills, invisible as the wind (John 3:8). Or is there any sense in which the new covenant—more specifically, an individual's entrance into the new covenant—is a visible, public affair?

In this chapter I will argue that baptism is the initiating oath-sign of the new covenant, and this makes baptism necessary for church membership. First, I'll survey the biblical covenants to set a backdrop for the new covenant. Second, I'll argue that baptism is a sign of the new covenant and that it embodies the newness of the new covenant. Third, I'll argue more specifically that baptism is the *initiating oath-sign* of the new covenant.[4] Fourth, I'll answer questions many readers will be asking by this point: Don't we enter the new

---

[3] There's some truth, therefore, in John Fesko's charge that the recent work edited by Schreiner and Wright pays only "nominal" attention to what Fesko calls "the doctrine of the covenant." He notes, "The term *covenant* appears in the subtitle, but there is little effort to set forth the doctrine of the covenant in the book" (*Word, Water and Spirit: A Reformed Perspective on Baptism* [Grand Rapids: Reformation Heritage Books, 2010], 2). Certainly, Wellum's essay in that volume presents an in-depth discussion of certain aspects of baptism's relationship to the new covenant. But its primary interest is polemical, not constructive. As such it passes over several crucial questions that are relevant to baptism and membership—such as the ones I raise in the paragraph above. Further, Brandon Jones's helpful book, *Waters of Promise: Finding Meaning in Believer Baptism* (Eugene, OR: Pickwick, 2012), proposes what he calls a "covenantal" understanding of baptism but does not engage the theological questions I address in this chapter.

[4] I'm qualifying "oath-sign" with "initiating" both to describe the function of baptism in relation to the covenant and to make room for what we'll see in chap. 6: the Lord's Supper is also an oath-sign of the new covenant, with a complementary function to baptism.

covenant by faith? How then can baptism initiate us into the covenant? Finally, I'll describe the ecclesial shape which baptism's role as initiating oath-sign of the new covenant uncovers and show why this means baptism is necessary for church membership.

Introduction to the Biblical Covenants

Covenants are the backbone of Scripture. They structure its entire plotline.[5] What is a covenant? Gordon Hugenberger defines a covenant as "an elected, as opposed to natural, relationship of obligation under oath."[6] A covenant can be made between people (e.g., Gen 14:3; 1 Sam 18:3), but our concern is with covenants between people and God.

The most prominent covenants in Scripture are God's covenants with Adam and Eve (Genesis 1–3), Noah (Gen 8:20–9:17), Abraham (Gen 12:1–3; 15:1–21; 17:1–14; 22:15–18), the nation of Israel (Exodus 19–24), and David (2 Sam 7:1–17). Finally, God promises to make a new covenant with Israel and Judah, which will differ radically from the covenant he made with them at Sinai (Jer 31:31–34). In this brief overview of the Bible's covenants, I'll highlight only what will shed light on our discussion of the new covenant.

In God's creation covenant with Adam and Eve, he granted them dominion over the earth and charged them to be fruitful and multiply, to fill the earth with his glory as they imaged his righteous rule (Gen 1:26–28).[7] Instead, Adam and Eve threw off God's rule, listened to the serpent, and ate from the tree

---

[5] Gentry and Wellum write, "The covenants form the backbone of the metanarrative of Scripture and thus it is essential to 'put them together' correctly in order to discern accurately the 'whole counsel of God' (Acts 20:27)" (Peter J. Gentry and Stephen J. Wellum, *Kingdom Through Covenant: A Biblical-Theological Understanding of the Covenants* [Wheaton, IL: Crossway, 201], 21; cf. 57, 226). My treatment of the covenants in this section is indebted to their in-depth work.

[6] Gordon P. Hugenberger, *Marriage as a Covenant: Biblical Law and Ethics as Developed from Malachi*, Biblical Studies Library (paperback ed., Grand Rapids: Baker, 1998), 11. Paul R. Williamson's definition is similar: "a solemn commitment, guaranteeing promises or obligations undertaken by one or both parties, sealed with an oath." In *Sealed with an Oath: Covenant in God's Unfolding Purpose*, New Studies in Biblical Theology 23 (Downers Grove, IL: InterVarsity Press, 2007), 43. See also the complementary discussion in Gentry and Wellum, *Kingdom Through Covenant*, 132–33.

[7] For an argument against viewing the original creation arrangement as a covenant, see Williamson, *Sealed with an Oath*, 52–58. For an argument in favor, see Gentry and Wellum, *Kingdom Through Covenant*, 179–233, 613–30.

of the knowledge of good and evil (Gen 3:1–7). As a result, they were exiled from Eden, sentenced to death, and the creation itself was cursed (Gen 3:8–24). Yet God promised that the woman's offspring would crush the serpent's head, delivering humanity from evil and all its consequences (Gen 3:15).

Over generations humankind grew so wicked that God wiped them all out, save the eight members of Noah's family, in a worldwide flood (Genesis 6–8; cf. 1 Pet 3:19–20). After the flood God made a covenant with Noah in which he promised never to flood the world again (Gen 8:20–22), and he reinstated the creation covenant, now adapted to a post-fall setting (Gen 9:1–17).

After Noah, people joined together in a rebellion against God (Genesis 11), so God confused their language and dispersed them over the earth (Genesis 10). Against this dark backdrop God solemnly promised Abram (later named Abraham) that he would give him the land of Canaan (Gen 12:1; 13:14–18), multiply his offspring beyond imagining (Gen 12:2; 15:1–6; 17:4ff.), bless him (Gen 12:2; 15:1), and bless all nations in him and in his offspring (Gen 12:3; 22:18). God's covenant with Abraham thus became the solid, unshakeable ground of all his future dealings with his people.

God ratified his promise to Abraham with an oath-sign, a solemn ceremony in which God bound himself to his word. In Genesis 15 God instructed Abraham to bisect a heifer, goat, ram, turtledove, and pigeon, and to lay the halves facing each other (vv. 7–11). Then God put Abraham into a deep sleep, repeated his promise to him, and passed between the animals, appearing as a smoking fire pot and flaming torch (vv. 12–17). Based on other biblical references to a ceremony like this (Ps 50:5; Jer 34:18) and parallels in extrabiblical covenants, this ritual seems to enact a conditional self-maledictory oath. That is, by passing through these halved animals, God symbolically swore that the animals' fate would befall him if he should fail to keep his promise to Abraham.[8]

Just as he said he would, God brought Abraham's descendents up out of slavery in Egypt (Exodus 1–18). Before planting them in the land he had promised to Abraham, God made a covenant with them at Sinai, often called the Mosaic covenant since Moses was its mediator. The core of this covenant is found in Exodus 19–24; its full stipulations are spelled out in the rest of Exodus, Leviticus, and Numbers and are reiterated to the next generation in Deuteronomy. This covenant constituted Israel as a nation (Exod 19:5–6). It

---

[8] See Hugenberger, *Marriage as a Covenant*, 195; Gentry and Wellum, *Kingdom Through Covenant*, 248–58.

specified the means by which they would continue to experience the blessings promised to Abraham, namely obedience to God's law, which governed every aspect of their life.[9] It promised blessing upon blessing if the people obeyed and curse upon curse if they disobeyed, culminating in exile from the land. Yet God will not forsake his people, even if—or rather, when—they utterly scorn him (see Lev 26:1–45; Deut 28:1–68; 30:1–10).

After punishing that generation for their rebellion (Num 14:20–35), God brought their children into the land, drove out their enemies, and eventually established a king over them. After deposing disobedient Saul, God enthroned David and gave him "rest from all his surrounding enemies" (2 Sam 7:1). In response to God's kindness, David was moved to build a house—a temple— for God (2 Sam 7:2–3). Instead, God promised to build David a house—that is, a dynasty (2 Sam 7:4–17). He promised David that his offspring would build a house for God's name (v. 13), find favor with God (vv. 14–15), and have his throne established forever (v. 16).

While 2 Samuel 7 doesn't use the word *covenant*, this promise is referred to as a covenant elsewhere in Scripture (e.g., Ps 89:3–4). This covenant implies that Abraham's great name will be realized through the great name of David's son (v. 9), and that the land promise will be permanently secured through him (v. 10). In addition, as Moses prophetically taught in Deuteronomy, the king was to devote himself to studying and obeying God's law (Deut 17:18–20), so that as God's "son" he might set the pace for all God's people. In sum, there-fore, "Just as the Mosaic Covenant was to administrate the promises of the Abrahamic Covenant, so the Davidic Covenant assigned the king the task of administrating the people's obedience of the Mosaic Covenant."[10] And just as the Davidic king was supposed to superintend the people's obedience, so also the people would fall with him if he disobeyed.

Of course, the latter is what actually happened. Just as Adam and Eve sinned and were expelled from the garden, so Israel and Judah also sinned, their kings leading the way, and were exiled from the land (2 Kgs 17:7–22; 24:10–25:30). Their problem was that their hearts were rotten to the core. Instead of walking in God's ways, they walked "in their own counsels and the stubbornness of their evil hearts" (Jer 7:24). What the people needed was not

---

[9] Exodus 19:5, "Now therefore, *if* you will indeed obey my voice and keep my cov-enant, you shall be my treasured possession among all peoples."

[10] Jonathan Leeman, *Political Church: The Local Assembly as Embassy of Christ's Rule* (Downers Grove, IL: InterVarsity Press, forthcoming), chap. 4.

finally a law, or even a king, but a new heart. And that's precisely what God promised in the new covenant:

> Behold, the days are coming, declares the Lord, when I will make a new covenant with the house of Israel and the house of Judah, not like the covenant that I made with their fathers on the day when I took them by the hand to bring them out of the land of Egypt, my covenant that they broke, though I was their husband, declares the Lord. For this is the covenant that I will make with the house of Israel after those days, declares the Lord: I will put my law within them, and I will write it on their hearts. And I will be their God, and they shall be my people. And no longer shall each one teach his neighbor and each his brother, saying, "Know the Lord," for they shall all know me, from the least of them to the greatest, declares the Lord. For I will forgive their iniquity, and I will remember their sin no more. (Jer 31:31–34)

We'll trace some of the key features of this new covenant in the rest of this chapter. For now it's enough to note that Jesus said his death would usher in this new covenant (Luke 22:20), and the rest of the New Testament confirms this (e.g., 2 Corinthians 3–4; Hebrews 8–10).[11]

Baptism, a Sign of the New Covenant

Another aspect of the biblical covenants we need to highlight is that many of them, though not all, come with signs. The sign of the Noahic covenant is God's "bow" in the cloud, a witness to all creation that he has laid down his weapon and will not destroy the earth again by flood (Gen 9:12–15). The sign of the Abrahamic covenant is circumcision, which consecrates Abraham's offspring as Yahweh's special possession (Gen 17:9–14). The sign of the Mosaic covenant is the Sabbath, in which Israel participates in God's own rest to remind them that he is the one who sanctifies them (Exod 31:13–17).

Is there a sign of the new covenant? It seems obvious that when Jesus says, "This cup . . . is the new covenant in my blood" (Luke 22:20), that's precisely what he's saying the Lord's Supper is. When God instituted circumcision, he

---

[11] See David G. Peterson, *Transformed by God: New Covenant Life and Ministry* (Downers Grove, IL: InterVarsity Press, 2012), for a helpful discussion of the new covenant in Jeremiah and its resonances throughout the New Testament.

said, "This is my covenant, which you shall keep, between me and you and your offspring after you" (Gen 17:10). So too with the Sabbath: "Therefore the people of Israel shall keep the Sabbath . . . as a covenant forever" (Exod 31:16). In both of these instances, the sign of the covenant is identified as the covenant, which seems to be a precedent Luke 22:20 follows.[12] We'll think more about the Lord's Supper and the new covenant in chapter 6. For now, though, we need to ask where this leaves baptism. Is baptism also a sign of the new covenant?

I'd argue it is, for four reasons. First, remember that Jesus' death inaugurates the new covenant (Heb 9:15), and baptism pictures a believer's union with Christ in his death, burial, and resurrection (Rom 6:1–4). If Jesus' death inaugurates the new covenant, it's fitting to infer that a sign of his death is a sign of that covenant. Second, consider that all of the spiritual realities baptism symbolizes are bound up with the new covenant: forgiveness (Jer 31:34), cleansing (Ezek 36:25), resurrection (Ezek 37:11–14), and the gift of the Spirit (Ezek 36:27). The new covenant is what baptism *means*. Third, note that baptism was instituted immediately after the death and resurrection of Christ (Matt 28:19). It wasn't a standing religious rite that just happened to make it into the new covenant era; instead, it began when the new covenant began. Fourth, while baptism doesn't exactly "replace" circumcision,[13] the two rites both identify God's covenant people and mark them off from the world. Just as circumcision was a one-time act which conferred a lasting covenantal identity, so also baptism is a one-time act which marks a person as belonging to the new covenant.[14] This is a point I'll develop throughout this chapter and the next.

Baptism is a sign of the new covenant because it is tied to Christ's covenant-inaugurating death, it pictures the realities of the new covenant, it was instituted along with the new covenant, and it picks up circumcision's covenantal boundary-marking function. For these reasons and more, baptists, along with

---

[12] The technical term for this is metonymy, a figure of speech in which one thing stands for another to which it is related. As we considered in the last chapter, synecdoche—part for whole or whole for part—is a specific kind of metonymy.

[13] See, e.g., Wellum and Gentry, *Kingdom Through Covenant*, 700–703.

[14] Cf. Schreiner's reference to baptism as the "boundary marker" of the church in Thomas R. Schreiner, "Baptism in the Epistles," in *Believer's Baptism: Sign of the New Covenant in Christ*, ed. Thomas R. Schreiner and Shawn D. Wright (Nashville: B&H, 2007), 91.

most Christians throughout history, have consistently identified baptism as a sign of the new covenant.

Baptism Embodies the Newness of the New Covenant

As a sign of the new covenant, baptism embodies the "newness" of the new covenant. Baptism pictures God's promises *fulfilled*. What the old, Mosaic covenant couldn't accomplish (Heb 8:6–7, 13), God has accomplished through the new covenant, and baptism portrays this redemptive-historical achievement. Baptism derives its meaning and character from the new age of fulfillment that the new covenant has ushered in.

One of the crucial differences between the new covenant and the old is that in the new covenant, the entire covenant community knows the Lord: "For they shall all know me, from the least of them to the greatest" (Jer 31:34; cf. Isa 54:13). Under the Mosaic administration the covenant community was an ethnic entity marked off by circumcision. To answer the question, Who's in the covenant?, you would point to all the circumcised offspring of Abraham and their families. Those families were part of the covenant community regardless of whether they knew the Lord. And the covenant itself was administrated by prophets, priests, and kings who were to mediate the knowledge of God to the people.[15]

Yet now the new covenant partakes of both a new nature and a new structure.[16] The new covenant's structure is new in that there's no need for a set of covenant mediators. Through the work of the covenant's *one* mediator, Jesus the Messiah (Heb 8:6; 9:15; 12:24; cf. 1 Tim 2:5), and the indwelling Holy Spirit (1 Cor 2:10–16), all the covenant people know the Lord. The other mediators are no longer necessary (1 John 2:20).

And the new covenant has a new nature in two ways. First, as we've already seen, instead of an ethnic people of mixed spiritual status, the new covenant creates a regenerate people, a people who all have new hearts (Jer 32:39–40). Second, in keeping with this, the new covenant is also open to all

---

[15] D. A. Carson, "Evangelicals, Ecumenism, and the Church," in *Evangelical Affirmations*, ed. Kenneth S. Kantzer and Carl F. H. Henry (Grand Rapids: Zondervan, 1990), 359–60.

[16] On the new covenant's new nature and structure, see Stephen J. Wellum, "Beyond Mere Ecclesiology: The Church as God's New Covenant Community," in *The Community of Jesus: A Theology of the Church*, ed. Kendell H. Easley and Christopher W. Morgan (Nashville: B&H, 2013), 183–212.

nations, without those Gentiles having to become Jews first. The entire book of Galatians argues this point, but it also rises to the surface in a number of Old Testament texts related to the new covenant. In Isaiah 56, which concludes Isaiah's reflection on the new covenant-inaugurating work of the Servant, God promises that foreigners will become his servants and offer acceptable sacrifices to him (vv. 6–7). He promises to "gather yet others" to Israel in addition to the outcast Israelites he has already gathered (v. 8). Foreigners *as foreigners* will become part of God's true people Israel in this new covenant age. This sheds light on passages such as Isaiah 19:24–25, where God refers to "Egypt my people, and Assyria the work of my hands" in the same breath as "Israel my inheritance."[17] Similarly, in Jeremiah 4:2 the Lord promises that when Israel returns to him the nations also will be included in the blessing of Abraham (cf. Jer 12:16).

All this is to say, the new covenant ushers in a decisive shift in the composition of God's covenant community. God's new covenant people are intrinsically multiethnic. The boundary that divided Israel from the nations is now torn down (cf. Eph 2:14–16). As such, the Old Testament implies and the New Testament explicitly states that in the new covenant era circumcision is no longer the boundary marker between the people of God and the world. Therefore, it is fitting that there be a new covenant sign to mark off this new covenant people. Baptism is just this sign since it signifies that its recipients have indeed entered into the new covenant. And insofar as baptism is applied to believing Jews *and* Gentiles, it vividly pictures the new nature of the new covenant community. In these two key ways, baptism embodies the newness of the new covenant.

The Initiating Oath-Sign of the New Covenant

With these foundations in place, we can put our previous point more precisely: baptism is the initiating oath-sign of the new covenant. That is, baptism is a solemn, symbolic vow which ratifies a person's entrance into the new covenant.

An oath is essential to a covenant. No oath, no covenant.[18] Recall that a covenant is a "relationship of obligation." An oath ratifies one's commitment to

---

[17] See also Isa 66:18–24 and Zech 2:11.
[18] See Hugenberger, *Marriage as a Covenant*, 182–84; Williamson, *Sealed with an Oath* 39, 43, and the literature cited therein.

the obligations of the covenant, and, typically, places one under the sanctions of the covenant should one fail to uphold its obligations. Thus, in order to ratify the covenant at Sinai, the people of Israel solemnly declared, "All that the Lord has spoken we will do, and we will be obedient" (Exod 24:7). And Scripture describes the Lord's promise to David as a covenant-constituting oath (2 Sam 23:5; Ps 89:3–4).

Yet an oath may be accompanied by, or even consist of, symbolic actions.[19] In ratifying the covenant at Sinai, the people were sprinkled with blood (Exod 24:8), and then Moses and the leaders of the people ate a meal in the presence of the Lord to solemnize their fellowship with him (Exod 24:11). These symbolic actions accompanied the verbal oath. Contemporary examples include a president raising one hand and putting the other on a Bible when he takes the oath of office and a bride and groom exchanging rings to symbolize the verbal vows of a wedding.

A symbolic action can also *constitute* an oath. That is, a symbolic act can function as an oath—an "oath-sign." The biblical idiom "to cut a covenant" apparently derives from the fact that an animal-cutting ceremony like the one we see in Genesis 15 was often used to ratify a covenant.[20] Circumcision was apparently a covenant-ratifying oath-sign. The Lord commanded Abraham, "You [pl.] shall be circumcised in the flesh of your foreskins, and it shall be a sign of the covenant between me and you" (Gen 17:11). And, "any uncircumcised male . . . shall be cut off from his people; he has broken my covenant" (Gen 17:14). Entrance into the covenant involved "cutting off" a male's foreskin. Any male descendent of Abraham who failed to undergo this rite would be "cut off" from his people—that is, put to death. The curse of the covenant was dramatized in its entrance rite. A sign of the covenant's sanctions was placed, quite literally, on those thereby consecrated to the Lord.[21]

This raises the question, if baptism is the initiating sign of the new covenant, is it also an oath? To answer that question, however, we first need to sort out whether the new covenant is inaugurated by an oath.

---

[19] Hugenberger, *Marriage as a Covenant*, 193–96. The following discussion is heavily indebted to Hugenberger's treatment.

[20] "Cut a covenant" literally renders the Hebrew of, e.g., Gen 15:18 and Deut 29:13.

[21] For fuller discussion, including the idea of circumcision as consecration, see Meredith G. Kline, *By Oath Consigned* (Grand Rapids: Eerdmans, 1968), 39–49, 86–89; Jason S. DeRouchie, "Circumcision in the Hebrew Bible and Targums: Theology, Rhetoric, and the Handling of Metaphor," *Bulletin of Biblical Research* 14 (2004): 182–89, 202–3.

Is the New Covenant Inaugurated by an Oath?

As we've seen, some of the Bible's covenants are inaugurated by divine oath. The Davidic covenant is the most obvious example of this: "You have said, 'I have made a covenant with my chosen one; I have sworn to David my servant: "I will establish your offspring forever, and build your throne for all generations"'" (Ps 89:3–4). And in Genesis 15 the Lord ratifies his covenant with Abraham with the oath-sign of passing between halved animals (Gen 15:18). Is the new covenant, like these two covenants, also inaugurated by a divine oath?

At first blush it would seem so since the new covenant, like these two covenants, is founded on divinely guaranteed promises: Jeremiah 31:31–34; 32:37–41, and so on. Yet there are crucial differences. Genesis 15:18 and Psalm 89:3–4 clearly indicate that the Abrahamic and Davidic covenants came into being on the day the Lord made those promises. Thus, while the fulfillment of the promises remained future, these two covenants were inaugurated by the word of Yahweh—and in the case of Genesis 15, an oath-sign which confirmed the word. However, when God promised the new covenant to his people, the day of its inauguration clearly remained future: "Behold, *the days are coming*, declares the LORD, when I *will make* a new covenant with the house of Israel and the house of Judah" (Jer 31:31, italics added). The promise of the covenant did not bring the covenant into existence. The new covenant is expressly contrasted with the Mosaic covenant (Jer 31:32), yet the Mosaic covenant remained in force for centuries after the Lord made this promise. Therefore, while the new covenant is certainly grounded in a promise like those made to Abraham and David, it differs from them in that it was not itself inaugurated by that promise.

How then does God "cut" the new covenant? By cutting off his Son, our Lord Jesus Christ. Recall Luke 22:20: "And likewise [he took] the cup after they had eaten, saying 'This cup that is poured out for you is the new covenant in my blood.'" The new covenant is inaugurated by Jesus' effective sacrifice. As Hebrews explains, "Therefore he is the mediator of a new covenant, so that those who are called might receive the promised eternal inheritance, since a death has occurred that redeems them from the transgressions committed under the first covenant" (Heb 9:15; cf. vv. 16–17). In his death Jesus simultaneously suffered the curse of the broken Mosaic covenant and unleashed the blessings of the new covenant.[22]

---

[22] See, e.g., Peter T. O'Brien, *The Letter to the Hebrews*, Pillar New Testament Commentary (Grand Rapids: Eerdmans, 2010), 326–28.

Thus, Meredith Kline is close to the mark when he concludes that "the New Covenant is not ratified by oath ritual, whether performed by men or by God, but rather by a decisive inbreaking of God in an eschatological act of judgment."[23] The cross was an eschatological act of judgment in that God brought the final, ultimate punishment for sin into the present, laying it on Jesus. As a result, all the blessings of the new covenant are now poured out on God's people. The new covenant is not inaugurated by sheer promise, or by the symbolic death of animals, but by the death of Christ which fulfills all of God's promises.[24]

Yet while the new covenant was not founded by an oath per se, God's promises in Jeremiah 31:31–34; 32:37–41, and other passages do seem to function as an oath once the covenant is inaugurated. In these promises God specifies the obligations he *will* fulfill for his people. Hear the drumbeat:

> I will gather them. . . . I will bring them back. . . . I will be their God.
> I will give them one heart. . . . I will make with them an everlasting
> covenant, . . . I will not turn away from doing good to them. . . . I will
> put the fear of me in their hearts. . . . I will rejoice in doing them good,
> and I will plant them in this land in faithfulness, with all my heart and
> all my soul. (Jer 32:37–41)

These glorious, whole-souled promises bind God to act toward his people in this way when he inaugurates the new covenant. And the New Testament tells us they take effect when God the Father cuts the new covenant by cutting off Jesus, raising him from the dead, and pouring out the Holy Spirit to effect the transformation of his people that the new covenant promises. Therefore, while the new covenant is not founded by an oath, it is nevertheless grounded on one.

---

[23] Kline, *By Oath Consigned*, 33. I say "close to the mark" because I'll qualify his statement about how the new covenant is ratified later on. As with the Abrahamic covenant (Genesis 15 and 17), with the new covenant we must distinguish between the covenant's initial establishment and the means by which each individual enters into it.

[24] Hebrews 8:6 might seem to argue otherwise, since it says that Christ's ministry "is as much more excellent than the old as the covenant he mediates is better, since it is enacted on better promises." The verb νενομοθέτηται, here translated "enacted," could also be rendered "legitimately established" or "legally founded." And the similar use of the term in 7:11 speaks about the giving of the law and hence the inauguration of the Mosaic covenant. However, the term here seems to refer to the promises of Jer 31:31–34 as the basis, rather than the means or occasion, of the inauguration of the new covenant.

Is Baptism an Oath?

Does this mean the only oath involved in the new covenant is God's promise, which takes effect through Jesus' saving work? I'd argue the answer is no and that baptism is in fact the oath-sign by which an individual is formally initiated into the new covenant.

It's helpful to remember that the Abrahamic covenant was inaugurated through a divine promise accompanied with an oath-sign (Gen 12:1–3; 15:1–18), *and* each male descendent of Abraham entered into the covenant by means of an oath-sign of his own (Gen 17:9–14). The Abrahamic covenant was founded by an oath and entered by an oath. In this section I'll argue that the new covenant is similar to the Abrahamic covenant in this respect. The new covenant is founded upon God's oath which comes into effect through Christ's saving act, and it is ratified by each believer in baptism.

We need to put three lenses in place in order to discern the Bible's teaching that baptism is the initiatory oath-sign of the new covenant. The first is that the new covenant replaces the old covenant—that is, the Mosaic covenant—in God's economy (Heb 8:6–7, 13). Recall what we briefly touched on above, that the Mosaic covenant was God's ordained means of administrating the Abrahamic covenant, and the Davidic covenant further specified the means by which the people would either fulfill or fail to meet the Mosaic covenant's demands. The new covenant, then, replaces the Mosaic covenant in that it becomes the means by which the Abrahamic covenant is finally fulfilled. Paul says Christ became a curse for us "so that in Christ Jesus the blessing of Abraham might come to the Gentiles, so that we might receive the promised Spirit through faith" (Gal 3:14). Through Christ bearing the curse of the old covenant, believers from all nations receive the promised Spirit of the new covenant; and Paul says this outpouring of the Spirit is the blessing promised to Abraham back in Genesis 12. Further, the new covenant and the Davidic covenant are fulfilled together since Jesus the Son of David is the one who mediates the new covenant (cf. Ezek 37:21–28). "After making purification for sins" and thereby inaugurating the new covenant, Jesus "sat down at the right hand of the Majesty on high," beginning his reign as David's heir (Heb 1:3; echoing Ps 110:1).

In brief the new covenant accomplishes what the old covenant never could (Gal 2:21–22; Heb 8:7). It assumes the office, as it were, formerly held by the Mosaic covenant; yet there's no danger of this covenant being removed from office.

The second lens we need to put in place is that, just as the old covenant provided a comprehensive, all-embracing rule of life for the people of God, so does the new. The old covenant governed not just whom Israel worshipped and how but also how they did business, what they wore, what they ate, whom they could marry, and just about everything else imaginable. Because the covenant bound them to observe all of God's laws—613 of them by the count of some rabbis—the people's pledge of obedience was their means of entering the covenant (Exod 24:7). The new covenant also provides a rule of life that is every bit as comprehensive as the old, though notably different in detail and focus. Consider Jesus' Great Commission: "All authority in heaven and on earth has been given to me. Go therefore and make disciples of all nations, baptizing them in the name of the Father and of the Son and of the Holy Spirit, teaching them to observe all that I have commanded you. And behold, I am with you always, to the end of the age" (Matt 28:18–20).

To become a disciple of Jesus is to commit to observe all that he has commanded. It is to submit to his rule, which extends not only to the farthest corners of the universe but also to the most intimate reaches of our hearts. The wonder of the new covenant is that it enables us to obey everything Jesus commands: "I will put my law within them, and I will write it on their hearts" (Jer 31:33; cf. Jer 32:39–40; Ezek 36:26–27). Augustine's prayer, "Command what you will and give what you command," is the cry of every new covenant believer. Our second lens, then, is this: the new covenant both dictates and enables a whole life of heart-deep obedience to God.

Building on this, our third lens is one we developed earlier in the chapter, namely, that baptism is a sign of the new covenant. But now we can go further: baptism both symbolizes and commits one to the new life of obedience the new covenant entails. Baptism symbolizes our new life in Christ (Col 2:12), and Paul appeals to baptism to remind us that we who have passed from death to life must now live for God (Rom 6:1–10). Paul's appeal presupposes that baptism involves a commitment to obey Christ. And both the symbolism and the pledge of obedience entailed in baptism have a new covenant context, as we see explicitly in Matthew 28:19 and implicitly in 1 Peter 3:21.

Regarding Matthew 28:19, notice first that baptism is "into the name" of the Father, Son, and Holy Spirit. Being baptized into God's "name" is an act of covenantal initiation and identification. When God makes a covenant with people, he identifies himself with them and they with him. This is at the heart of the "covenant formula" which echoes through Scripture: "I will be their

God, and they shall be my people."[25] Another way Scripture describes this mutual identification is to say that by virtue of his covenants, God puts his name on his people, and they are called by his name.[26] Thus, to be baptized into the name of the Triune God is to be initiated into covenantal identification with him. And this covenant identification entails ownership: we now belong to God.[27] D. A. Carson ties all these threads together when he writes of Matthew 28:19 that "the preposition 'into' strongly suggests a coming-into-relationship-with or a coming-under-the-Lordship-of. . . . [Baptism] is a sign of both entrance into the Messiah's covenant community and of pledged submission to his lordship."[28]

In sum, we see in Matthew 28:19 that the new covenant commands comprehensive obedience to Jesus' teaching, and baptism pledges us to this obedience. Further, baptism into the Triune name is a new-covenantal identification with the Lord of the covenant, with the result that we now belong to him. As a pledge of submission to Christ's lordship, baptism is a covenant oath-sign, an enacted vow analogous to Israel's "all that the LORD has spoken we will do" (Exod 24:7). This doesn't necessarily require that the one being baptized must verbally pronounce a vow to obey all of Jesus' teaching—though that is certainly allowable, even advisable. Instead, as with Old Testament covenant-cutting ceremonies, the act is the oath.

Baptism's function as a covenantal oath-sign is implicitly confirmed in 1 Peter 3:21. After speaking about how Noah's family was brought safely through the judgment of the flood, Peter writes, "Baptism, which corresponds to this, now saves you, not as a removal of dirt from the body but as an appeal to God for a good conscience, through the resurrection of Jesus Christ." Two issues in this verse are particularly disputed. The first is whether the word the ESV translates as "appeal"[29] should instead be translated "pledge," as in

---

[25] See, e.g., Gen 17:7–8; Exod 6:7; Lev 26:12; Jer 31:33; 2 Cor 6:16; and Rev 21:3.

[26] See Num 6:27; Deut 28:10; 2 Chr 7:14; and Dan 9:18–19.

[27] See, e.g., G. R. Beasley-Murray, *Baptism in the New Testament* (repr., Grand Rapids: Eerdmans, 1973), 91.

[28] D. A. Carson, *Matthew*, in *The Expositor's Bible Commentary*, vol. 8, ed. Frank Gaebelin (Grand Rapids: Zondervan, 1984), 597. Also commenting on Matt 28:18–20, Grant Macaskill writes, "Baptism represents initiation into the covenant presence of a God now considered Triune" (*Union with Christ in the New Testament* [Oxford: Oxford University Press, 2013], 201; cf. 217).

[29] Gk. ἐπερώτημα.

"vow" or "promise." While translating the word as "pledge" would actually strengthen my overall case, I think "appeal" is the most likely meaning.[30] If that's the case, then Peter describes baptism as a solemn request, an acted prayer.

The second disputed issue is whether the appeal is *for* a good conscience or *from* a good conscience.[31] If the appeal is *from* a good conscience, the phrase may simply indicate that the request is sincere or that it is offered by one whose sins have been forgiven. This is both theologically and contextually possible. However, we saw in the last chapter that baptism is where faith goes public. It embodies the decision to repent and believe. As such, it is closely associated with the forgiveness of sins: "Repent and be baptized every one of you in the name of Jesus Christ for the forgiveness of your sins" (Acts 2:38; cf. Acts 22:16). It seems more likely, then, that Peter is portraying baptism as an act of faith, an embodied appeal for salvation. As such, I think "appeal to God for a good conscience" is probably the most accurate translation of the whole phrase, though nothing crucial is at stake in either of these decisions.

If Peter presents baptism as an appeal to God for a good conscience, what does this tell us about baptism's relationship to the new covenant? I'd suggest it tells us that baptism dramatizes the decision of faith—the faith by which we lay hold of Christ's new covenant promises. Baptism embodies an appeal to God that says, in effect, "O Lord, accept me on the terms of your new covenant." Since the new covenant brings forgiveness, cleansing, and a new heart, a good conscience is a new covenant blessing. Christ's new covenant-inaugurating sacrifice purifies our conscience in a way the Levitical rites never could (Heb 9:13–14). That's why, after expounding Christ's inauguration of the new covenant, the author of Hebrews exhorts us to draw near to God "with a true heart in full assurance of faith, with our hearts sprinkled clean from an evil conscience and our bodies washed with pure water" (Heb 10:22).

Further, remember that Peter says, "Baptism now saves you . . . through the resurrection of Jesus Christ." Christ's resurrection is what brings the power of the age to come into the present, and that same power is what fuels the new covenant (cf. Ezek 37:11–14, 24–28). In sum, baptism is an appeal to God *for* the new covenant blessing of a good conscience, *on the basis of* Jesus' resurrection, the new covenant's eschatological power source. Baptism may not be

---

[30] See, e.g., Thomas R. Schreiner, *1, 2 Peter, Jude*, New American Commentary 37 (Nashville: B&H, 2003), 195–96.

[31] In terms of the Greek syntax, the question is whether the phrase συνειδήσεως ἀγαθῆς is a subjective or an objective genitive.

explicitly described as a covenant oath in 1 Peter 3:21, but it is a covenantal appeal, the solemnizing of one's decision to relate to God on the terms of his new covenant. As such, it nicely complements Matthew's depiction of baptism as entering into a new life of obedience to Jesus' commands. In the same act we both submit to Jesus as Lord (Matt 28:19) and call on him as Savior (1 Pet 3:21), twin aspects of our entrance into the new covenant.

More broadly, think back to texts such as Acts 2:38–41; Romans 6:1–4; and Colossians 2:11–12. These passages show that baptism symbolizes our union with Christ in his death, burial, and resurrection. It publicly commits us to Christ and his cause. Baptism therefore marks a decisive break with our pre-Christian life. Together with the more detailed rationale provided by texts like Matthew 28:19 and 1 Peter 3:21, this is why countless writers, baptist and otherwise, have argued that baptism is an oath of allegiance to Christ.

For example, eighteenth-century Baptist pastor Andrew Fuller argued that for the first believers baptism was an "oath of allegiance to the King of Zion; by which they avowed the Lord to be their God."[32] The late Baptist theologian Stanley Grenz made the same basic point but brought the covenant to the foreground: "Bound up with our confession of faith is a transfer of loyalties—the replacement of former allegiances by a new allegiance to Christ as Lord. . . . Finally, as a sign of our union with Christ in his resurrection, baptism symbolizes the confirming of a covenant with God."[33] John Owen similarly wrote that baptism "is the solemn pledge of our entrance into Covenant with God, and of our giving up ourselves unto Him in the solemn bond of religion."[34]

Michael Horton makes the more explicit point that baptism is a covenant oath-sign. He writes concerning both sacraments:

---

[32] Andrew Fuller, "The Practical Uses of Baptism," in *The Complete Works of the Rev. Andrew Fuller With a Memoir of His Life by Andrew Gunton Fuller*, vol. 3, ed. J. Belcher (Philadelphia: American Baptist Publication Society, 1845; repr., Harrisonburg, VA: Sprinkle, 1988), 339. Further, in baptism, "We have solemnly surrendered ourselves up to Christ, taking him to be our prophet, priest, and king; engaging to receive his doctrine, to rely on his atonement, and to obey his laws. The vows of God are upon us. We have even sworn to keep his righteous judgments; and without violating the oath of God, we cannot go back" (ibid., 339–40).

[33] Stanley J. Grenz, *Theology for the Community of God* (Nashville: B&H, 1994), 679–80.

[34] John Owen, *ΠΝΕΥΜΑΤΟΛΟΓΙΑ or A Discourse Concerning the Holy Spirit*, in *The Works of John Owen*, vol. 3, ed. William H. Goold (repr., Edinburgh: Banner of Truth Trust, 1965), 73.

The ritual is inseparable from the treaty [i.e., covenant] itself, establishing and not merely symbolizing a new relationship between two parties. . . . In the covenantal economy, the function of signs is not primarily to express an inner experience or wish. Nor is it primarily to refer symbolically to a state of affairs that transcends it. Rather, it is an obligation-creating act in the present that can only obtain in a relationship of persons.[35]

Finally, one of the clearest expositions of baptism as an oath is given by the sixteenth-century Anabaptist Balthasar Hubmaier, who wrote concerning the baptismal vow:

It is a commitment made to God publicly and orally before the congregation in which the baptized person renounces Satan and all his imaginations and works. He also vows that he will henceforth set his faith, hope, and trust solely in God and regulate his life according to the divine Word, in the strength of Jesus Christ our Lord, and if he should fail to do so, he thereby promises the church that he would dutifully accept brotherly discipline from it and its members.[36]

Many others have argued that baptism constitutes a vow of allegiance to the Lord Jesus, including some who rightly highlight this vow's covenantal context and therefore label it a covenant oath.[37]

---

[35] Michael S. Horton, *People and Place: A Covenant Ecclesiology* (Louisville: WJK, 2008), 101–2. As we've seen, 1 Pet 3:21 indicates that "expressing a wish," or more properly a solemn petition, plays a more prominent role in baptism than Horton, as a paedobaptist, is willing to grant. Besides this, his statement is on target.

[36] Balthasar Hubmaier, "A Christian Catechism," in *Balthasar Hubmaier: Theologian of Anabaptism*, ed. H. Wayne Pipkin and John Howard Yoder, Classics of the Radical Reformation, vol. 5 (Scottdale, PA: Herald Press, 1989), 350–51. See discussion in Eddie Mabry, *Balthasar Hubmaier's Doctrine of the Church* (Lanham, MD: University Press of America, 1994), 140–42.

[37] See, e.g., James D. G. Dunn, *Baptism in the Holy Spirit: A Re-Examination of the New Testament Teaching on the Gift of the Spirit in Relation to Pentecostalism Today,* 2nd ed. (London: SCM Press, 2010), 97, 117–18; James Bannerman, *The Church of Christ*, vol. 2 (Edinburgh: T&T Clark, 1868), 12, "[The Sacraments] presuppose and imply a covenant transaction between the man who partakes of them and God; and they are the attestations to and confirmations of that transaction, pledging God by a visible act to fulfill His share of the covenant, and engaging the individual by the same visible act to perform his part in it." From a baptist perspective, R. Stanton Norman writes, "Baptism as the 'seal of the covenant' was the basis for the early Baptist understanding of the church as a covenant

The new covenant which baptism signifies both mandates and empowers all-embracing obedience to the Lord Jesus. Baptism both symbolizes our new life in the new covenant and commits us to fulfill its demands, through faith in Christ and by the power of the Spirit. Baptism covenantally identifies us with the name of the Triune God (Matt 28:19). It embodies our appeal to God to accept us on the basis of the new covenant (1 Pet 3:21). Taking all this together, Scripture teaches that baptism is the initiating oath-sign of the new covenant. Is the enacted word by which we formally, publicly ratify our entrance into God's covenant of peace (Ezek 37:26).[38]

Two Crucial Differences Between Baptism and Circumcision

Now we need to note two crucial differences between baptism as the initiating oath-sign of the new covenant and circumcision as the initiating oath-sign of the Abrahamic covenant.[39] The first is that whereas circumcision threatened judgment for disobedience, baptism pictures the full, final judgment which already fell on Christ. Circumcision was, in part, a sign of the sanctions which would apply to anyone who disobeyed the covenant: they would be "cut off" from the people (Gen 17:14). Yet baptism beautifully portrays the truth that Jesus already has been "cut off out of the land of the living" (Isa 53:8) so that we would have eternal life in him. Christ has already suffered the sanctions to which circumcision pointed; there are none left over for us. Baptism does picture judgment, but it is judgment satisfied, judgment exhausted, judgment we will never taste because Christ drained the cup to

---

community" (*The Baptist Way: Distinctives of a Baptist Church* [Nashville: B&H, 2005], 135). Also Brandon C. Jones: "The first covenantal role of baptism is that God designed baptism as a one-time event, or seal, that confirms initiation into his new covenant, carrying with it lasting effects for the individual believer's life" (*Waters of Promise: Finding Meaning in Believer Baptism* [Eugene, OR: Wipf and Stock, 2012], 136).

[38] Brandon Jones describes his position on baptism similarly: "The covenantal view presents baptism as the divinely ordained normative confirming sign and seal of initiation into God's new covenant and his covenant community, without which the normative process of Christian initiation is incomplete" (ibid., 142).

[39] More specifically, from the time of its inception until the dawn of the new covenant, circumcision initiated one into the Abrahamic covenant. Further, since the Mosaic covenant administrated the Abrahamic covenant, during the time of the Mosaic administration one would have simultaneously entered both covenants by means of circumcision (cf. Josh 5:1–9).

its dregs. Circumcision pictures a sanction threatened, baptism a sanction satisfied.[40]

Second, circumcision implicitly demanded that the people renew their hearts: "Circumcise therefore the foreskin of your heart, and be no longer stubborn" (Deut 10:16; cf. Jer 4:4). Circumcision called Israel to consecrate themselves so that their lives matched their status as God's covenant people. Baptism, on the other hand, proclaims that God *has* circumcised our hearts (Col 2:12). He *has* poured out his Spirit, cleansed us, and renewed us.

Therefore, while baptism is an oath, and it does commit one to the obligations of the new covenant, it is *not* a self-maledictory oath—that is, a conditional curse.[41] Baptism is more like an exchange of wedding rings than, say, the covenant-inaugurating ceremonies of Genesis 15 and Exodus 24. In complementary ways these two rituals portray death as the threat for covenant faithlessness.[42] On the other hand, the purpose of exchanging wedding rings is the solemn commitment of groom to bride and bride to groom. Certainly this commitment entails a new set of obligations: the vows themselves. And both husband and wife will answer to God for how they fulfill those new obligations. But the ceremony symbolizes promised commitment, not threatened judgment.

The same goes for baptism, which pictures the Christian life in microcosm.[43] Baptism proclaims that in Christ we have already passed through judgment and emerged safely on the other side.[44] As we rise from the waters of

---

[40] On the latter point see Justyn Terry, *The Justifying Judgment of God: A Reassessment of the Place of Judgment in the Saving Work of Christ*, Paternoster Theological Monographs (Eugene, OR: Wipf and Stock, 2007), 181–87.

[41] In *Marriage as a Covenant*, 200–214, Hugenberger discusses several covenantal oath-signs—such as raising a hand, giving a hand in pledge, and eating together—which are not self-maledictory.

[42] Just as circumcision pictures both consecration to the Lord and the threat of judgment for faithlessness, so, I would suggest, the covenant initiation of Exod 24:3–8 pictures both elements as well. For a fine discussion of Exod 24:3–8 that treats consecration to the Lord as the primary theme, see W. Ross Blackburn, *The God Who Makes Himself Known: The Missionary Heart of the Book of Exodus*, New Studies in Biblical Theology 28 (Downers Grove, IL: InterVarsity, 2012), 95–99.

[43] Beasley-Murray, *Baptism in the New Testament*, 144.

[44] C. F. D. Moule writes, "By baptism an individual, or indeed the whole Church corporately, is (in a sense) brought past the great assize, past the final judgment of the last day, into the life of the new age. . . . In this sense, a baptized person has undergone the final judgment, and risen into new life; for such the 'second death' of Rev xx. 6, 14 has

judgment and step onto the shore of God's new creation, we commit to obey all that the Lord Jesus commands through the grace which he gives. As John Webster says, "The reality out of which the church emerges, and in which alone it always stands, is: You he made alive."[45] Baptism pictures this stunning indicative even as it commits us to the imperative.[46]

Like circumcision baptism is a covenant-initiating oath-sign. Unlike circumcision baptism is not a conditional self-malediction but instead pictures the full satisfaction of God's wrath in the death of Christ. Therefore, baptism's meaning as an oath-sign, like every other aspect of its significance, is determined by the newness of the new covenant.

But Don't We Enter the New Covenant by Faith?

All this raises important questions: Don't we enter the new covenant by faith? How then can we say that baptism initiates us into the covenant?

The first thing to say is, yes, we do enter the new covenant by faith. We are justified by faith (Rom 3:21–26; Gal 2:15–16)—there's the foundational new covenant blessing of forgiveness (Jer 31:31–34). We receive the Spirit by faith (Gal 3:14), another new covenant blessing (Ezek 36:27; 37:26). Through faith we're adopted by God, becoming heirs of all the blessings of the covenant (Gal 3:26).

Yet the new covenant creates a new people, not just new persons. Alluding to Exodus 19:5–6 and Hosea 2:23, Peter tells believers scattered throughout Asia Minor: "But you are a chosen race, a royal priesthood, a holy nation, a people for his own possession, that you may proclaim the excellencies of him who called you out of darkness into his marvelous light. Once you were not a people, but now you are God's people; once you had not received mercy, but now you have received mercy" (1 Pet 2:9–10).

---

no power" ("The Judgement Theme in the Sacraments," in *The Background of the New Testament and Its Eschatology*, ed. W. Daube and W. D. Davies [Cambridge: Cambridge University Press, 1954], 467).

[45] John B. Webster, "'The Visible Attests the Invisible,'" in *The Community of the Word: Toward an Evangelical Ecclesiology*, ed. Mark Husbands and Daniel J. Treier (Downers Grove, IL: InterVarsity, 2005), 102.

[46] Grant Macaskill argues that the covenantal dimension of baptism explains how baptism formally identifies a believer with the life and death of Christ: "The believer, in baptism, identifies him/herself as dead and risen under the terms of the covenant on account of the representative work of Jesus" (*Union with Christ*, 196).

Notice how Peter piles up corporate and even political terms to describe God's new covenant people. We're a chosen race, a race that includes people from every ethnicity. We're a royal priesthood, called to portray God's holiness to the world. We're a holy nation, even though we're spread through every nation. We who formerly were not a people have been made a people for God's possession.

In applying these old covenant terms to God's new covenant people, Peter demonstrates that the new covenant creates a body of people who are distinct from the world. In fact, distinguishing God's people from the world is one of the key purposes of the covenants throughout Scripture, not least the new covenant.[47] In Exodus 19:5, immediately prior to what Peter quotes, the Lord tells Israel, "If you will indeed obey my voice and keep my covenant, you shall be my treasured possession among all peoples." God's covenant with Israel formally enacted and publicized his distinguishing, electing love for them. Out of all the peoples of the earth, he made *them* his own (Amos 3:2). As such, God's covenant signs of circumcision and Sabbath distinguished his people from the nations, as did his laws more broadly.

To what end? That they would display his glory to the nations. In Deuteronomy 4:5–8, Moses commands the people of Israel to keep God's law in order that the nations would marvel at the wisdom of their laws and the glory of their God. Israel failed in this task, but God would accomplish it through the new covenant. Introducing his new covenant promises in Ezekiel, the Lord proclaims:

> Therefore say to the house of Israel, Thus says the Lord God: It is not for your sake, O house of Israel, that I am about to act, but for the sake of my holy name, which you have profaned among the nations to which you came. And I will vindicate the holiness of my great name, which has been profaned among the nations, and which you have profaned among them. And the nations will know that I am the Lord, declares the Lord God, when through you I vindicate my holiness before their eyes. (Ezek 36:22–23)

---

[47] See Jonathan Leeman, *The Church and the Surprising Offense of God's Love: Reintroducing the Doctrines of Church Membership and Discipline* (Wheaton, IL: Crossway, 2010), 253–56.

Through the new covenant the Lord vindicates his glory before the nations. How? By enabling his people to keep his word and display his glory (Ezek 36:24–32). The new covenant creates a people who are distinct from the world.

And in order to be distinct from the world, God's new covenant people have to be visible to the world. Certainly our corporate life as a whole is the fullest witness to our difference from the world (John 13:34–35), but I'd also suggest this is precisely where baptism enters the picture. Just as circumcision marked off the descendents of Abraham from the nations, so baptism marks off those who are Abraham's true children (Gal 3:25–29). Just as circumcision was a verifiable status, so also baptism is a one-time act that can be verified by asking who performed it and who saw it. To be sure, we must love God and love our neighbors in order to show God's glory to the world, but baptism trains the spotlight on each of God's people and says to the watching world, "Want to see what God is like? Look here! This one belongs to him."

The new covenant is more than an invisible, spiritual reality. It has a visible, public shape, and baptism draws the edges of that shape. To enter the new covenant necessarily entails entering the new covenant community. As we've seen, there's more to becoming a Christian than a private, invisible decision to believe. So too with entering the new covenant, which is simply another biblical description of "becoming a Christian." Since the new covenant creates a public people, entrance into the covenant requires a public promise, namely baptism.[48]

Marriage provides a helpful analogy at this point, especially since marriage is also a covenant.[49] When does a couple become "married"? Is it when they say "I do"? Or when the minister pronounces them husband and wife? Or when they consummate the marriage? There's a sense in which the minister's pronouncement of marriage is performative: it enacts what it declares. And yet without the man and woman pledging themselves to each other by vows, a minister's mere declaration would accomplish nothing. Further, if the first two components occur but the marriage is never consummated, there's a sense

---

[48] Eddie Mabry writes concerning Balthasar Hubmaier's doctrine of baptism, "Water baptism for Hubmaier is a public witness, a sign which all can see. Since the church cannot see into the heart of the regenerated person, his or her faith and regeneration cannot be known without some outward sign" (*Balthasar Hubmaier's Doctrine of the Church*, 138).

[49] Cf. Robert H. Stein, "Baptism and Becoming a Christian in the New Testament," in *Southern Baptist Journal of Theology* 2, no. 1 (1998): 13.

in which the couple is not "fully" married.[50] Traditionally, therefore, the legal dissolution of such a bond amounts to an annulment, not a divorce. Marriage is a comprehensive union, and constituting a marriage is a correspondingly complex act.

Similarly, the new covenant is a comprehensive divine-human relationship, and entering it is a correspondingly complex act. Certainly someone who is spiritually regenerate but not yet baptized participates in the "invisible" realities of the new covenant: forgiveness, receiving the Spirit, and so on. Again, if someone dies five minutes after coming to faith, they go to heaven. Yet, just as we saw in the last chapter with "becoming a Christian," if someone believes but has not yet been baptized, he has not yet *fully* entered the new covenant. That entry is completed—formalized, ratified—in baptism. You might say that an as-yet-unbaptized believer belongs to the new covenant privately but not yet publicly, and God intends the two to be inseparable. The new covenant, as we've seen, is more than an invisible register of the redeemed; it has a public shape. And the way you enter the space on earth which the new covenant occupies is baptism, its initiating oath-sign.

Covenant Shaped, Therefore Church Shaping

The new covenant creates a visible people, and one becomes a visible member of that people through baptism. Thus, baptism is required for church membership. One may not belong to God's visible people without bearing the sign which makes that people visible. One may not be counted among the people of the new covenant until one has undergone its initiating oath-sign.

So when the church asks, "Who belongs to the new covenant?" one part of the answer is, "Who has sworn the oath? That is, who has been baptized?" Because baptism is the means by which one is initiated into the new covenant, it is also a necessary, though not sufficient, means by which new covenant members are known to one another. In keeping with its role as the place where faith goes public, baptism is also a badge of belonging. It is a boundary marker

---

[50] On the role of conjugal union in constituting a marriage, see Sherif Girgis, Ryan T. Anderson, and Robert P. George, *What Is Marriage? Man and Woman: A Defense* (New York: Encounter Books, 2012). For example, "Only in the generative act do two people thus become 'one flesh' to seal a marriage" (100).

for the new covenant people of God. It is God's appointed means of drawing a line between the church and the world.

This subverts the common open-membership argument that baptism is simply a matter of personal obedience and has no theological connection to the church. Consider, for example, John Bunyan's claim that baptism is "no characteristical note to another of my sonship with God."[51] Bunyan claims that baptism has nothing to do with how you know someone else is a Christian. Yet baptism's relationship to the new covenant argues otherwise, to say nothing of the fact that immersion in water is a visible, public symbol that can't help but send a message to everyone who sees it. Just as circumcision marked the Israelites off from the nations, so also baptism identifies the new covenant people, both to one another and to the world. As Andrew Fuller argued, "The importance of this ordinance . . . arises from its being the distinguishing sign of Christianity—that by which they were to be known, acknowledged, and treated as members of Christ's visible kingdom. . . . It is analogous to a soldier on his enlisting into his Majesty's service putting on the military dress."[52]

Baptism is like a soldier's uniform, identifying him to his commander and fellow soldiers. It's like a wedding ring, signifying that God's people have pledged themselves wholly to Jesus. Yet baptism is also like a soldier's oath of allegiance, or a bride and groom's vows: baptism doesn't just represent an oath; it *is* an oath.

Because baptism marks entry into the covenant, it draws the shape of the covenant community on earth. Because baptism is covenant shaped, it is also church shaping. Baptism, therefore, has an ecclesial shape. It is not merely an individual ordinance but an ordinance which brings an individual into a new whole of which he is now a part. The ordinance which seals covenant entry opens the door of the church.

Baptism is the initiating oath-sign of the new covenant. Therefore it is necessary for entry into the new covenant community on earth—the membership of a local church.

---

[51] John Bunyan, *Differences in Judgment about Water-Baptism, No Bar to Communion*, in Underwood, *The Miscellaneous Works of John Bunyan*, 216.

[52] Andrew Fuller, "Thoughts on Open Communion," in Belcher, *Complete Works*, 3:504–5.

The First Pillar

We've seen in this chapter that baptism is a sign of the new covenant that embodies the newness of the new covenant. More precisely, it is the oath-sign by which one ratifies one's entrance into the new covenant. It is the symbolic, public act by which one confesses Christ as Savior and submits to him as Lord according to the terms of the new covenant. It is the means by which one pledges before God, the church, and the world to fulfill the demands of the new covenant, which the new covenant itself enables.

As such, baptism is the initial means by which the new covenant people become visible, both to the world and to one another. Because baptism is a covenant oath, it marks the boundaries of the covenant community. It is a badge of belonging. Therefore, it is required for local church membership.

Baptism's function as the initiating oath-sign of the new covenant is the first pillar in my case for why baptism is required for church membership. No one may enter the covenant community who has not ratified the covenant. I'd suggest that, even on its own, this is decisive. Yet this is far from the only pillar holding up this particular roof. We'll add another in the next chapter, where we'll investigate baptism's role in how the kingdom of heaven shows up on earth.

Headlines
Baptism is a sign of the new covenant and embodies the newness of the new covenant (Isa 54:13; Jer 31:33). Baptism pictures God's promises fulfilled.
More specifically, baptism is the initiating oath-sign of the new covenant. It is an enacted vow whereby a person formally submits to the Triune Lord of the new covenant and pledges to fulfill the requirements of the new covenant (Matt 28:19; 1 Pet 3:21).
The new covenant creates a visible people, and one becomes a visible member of that people through baptism. One may not be counted among the people of the new covenant until one has undergone its initiating oath-sign.

Chapter 5

The Passport of the Kingdom

Whom do you speak for? Whether in your family, work, church, or any other sphere, whom do you represent—and how?

"Son, remember that you're a Peterson." "Views expressed on this blog are solely my own and do not represent the positions of First Baptist Church of Fairfield." "This isn't an official recommendation, but speaking as a friend, if I were in your shoes, here's what I'd do."

We've all said or heard things like these. Everyone is in some way responsible for someone else's reputation. Our names tell the world whom we've come from, whom we belong to. Our jobs, whatever they may be, involve delegated authority that we must steward well in order to accomplish our work and honor those to whom we are accountable.

Delegated authority, representation, and reputation are all bound together. When I teach a Sunday school class at my church, the elders delegate to me a measure of authority. For several weeks I get to explain and apply God's Word to whomever shows up for those fifty minutes before church. By and large what I say represents the church since the class is a formal means by which the church is striving to present everyone complete in Christ. And my teaching will impact the church's reputation for good or ill.

In this chapter I'm going to argue that delegated authority, representation, and reputation aren't just practical lenses on the life of the church. Instead they go to the heart of what makes a church a church. They also shed light on the ecclesial shape of baptism and how baptism relates to church membership.

This chapter aims in the same direction as the previous one though it takes a different route there, and it goes a step further. In order to discern whether baptism is required for church membership, we need to discern whether baptism itself has an ecclesial shape. What we discovered in the previous chapter is that baptism is the initiating oath-sign of the new covenant, the visible means by which someone is ushered into the body politic of God's new covenant people. Because baptism is covenant shaped, it is also church shaping.

Throughout Scripture, God uses covenants to establish his kingdom. Kingdom is the goal of covenant.[1] So in this chapter we're going to consider baptism in light of the kingdom. We're going to see that when Jesus inaugurated the kingdom of God, he established the church as an embassy of that kingdom in order to identify its citizens before the world.[2] And the initial and initiating means by which the church identifies individuals as kingdom citizens is baptism. The individual isn't the only one speaking in baptism; the church speaks too.

From another angle the previous chapter leaves us with a question: If baptism is the new covenant-initiating oath-sign, who has the authority to transact this oath? That is, who is authorized to administer baptism, and by what authority? This chapter goes a step further than the previous by naming the local church as the institution responsible to mark off God's new covenant people from the world. The church has authority to represent the kingdom of heaven on earth by marking off kingdom citizens, and it derives this authority from Jesus' grant of the keys of the kingdom.

The local church's responsibility to identify kingdom citizens shines a brighter light on the ecclesial shape of baptism, its role as the identifying badge of God's people. Since local churches are embassies of the kingdom, a local church constitutes the visible, institutional shape of the kingdom of heaven on earth. The institutional space the kingdom of heaven occupies on earth is the local church, and the way you enter that space is baptism.

Two moves in this chapter will take us to this goal. First, we'll trace crucial connections between Jesus, the kingdom, and the church. Jesus is the kingdom in person, and he grants the keys of the kingdom to the local church. Second,

---

[1] This is the thesis of Peter J. Gentry and Stephen J. Wellum, *Kingdom Through Covenant: A Biblical-Theological Understanding of the Covenants* (Wheaton, IL: Crossway, 2012).

[2] For a fuller defense of this idea, see chap. 6 of Jonathan Leeman, *Political Church: The Local Assembly as Embassy of Christ's Rule* (Downers Grove, IL: InterVarsity, forthcoming).

we'll see that baptism is the passport of the kingdom and a kingdom citizen's swearing-in ceremony. It is how the church officially recognizes and affirms one's citizenship in the kingdom of heaven. It is how the church speaks a word of affirmation over a Christian profession. After establishing these two points, we'll tally up their cash value for our overall argument that baptism is required for church membership.

Jesus, the Kingdom, and the Church

Jesus' ministry opens with a stunning claim: "The time is fulfilled, and the kingdom of God is at hand" (Mark 1:15). With these words Jesus claims to be the hinge of history, the fulfillment of God's promises through the prophets, the satisfaction of long centuries of longing. This claim to be the agent of God's kingdom flies as a banner over Jesus' ministry, and the entire New Testament unpacks precisely how Jesus inaugurates the kingdom and what that means for us.

In this first main section of the chapter, we're going to trace crucial connections between Jesus, the kingdom, and the church, ultimately zeroing in on the church's role in the kingdom. We'll begin by seeing that Jesus is the kingdom in person. He executes God's rule on earth and speaks on earth with all the authority of heaven.[3]

The Kingdom in Person

How can Jesus say, "The kingdom of God is at hand"? Is some decisive political upheaval imminent? Will the Jews finally throw off their Roman yoke? Not exactly. What enables Jesus to say that the kingdom of God is at hand is that *he* is among them.[4]

His powerful deeds are proof of this: "But if it is by the Spirit of God that I cast out demons, then the kingdom of God has come upon you" (Matt 12:28).

---

[3] While he doesn't draw all the connections I do below, Miroslav Volf does connect Jesus as the kingdom in person with the founding of the church when he writes, "According to the message of Jesus, the gathering of the people of God is grounded in the coming of the Kingdom of God in his person" (*After Our Likeness: The Church as the Image of the Trinity* [Grand Rapids: Eerdmans, 1999], 128).

[4] My argument in this section is indebted to Dan G. McCartney, "*Ecce Homo*: The Coming of the Kingdom as the Restoration of Human Vicegerency," in *Westminster Theological Journal* 56, no. 1 (1994): 9–10.

Ultimately, Jesus is the kingdom in person because he is God himself, come to his people as a man (Matt 1:21). He proves this by doing what only God can do: he forgives sins (Matt 9:6); he stills a storm with a word (Matt 8:26); he comes to gather the lost sheep of Israel (Matt 15:24), which God had promised to do himself (Ezek 34:15). As all four Gospels demonstrate, Jesus isn't merely a prophet or a king but is God the Son incarnate.[5]

Because Jesus is the kingdom in person, he speaks on earth with all the authority of heaven. In Matthew's Gospel Jesus unilaterally revises not just traditional accretions to the law but even some of Moses' own prescriptions when he states, "You have heard that it was said . . . but I say to you" (Matt 5:21–22, 27–28, 31–32, 33–34, 38–39).[6] No wonder the people marvel: "When Jesus finished these sayings, the crowds were astonished at his teaching, for he was teaching them as one who had authority, and not as their scribes" (Matt 7:28–29; cf. Mark 1:27). Further, Jesus authoritatively declares who will and won't inherit the kingdom of heaven (Matt 5:3; 7:21–23; 8:11–12; 25:31–46). He claims the power to reveal the secrets of the kingdom to those he chooses (Matt 11:27). God the Father twice speaks from heaven, affirming Jesus as his "beloved Son" (Matt 3:17) and urging those on earth to "listen to him" (Matt 17:5). And after his resurrection Jesus declares, "All authority in heaven and on earth has been given to me" (Matt 28:18).

In Jesus, God's kingdom has come to earth because God has come to earth as a man. Therefore, Jesus speaks for heaven on earth. Want to know what God thinks? Ask Jesus.

Jesus Delegates Kingdom Authority to the Local Church

But what about when Jesus isn't around anymore? Who on earth will speak for heaven when Jesus returns there?

---

[5] For one illuminating study of the New Testament's witness to the deity of Christ, see Richard Bauckham, *Jesus and the God of Israel: God Crucified and Other Studies on the New Testament's Christology of Divine Identity* (Grand Rapids: Eerdmans, 2008), especially chap. 1.

[6] I'm focusing on Matthew in this section because the relationship between heaven and earth is uniquely prominent in this Gospel. For a full-scale treatment see Jonathan T. Pennington, *Heaven and Earth in the Gospel of Matthew* (Grand Rapids: Baker, 2009). My argument in this paragraph is informed by Jonathan Leeman, *The Church and the Surprising Offense of God's Love* (Wheaton, IL: Crossway, 2010), 175–76.

In the Gospel of John, Jesus teaches that the Holy Spirit will come and teach Jesus' apostles on his behalf: "But the Helper, the Holy Spirit, whom the Father will send in my name, he will teach you all things and bring to your remembrance all that I have said to you" (John 14:26). Further:

> I still have many things to say to you, but you cannot bear them now. When the Spirit of truth comes, he will guide you into all the truth, for he will not speak on his own authority, but whatever he hears he will speak, and he will declare to you the things that are to come. He will glorify me, for he will take what is mine and declare it to you. All that the Father has is mine; therefore I said that he will take what is mine and declare it to you. (John 16:12–15)

When the Holy Spirit comes, he will glorify Jesus by declaring Jesus' divine knowledge of the Father—including "the things that are to come"—to Jesus' apostles. Jesus promises that the Spirit will enable the apostles to faithfully remember Jesus' teaching—teaching that is now preserved in the four Gospels. And he promises that the Spirit will guide them into "all the truth," including the truth about the future. This promise of revelation undergirds the apostles' authority in the church, and it guarantees the truthfulness of their teaching, which is preserved in the New Testament.[7] To put it in governmental terms—remember, we're talking about a kingdom—Jesus' promise of the Spirit to the apostles guarantees the total trustworthiness of his kingdom's written constitution. Today Jesus speaks to his churches, and to all people everywhere, through the Spirit-inspired apostolic writings of the New Testament, together with the Spirit-inspired prophetic writings of the Old.

But this isn't the only way Jesus intends to be represented on earth during the interval of his physical absence from us. Let's return to Matthew's Gospel. Remember that God charged Israel to represent his rule on earth as a kingdom of priests (Exod 19:5–6) in order to display his glory to the nations (Deut 4:5–8). Yet by and large Israel rejected Jesus, the living embodiment of God's glory and rule. Their leaders hardened themselves against John the Baptist's call to repent, trusting instead in their Abrahamic ancestry (Matt 3:9; cf. 21:32). Instead of recognizing Jesus' authority, they indicted him for neglecting their

---

[7] See Scott Swain's discussion of "The Inspiration and Perfection of Holy Scripture" in *Trinity, Revelation, and Reading: A Theological Introduction to the Bible and Its Interpretation* (London: T&T Clark, 2011), chap. 3.

traditions (Matt 12:10; 15:2). Therefore Jesus warned his disciples not to heed them (Matt 16:5–12) and announced that they would soon be removed from office. Because these tenant farmers of God's vineyard would eventually kill not only his messengers the prophets but even God's own Son, Jesus declares: "Therefore I tell you, the kingdom of God will be taken away from you and given to a people producing its fruits" (Matt 21:43).

Notice that last phrase: the kingdom will not just be taken away from Israel and its representative leaders but will be *given* to a new people. Dan McCartney helpfully explains that the kingdom anticipated in Israel and inaugurated by Jesus is the restoration of humankind's "vicegerency": Adam's dominion over the earth as God's appointed representative.[8] Therefore, when Jesus says the kingdom will be taken away from the chief priests and Pharisees and given to another nation, "it is not that they are no longer subject to God's sovereign control, but that they have been disinherited from their vicegerency. On the other hand, the disciples of Jesus are given sovereignty. He tells them, 'I will give you the keys of the kingdom,' and he confers on them powers of binding and loosing."[9] To these keys of the kingdom, these powers of binding and loosing, we now turn.[10]

In Matthew 16:13 Jesus asks the disciples who people say he is, and then he asks the disciples who *they* say he is. Peter, probably on behalf of all, answers in verse 16, "You are the Messiah, the Son of the living God!" Jesus affirms Peter's answer and explains that Peter came to this right understanding because God himself revealed it to him. He continues in verses 18 and 19: "And I tell you, you are Peter, and on this rock I will build my church, and the gates of hell shall not prevail against it. I will give you the keys of the kingdom of heaven, and whatever you bind on earth shall be bound in heaven, and whatever you loose on earth will be loosed in heaven."

How will Jesus build his church? He will build it "on this rock," a play on Peter's name. Jesus probably means that he will build the church on Peter as one rightly confessing Jesus' identity. As Edmund Clowney puts it, "The

---

[8] McCartney, "Ecce Homo," 1–21.

[9] Ibid., 18.

[10] For more thorough exegesis in support of the following argument, see Leeman, *The Church and the Surprising Offense*, 174–94; also *Political Church*, chap. 6. My presentation of the issues here is also indebted to Leeman's concise discussion in *Church Membership: How the World Knows Who Represents Jesus* (Wheaton, IL: Crossway, 2012), chap. 3.

confession cannot be separated from Peter, neither can Peter be separated from his confession."[11]

Jesus then gives to Peter and the apostles the "keys of the kingdom of heaven" (v. 19). This grants them the authority to act as God's authorized representatives on earth for affirming those who, like Peter, truly confess that Jesus is the Messiah. When the apostles "bind and loose," they are affirming that a true confession of faith in Jesus has been uttered. In other words, they are formally recognizing both a *what* (a true confession) and a *who* (the person uttering it). In light of Matthew 18:15–20, to "bind" someone is to affirm that person's profession and hence add them to the church. And to "loose," as we'll see, is the opposite: it is to reject the credibility of their confession and hence remove them from the church. Both of these acts, Jesus says, represent a heavenly verdict: "Whatever you bind on earth shall be bound in heaven, and whatever you loose on earth shall be loosed in heaven" (Matt 16:19). In other words, "the apostles had heaven's authority for declaring who on earth is a kingdom citizen and therefore represents heaven."[12]

Two chapters later, in Matthew 18:15–20, we see an application of this power of the keys.[13] How should Jesus' disciples react when sinned against? First, confront the person privately, aiming for repentance and reconciliation (v. 15). If the person doesn't repent, bring along one or two others (v. 16). If the person won't hear them, involve the whole church. And if the person won't listen to the entire church, then the church is to exclude that person from their fellowship, treating him or her as an outsider (v. 17).

Immediately following, Jesus again introduces the keys of the kingdom of heaven: whatever the congregation binds on earth will be bound in heaven, and whatever it looses on earth will be loosed in heaven (18:18). Jesus is not speaking here about the apostles or a scattered, noninstitutional, universal church. He's describing a local church, a concrete gathering of believers. Therefore, the keys of the kingdom Jesus gave to the apostles are ultimately handed to the local church. This means that "the local church has heaven's authority for

---

[11] Edmund P. Clowney, *The Church*, Contours of Theology (Downers Grove, IL: InterVarsity, 1995), 40.

[12] Leeman, *Church Membership*, 59.

[13] On 18:18 as an application of the authority of the keys, see D. A. Carson, *Matthew*, in The Expositor's Bible Commentary, vol. 8, ed. Frank Gaebelin (Grand Rapids: Zondervan, 1984), 374.

declaring who on earth is a kingdom citizen and therefore represents heaven."[14] In so doing, the local church makes Jesus' heavenly kingdom visible on earth. By identifying and uniting kingdom citizens, the local church constitutes kingdom territory on earth.[15]

This church-commissioning work of Matthew 16 and 18 culminates in Matthew 28:18–20. As in chapters 16 and 18, Jesus here invokes the authority of heaven: "All authority in heaven and on earth has been given to me" (v. 18). As in the other two passages, Jesus authorizes his disciples to act as heaven's representatives, that is, to act *in his name*: "Go therefore and make disciples of all nations, baptizing them in the name of the Father and of the Son and of the Holy Spirit" (v. 19). So we see that the church's founding charter includes not merely affirming disciples but making disciples—by proclaiming the gospel to them, baptizing them, and instructing them to obey all of Jesus' teachings.[16]

To put all this together, think of the local church as the divinely appointed embassy of the kingdom of heaven. An embassy "declares its *home nation*'s interests to the *host nation*, and it protects the citizens of the home nation who happen to be visiting the host nation."[17] As an embassy, the church is subject to the authority of its home nation: the kingdom of Christ. As we've seen, this kingdom's written constitution is Spirit-inspired Scripture. In submission to this authority, the church is authorized to announce to its host nation—that is, all the nations of the earth—who does and does not belong to its home nation, the kingdom of heaven.

---

[14] Leeman, *Church Membership*, 61.

[15] John Owen similarly wrote: "The *institution of these churches* is the way which Christ hath ordained to render his kingdom visible or conspicuous, in distinction from and opposition unto the kingdom of Satan and the world. And he doth not, in a due manner, declare himself a subject in or unto the kingdom of Christ who doth not solemnly engage in this way" (*An Inquiry into the Original, Nature, Institution, Power, Order, and Communion of Evangelical Churches*, in *The Works of John Owen*, ed. William H Goold, vol. 15 [repr., Edinburgh: Banner of Truth Trust, 1965], 326, emphasis original). Note how Owen correlates churches' representative authority with the necessity of church membership. Because local churches make the kingdom visible, Christians who do not join a church fail to "in a due manner" declare themselves kingdom citizens.

[16] For discussion of Matt 28:18–20 in relation to 16:18–19 and 18:15–20, see Leeman, *The Church and the Surprising Offense*, 182–83, 191. See also Pennington, *Heaven and Earth*, 205: "The authority given to Jesus in 28:18 likely echoes and grounds the authority given to the church by Jesus as found in 16:19 and 18:18, texts that famously use the same type of heaven and earth language."

[17] Leeman, *Church Membership*, 27, emphasis original.

Of course, the church does not *make* anyone a citizen. We become citizens of the kingdom through faith in the king. Yet an embassy does have the authority to formally affirm one's citizenship. If you're traveling abroad and your passport expires, the US embassy can renew your passport, officially validating your claim to be an American citizen.

This is precisely the kind of authority Jesus has granted to the local church. The local church hears a confession, considers the life of the confessor, and by including or excluding that person the church delivers a judgment to both the church and the world that bears the authority of heaven. In that sense a local church is also like a president's press secretary. The press secretary does not make up the president's mind for him. He cannot create executive policy. But he does formally, publicly declare the mind of the president. Is it possible for him to slip up in the press room and then issue a retraction? Absolutely. But mistakes on his part do not dissolve the authority by which he speaks for the president.

A Church-Constituting Charter

This grant of authority from Jesus is what makes a church a church, what makes "church" mean something more than "Christians" in the plural. In other words the keys of the kingdom are an institutional charter. Seventeenth-century Congregationalist Thomas Goodwin said as much when he described Matthew 16:19 as "the first Charter granted by the Founder" of the church.[18]

In addition to giving a church its churchness, this institutional charter also gives a church its marching orders. The keys of the kingdom give the local church the authority and the responsibility to affirm as kingdom citizens those who credibly profess faith in Christ, identifying them with God and God's people; to oversee the discipleship of those so affirmed by teaching them to obey Christ's commands; to exclude those whose lives render their professions incredible; and to make new disciples, identifying them with the Father, Son, and Holy Spirit through baptism.[19]

---

[18] Cited in Hunter Powell, *The Dissenting Brethren and the Power of the Keys, 1640–1644* (PhD diss., University of Cambridge, 2011), 75. See also Goodwin's statement that the "grand charter of the power of the keys" is granted only to a local, congregational church (Thomas Goodwin, *Of the Constitution, Right Order, and Government of the Churches of Christ, in The Works of Thomas Goodwin*, vol. 11 [repr., Eureka, CA: Tanski, 1996], 8).

[19] Leeman, *The Church and the Surprising Offense*, 194–95.

We began this section by seeing that Jesus is the kingdom in person. He speaks on earth with all the authority of heaven. But when Jesus inaugurated his kingdom on earth and returned to heaven for a time (Acts 1:11; 3:21), he did not leave himself without a witness. He sent the Spirit to impart his authoritative teaching to his apostles and through them to the church across time and space. And he also delegated authority to the church to act as the embassy of the kingdom.

In submission to Scripture, the kingdom's authoritative constitution, the local church is responsible to affirm true gospel professions by uniting to itself true gospel professors. Conversely, the church is responsible to protect the name of Christ by removing from its number those who say "Lord, Lord" but do not do the will of Jesus' Father in heaven (Matt 7:21). The church represents Christ's kingdom on earth in order to display Jesus' glory and guard his reputation until he comes again.

The Passport of the Kingdom and the Citizen's Oath of Office

If the keys of the kingdom are a church-constituting charter, how is this charter enacted on earth? How does this blueprint become a reality? We'll answer this question in two steps. The first focuses on the church as a corporate whole and the second on the individual's entrance into that whole. Together these two steps comprise the second main move of the chapter. We've seen that the church is the kingdom's embassy; now we'll discover that baptism is its passport. And, from the opposite angle, baptism is a kingdom citizen's swearing-in ceremony.

How Is This Heavenly Charter Enacted on Earth?

In order to see how this heavenly charter is enacted on earth, we first need to ask, how does a church come into existence?

In brief, a church comes into existence through the mutual, covenant-like commitment of its members to exercise the keys of the kingdom.[20] Consider

---

[20] Throughout the economy of redemption, God's action precedes and enables human action. Thus John Webster is exactly right to say, "First, the church is a human assembly or form of association. But its human act of assembly follows, signifies, and mediates a divine act of gathering; it is a moved movement of congregation" (John Webster, "'In the Society of God': Some Principles of Ecclesiology," in *Perspectives on Ecclesiology and Ethnography*,

what Jesus says in Matthew 18:19–20. After repeating his promise that whatever the church binds on earth will be bound in heaven, he says, "Again I say to you, if two of you agree on earth about anything they ask, it will be done for them by my Father in heaven. For where two or three are gathered in my name, there am I among them." The "asking" here is related to the exercise of the keys of the kingdom, as the context makes clear. Further, note that Jesus speaks of two or three who are gathered in his name, that is, in his authority. This passage isn't about two Christians who happen to run into each other in the grocery store. Instead, it's about believers who have formally joined together to carry out the charter Jesus has granted to his people.

Since the English Reformation, Baptists and other proponents of a free-church ecclesiology have described this church-constituting pact as a covenant. Consider, for instance, how the Charleston Baptist Association's 1774 *Summary of Church Discipline* defines a local church: "A particular gospel church consists of a company of saints incorporated by a special covenant into one distinct body, and meeting together in one place, for the enjoyment of fellowship with each other and with Christ their head, in all his institutions, to their mutual edification and the glory of God through the Spirit, *2 Cor. 8:5, Acts 2:1.*"[21]

According to this Baptist network, a church becomes a church when its members covenant with one another, bringing into being "one distinct body." This echoes the Congregationalist confession of 1648 known as the Cambridge Platform, which states: "A congregational church, is by the institution of Christ a part of the militant visible church, consisting of a holy company of saints by calling, united into one body, by a holy covenant, for the public worship of God, and the mutual edification of one another, in the fellowship of the Lord Jesus."[22]

The "holy covenant" is what unites the church "into one body." And, although seventeenth-century Congregationalists distanced themselves from the earlier Separatists, their language agrees with Separatists such as Robert Browne:

---

ed. Pete Ward [Grand Rapids: Eerdmans, 2012], 216). In this section I assume God's action whereby he regenerates people through the Spirit's application of the gospel. I attempt to describe only the human element in the "moved movement of congregation" whereby a local church comes into existence.

[21] The Baptist Association in Charleston, South Carolina, *A Summary of Church Discipline* (Charleston: David Bruce, 1774) in *Polity: Biblical Arguments on How to Conduct Church Life*, ed. Mark Dever (Washington, DC: Center for Church Reform, 2001), 118.

[22] Reprinted in *The Reformation of the Church: A Collection of Reformed and Puritan Documents on Church Issues*, ed. Iain H. Murray (Edinburgh: Banner of Truth, 1965), 245.

"The Church planted or gathered, is a company or number of Christians or believers, which by a willing covenant made with their God, are under the government of God and Christ, and keep his laws in one holy communion."[23]

Sometimes this act of covenanting has been explicitly tied to the power of the keys of the kingdom. For instance, not long after Browne wrote, during his Separatist period John Smyth grounded the exercise of the keys in this church-constituting covenant: "The power of binding and loosing is given to the body of the Church, even to two or three faithful people joined together in covenant, and this we prove evidently in this manner. Unto whom the covenant is given, unto them the power of binding and loosing is given."[24]

What all these definitional statements have in common is that a church becomes a church through the mutual pledge of its members. The line between "not yet a church" and "now a church" is crossed by the "covenant" Christians make with one another. This solemn commitment is what invests a group of believers with the keys of the kingdom. Before this covenant, they have no authority over one another and do not formally represent Christ's kingdom to the world. When they covenant, they assume responsibility for one another's lives and doctrine, and they create a new embassy of Christ's kingdom on earth.

Baptism as Passport of the Kingdom and Oath of Office

I think this classical free church account of how a church comes into being basically hits the mark because it works out the implications of a passage like Matthew 18:19–20. Yet given the existence of a local church so constituted, how does a new believer come to have his kingdom citizenship recognized and affirmed by a church? Given the existence of a kingdom embassy, by what means does that embassy grant legal standing to an individual? I'd argue that the initial mechanism for this is baptism. To stretch our embassy metaphor slightly, baptism is the passport of the kingdom. It's how the church identifies

---

[23] Robert Browne, *The Writings of Robert Harrison and Robert Browne*, ed. Albert Peel and Leland H. Carlson (London: Allen & Unwin, 1953), 253 (spelling modernized). See discussion of this passage in Jason K. Lee, *The Theology of John Smyth: Puritan, Separatist, Baptist, Mennonite* (Macon, GA: Mercer University Press, 2003), 128–29.

[24] *The Works of John Smyth, Fellow of Christ's College, 1594–1598*, 2 vols., ed. William Thomas Whitley (London: Cambridge University Press, 1915), 2:388–89 (spelling modernized). See discussion in Lee, *Theology of John Smyth*, 143.

someone as a kingdom citizen. It's also an oath of office, the means by which a kingdom citizen pledges loyalty to the king and to his fellow citizens.

Many scholars have pointed out that three parties are active in baptism: God, the church, and the one being baptized.[25] To discern baptism's function as passport of the kingdom and oath of citizenship, we need to consider baptism from the standpoint of the church, then of the individual being baptized.

From the standpoint of the church, consider again that baptism is into the "name" of the Father, Son, and Holy Spirit (Matt 28:19). As we saw in the previous chapter, this is the language of covenantal identification. And who on earth has the authority to identify a person with the God of heaven? As we've just seen, that's precisely the authority Jesus has granted to the local church. When a church baptizes someone, they identify him or her as a member of the new covenant, a citizen of the kingdom, someone who belongs to God and God's people. Jonathan Leeman says it well:

> Through baptism people are formally reinstated to Adam's original political office and the body politic of Jesus' church. The keys of the kingdom are exercised first *through* baptism. Baptism is the recognition of kingdom citizenship. . . . In the same way that good works function as a badge or passport of authentic faith, so baptism functions as the public badge or passport among Christ's people and the nations now.[26]

When the church baptizes a person, it affirms him as a true confessor making a true confession. It publicly endorses that person's kingdom citizenship.[27] Thus, the initial and initiating means by which the church enacts its institutional charter and exercises the keys of the kingdom is baptism. Just as a passport attests someone's citizenship *in this country* as opposed to all others, so baptism declares a person's citizenship in God's kingdom over against all competing powers.

---

[25] E.g., James D. G. Dunn, *Baptism in the Holy Spirit: A Re-Examination of the New Testament Teaching on the Gift of the Spirit in Relation to Pentecostalism Today,* 2nd ed. (London: SCM, 2010), 101, 224.

[26] Leeman, *Political Church*, chap. 6. Cf. also *The Church and the Surprising Offense*, 191, 267–68.

[27] Brandon Jones writes: "Thus, the local church's decision to baptize a believer represents God's and his one people's reception, acceptance, and support of the believer. . . . Baptism marks confirmation that one is now part of God's universal church, and it assures believers that they are part of the communion of the saints" (*Waters of Promise: Finding Meaning in Believer Baptism* [Eugene, OR: Pickwick, 2012], 138).

This brings us to the perspective of the one being baptized. If we become citizens of the kingdom through faith in the king, then baptism is like a swearing-in ceremony for the office of "citizen."[28] As we saw last chapter, in baptism you pledge allegiance to Christ as king, declaring supreme loyalty to the Triune God. To be baptized into Jesus' name is to submit to his authority, to commit to obey him as Lord (Matt 28:19). Thus, in baptism, you swear an oath of citizenship and are thereby formally recognized as a citizen of the kingdom of Christ.

Recall that baptism is the initiating oath-sign of the new covenant and that the new covenant creates a new people. When an individual swears this oath, he joins the company of all who have sworn the same oath. And as we've seen, this company's institutional shape is defined by the keys of the kingdom. The keys of the kingdom give the new covenant a visible shape on earth by creating the public space it occupies: the local church. Thus, in the same act by which a new believer pledges allegiance to Christ as Lord, he also pledges his submission to Christ's people. In coming under Christ's rule, he steps into his realm. In baptism a new convert not only ratifies a covenant with God; he also makes a covenant with God's people.[29] Normally, the two are not only inseparable but coincident. Balthasar Hubmaier described this richly:

> Where there is no water baptism, there is no church nor minister, neither brother nor sister, no brotherly admonition, excommunication, or reacceptance. I am speaking here of the visible church as Christ did in Matthew 18:15ff. There must also exist an outward confession or testimony through which visible brothers and sisters can know each other, since faith exists only in the heart. But when he receives the baptism of water the one who is baptized testifies publicly that he has pledged himself henceforth to live according to the Rule of Christ. By virtue of this pledge he has submitted himself to sisters, brothers, and to

---

[28] "And baptism, like a presidential inauguration ceremony, formally establishes a believer in office, even though it is not what *makes* one a believer, just like the inauguration ceremony does not *make* one president" (Leeman, *Political Church*, chap. 6).

[29] To borrow a term from historic Congregational and Baptist discussions, baptism may be viewed as an "implicit" covenant between the individual and the church since the act itself does not necessarily involve an explicit verbal commitment to the church. However, in chap. 4 we saw that symbolic acts can take the place of verbal oaths in covenant ratification, and baptism is just such an oath-sign. Thus, insofar as baptism pledges one's fidelity to both Christ and the church, it can legitimately be described as making a covenant with the church—with or without the qualifier "implicit." We'll revisit this issue in chap. 7.

the church so that when he transgresses they now have the authority to admonish, punish, ban, and reaccept him. But this is not the case with those who are still outside. . . . Where does this authority come from, if not from the pledge of baptism?[30]

Notice how Hubmaier weaves together all the main points we've developed in the past three chapters. Since "faith exists only in the heart," Hubmaier argues that baptism is where faith goes public. It is the means by which Christians are first able to recognize one another as brothers and sisters (chap. 3). In speaking about baptism as a pledge of obedience, he implicitly treats it as a covenant oath (chap. 4).[31] And he sets all this in the context of the church's authority to assess the confessions and lives of those who profess to be Jesus' disciples. Though he doesn't use the term "keys of the kingdom," Hubmaier does refer to Matthew 18:15ff., and he speaks of the church's responsibility to admonish and even excommunicate its erring members.

Crucially, Hubmaier roots this authority in the submission enacted in baptism: "Where does this authority come from, if not from the pledge of baptism?" In baptism one pledges to obey God and submit to the church. In baptism one enters the company of the saints and invites their admonition. Baptism is the means by which one acknowledges the sovereign authority of God *by* coming under the authority of the church.

To come full circle, Hubmaier addresses the question, "What makes a church a church?" when he writes, "Where there is no water baptism, there is no church." Without a public pledge of loyalty to God and submission to God's people, there is no public people. Without baptism, there may be self-proclaimed kingdom persons, but there is no kingdom *people*—no body politic. Given the church's responsibility to wield the keys of the kingdom, without a means of marking off its members, the church itself simply does not exist.

From the viewpoint of an individual believer, baptism is analogous to an oath of office. It is the means by which one pledges to fulfill one's responsibilities to King Jesus and one's fellow citizens of the kingdom. And insofar as baptism is the act of a local church toward an individual believer, it's analogous to

---

[30] Balthasar Hubmaier, "On the Christian Baptism of Believers," in *Balthasar Hubmaier: Theologian of Anabaptism*, ed. H. Wayne Pipkin and John Howard Yoder, Classics of the Radical Reformation, vol. 5 (Scottdale, PA: Herald, 1989), 127.

[31] Cf. also Hubmaier's statement that baptism is a "sacramental oath" ("On Fraternal Admonition," in Pipkin and Yoder, *Balthasar Hubmaier*, 384).

a passport which demonstrates citizenship in the kingdom. It formally affirms a person as a kingdom citizen, and it grants proof of their citizenship to the nations and to every other embassy of the kingdom scattered across the globe. In baptism the individual speaks to God and the church, and the church speaks for God to the individual. This is one sense in which baptism and a passport correspond closely. If a Christian is baptized in Chicago and then moves to Detroit, he does not need to be rebaptized in order to join a church in Detroit. He brings his baptism with him and reports it to the church like a tourist handing his passport to an embassy official.

Three Payoffs

In this chapter I've made two main moves. First, I've argued that Jesus is the kingdom in person and that he has authorized local churches to serve as embassies of his kingdom. This grant of the keys of the kingdom is the institutional charter for the local church. It's what makes a church a church.

Second, I've argued that this institutional charter is exercised through baptism. Baptism is the swearing-in ceremony for citizens of the kingdom. It's the means by which one pledges to obey God and submit to God's people. And from the church's standpoint, baptism is the passport of the kingdom. It's a badge of identity the church grants to a new believer as a public affirmation of that person's confession of faith in Jesus. Both the church and the individual speak in baptism.

This chapter's survey of baptism's relationship to the keys of the kingdom has three primary payoffs for this book's argument that baptism is required for church membership: First, it helps us unite, and rightly relate, the kingdom, the new covenant, and the local church. Second, it provides a thicker account of the ecclesial shape of baptism, confirming the conclusion that baptism is required for church membership. Third, it demonstrates that baptism confers church membership; it constitutes someone a "church member." Therefore, it is an effective sign of church membership.

Rightly Relating Kingdom, New Covenant, and Local Church

First, understanding baptism as the initial exercise of the keys of the kingdom helps us unite, and rightly relate, the kingdom, the new covenant, and the local church. The keys of the kingdom define the earthly, institutional shape of the new covenant, which is the local church. From another angle we can say that the new covenant is representatively, institutionally enacted on earth by the local church's exercise of the keys of the kingdom.

As we saw in chapter 4, the new covenant is not merely an invisible register of the redeemed but a public pact which creates a body politic. Even as the new covenant consists, in part, in invisible, spiritual realities, its existence on earth is visibly manifested in local churches. The local church is the public administration of the new covenant.[32]

But what about those who profess to believe in Christ, and belong to the church, but are not spiritually regenerate? Doesn't their inevitable presence sever any real relationship between the new covenant and local church membership? Or what about those who truly believe in Christ but haven't been baptized and don't belong to a local church? In response I'd simply return to the idea of representation that inheres in the keys of the kingdom. An embassy that mistakenly affirms a noncitizen as a citizen does not thereby cease to be an embassy. And a citizen without a passport is still a citizen, though certain privileges of citizenship might be withheld until he obtains one.

Proponents of regenerate church membership, myself included, freely admit that the membership of the new covenant—those written in the Lamb's book of life (Rev 21:27)—does not equal the sum total of the members of all churches throughout all time. Yet that doesn't mean new covenant membership and local church membership are hermetically sealed off from each other. Instead, to adapt a term from John Webster, there exists between them a "relation-in-distinction."[33] The distinction, of course, is that they're not identical: some church members are false professors, and some true Christians are not church members. The relation is the representative link established by the keys of

---

[32] John Owen writes, "*The visible administration of the kingdom of Christ* in this world consists in this church-state, with the administration of his institutions and laws therein" (in Goold, *Inquiry*, 333, emphasis original). And the new covenant is not far from view since "God's covenant with his people is the foundation of every church-state, of all offices, powers, privileges, and duties thereto belonging" (ibid., 329).

[33] Webster writes, "Much of the particular character of evangelical ecclesiology turns upon articulating in the right way the relation-in-distinction between the gospel and the church—'relation,' because the gospel concerns fellowship between God and creatures; 'distinction,' because that fellowship, even in its mutuality, is always a miracle of unilateral grace" (John B. Webster, "The Church and the Perfection of God," in *The Community of the Word: Toward an Evangelical Ecclesiology*, ed. Mark Husbands and Daniel J. Treier [Downers Grove, IL: InterVarsity, 2005], 76).

the kingdom: what the church declares on earth is backed by the authority of heaven (Matt 16:19). The church's authority is representative and declarative. It is commissioned by Jesus to mark off the boundaries of the new covenant's earthly shape—to identify the people of the new covenant, the citizens of the kingdom. And the initial and initiating means by which it does this is baptism.

In order to rightly define baptism's relationship to church membership, we need to discern whether baptism has an ecclesial shape—that is, whether there are any intrinsic links between baptism and the church. But it's equally true that we need to make sure our doctrine of the church is in working order in the first place. Hubmaier was right to argue, "Where there is no baptism, there is no church." But we can only grasp his point if we already understand the public, representative, embassy-like authority of the local church. If church is nothing more than "Christians" plural, what does membership mean in the first place?

The church's delegated authority to mark off kingdom citizens before the world is a crucial piece of ecclesiology to put in place before we can understand baptism's relation to membership. And when we do, and we then go on to see that baptism is that means of marking off kingdom citizens, we can rightly relate the kingdom, the new covenant, and the local church.

A Thicker Account of the Ecclesial Shape of Baptism

A second payoff of this chapter's argument is that it gives a thicker account of baptism's ecclesial shape. It clarifies that baptism is not merely an individual ordinance but a badge of belonging. It makes baptism's identity-defining, church-shaping role that much more explicit.

The keys of the kingdom are the church's institutional charter. What are the keys for? Identifying who is and is not a Christian. And baptism is the initial exercise of the keys. Thus baptism identifies someone as a Christian before the church and the world. Contra Bunyan's assertion that baptism is "no characteristical note to another of my Sonship with God,"[34] the keys of the kingdom teach us that baptism is nothing less than a church's formal, public endorsement of someone's claim to be a Christian.

---

[34] John Bunyan, *Differences in Judgment about Water-Baptism, No Bar to Communion*, in *The Miscellaneous Works of John Bunyan*, vol. 4, ed. T. L. Underwood (Oxford: Clarendon Press, 1989), 216.

How can kingdom citizens tell one another apart from the world? Materially, by their professions of faith and godly lives; formally, by their baptism. And how does a church identify those for whose professions it assumes responsibility? By baptizing them. How can a church tell whether someone new to town who claims to be a kingdom citizen really is? The answer includes, though isn't limited to, asking, "Do they have a passport?"[35]

Because baptism is the passport of the kingdom, baptism is a necessary though not sufficient criterion by which the church is to recognize someone as a Christian. Think of baptism as Christianity's team jersey; it publicly identifies which side you're on.[36] And identification is for recognition: the players on a football team identify themselves with a red jersey for the purpose of recognizing one another when they're mixing it up on the field with a blue-jerseyed team. Because baptism is how a church publicly identifies someone as a Christian, it's also the formal criterion by which it recognizes someone as a Christian.[37]

Church membership is a relationship in which the church affirms an individual's profession of faith and oversees his discipleship, and the individual submits to and serves the church. If baptism is a necessary criterion for recognizing and affirming someone's profession of faith, then by definition it is necessary for church membership. Church members and leaders might be convinced in their own private judgment that an unbaptized (or paedo-"baptized") applicant for membership is a Christian, but Jesus has bound the

---

[35] Augustus Strong makes a similar point when he writes in support of requiring baptism for participation in the Lord's Supper, "A foreigner may love this country, but he cannot vote at our elections unless he has been naturalized" (Augustus H. Strong, *Systematic Theology* [repr., Valley Forge, PA: Judson Press, 1977], 978).

[36] Stanley Fowler writes, "Within the New Testament it seems to be assumed that those who believe in Christ are an identifiable group, which implies the existence of some definitive mark of identification, and baptism is apparently that mark" (*More than a Symbol: The British Baptist Recovery of Baptismal Sacramentalism*, Studies in Baptist History and Thought 2 [Carlisle: Paternoster, 2002], 202).

[37] While he doesn't address baptism per se, John Owen makes a corroborating point when he argues, "Farther, Mark viii. 34–38, Matt x. 33, he hath appointed this church-state as the way and means whereby they may jointly and visibly make profession of this their subjection to him, dependence on him, and freedom in the observation of all his commands. He will not have this done singly and personally only, but in society and conjunction" (in Goold, *Inquiry*, 264). In other words, Christians declare themselves Jesus' subjects not as isolated individuals but by entering into church membership. All I am adding to Owen is that baptism is the initial, initiating form of this profession and entry.

church's judgment to baptism. Churches are to recognize as Christians those who have gone public with their faith. And the means Jesus has appointed for that is baptism.

Baptism Confers Church Membership—It Constitutes One a "Church Member"

The third payoff is that, normally speaking, baptism confers church membership; it constitutes someone a "church member." Therefore, baptism is an effective sign of church membership: it creates the ecclesial reality to which it points.

Consider Acts 2:41: "So those who received his word were baptized, and there were added that day about three thousand souls." What were these 3,000 added to? The Jerusalem church.[38] Luke writes of pre-Pentecost days that "the company of persons was in all about 120" (Acts 1:15). So these new believers are being added to a distinct, identifiable, local body. Note that Luke uses the passive voice here in Acts 2:41 (cf. 5:14; 11:24), but in 2:47 says, "And *the Lord* added to their number day by day those who were being saved." This seems to indicate that when Luke says in Acts 2:41 that "there were added that day," he's not referring to being "added to the church" as a distinct step in the process, following faith and baptism. Instead, he is emphasizing the Lord's sovereign work in saving sinners, which enables their decision to believe and be baptized (cf. 16:14).

How then were these 3,000 people added to the church? The only answer the context offers is baptism. If they had privately believed in Jesus but not been baptized, no one would have known of their faith, and they certainly wouldn't have been added to the church. And the text doesn't show us a distinct step of "joining the church" after baptism. So Luke's summary "were added" seems to tell us that baptism was the means by which people entered the church in its

---

[38] Cf. Beasley-Murray's comments on this passage: "Apart from an explicit statement, words could hardly have expressed more clearly the conviction that by baptism the convert forsakes the Israel that had rejected the Messiah, to join the community that owned His sovereignty." He writes further, "In such circumstances baptism was a genuine demarcation of the Church from the world which none would consider passing through without strong conviction" (George R. Beasley-Murray, *Baptism in the New Testament* [repr.; Grand Rapids: Eerdmans, 1973], 104, 283). Further, Beasley-Murray argues that the New Testament presents baptism "as entrance into the church in the fullest sense—that is, as initiating local church membership" (ibid., 283).

earliest days. And we have no reason to think that any New Testament church departed from this pattern.

Of course, there's at least one instance of baptism which departs from this pattern: the Ethiopian eunuch in Acts 8:26–40. The salient point here is that the Ethiopian eunuch doesn't live in Jerusalem, and there's no church where he lives. If a church doesn't yet exist, it's impossible for baptism to add someone to the church. The discrepancy between those added to the Jerusalem church and the Ethiopian eunuch's baptism is explained by the fact that baptism follows the gospel even more closely than the church does, by a factor of one or two people. When the Ethiopian eunuch was baptized, the church had not yet caught up with the gospel.

As the gospel spreads into a totally "ungospeled" area, whoever first believes will be baptized but will not yet be a member of a church because there are no fellow believers with whom to constitute a church. Yet as soon as even one or two others are converted and baptized, they can and should form a church (Matt 18:20). On the front lines of gospel expansion, baptism immediately follows an individual's profession, and the church follows as soon as there are multiple Christians to constitute it. Thus, one could say that the Ethiopian eunuch's baptism gained its full, ecclesial meaning when the gospel brought a church into being in Ethiopia.

Yet normally speaking, baptism initiates and confers church membership. For new converts baptism is the New Testament way to join a church.[39] If baptism is the new covenant's initiating oath-sign, and if it is the swearing-in ceremony in which believers pronounce their oath of office, then *by that very act* those who undergo baptism are united to the church. If in baptism the believer submits to the church, and the church affirms and commits themselves to the believer, then baptism constitutes someone a "church member." There's no missing step for which we need an extra category with its own label. Church membership is a relationship of affirmation, oversight, and submission between a church and a

---

[39] Recall Beasley-Murray's comments in the previous note; also Robert H. Stein, "Baptism and Becoming a Christian in the New Testament," in *Southern Baptist Journal of Theology* 2, no. 1 (1998): 14. Cf. Jason Lee, summarizing John Smyth, "To enter the public body of the church, the covenant offered by God must be agreed upon by the individual. The individual makes his consent visible to fellow believers through the sign of baptism" (Jason K. Lee, "Baptism and Covenant," in *Restoring Integrity in Baptist Churches*, ed. Thomas White, Jason G. Duesing, and Malcolm B. Yarnell III [Grand Rapids: Kregel, 2008], 135).

believer, and baptism begins that relationship. Just like walking through a door initiates your presence in a house, baptism initiates the relation we call "church membership." Baptism is therefore an effective sign of church membership.[40]

What if someone were to argue that baptism initiates one into the universal church, not a local church? I agree that there is a sense in which baptism initiates one into the universal church as it is visibly, publicly expressed on earth. Just as Christians all share one faith and one Lord, so also there is one and only one baptism (Eph 4:5). And as I said, when a Christian converted in Chicago moves to Detroit, he need not be baptized again; he brings his baptism with him. Baptism is an affirmation of kingdom citizenship. And local churches, as embassies of the kingdom, are bound to affirm all the kingdom citizens they are presented with. Thus, insofar as baptism is an affirmation of kingdom citizenship, it confers a status which transcends the local church that grants it.

However, the universal church exists institutionally on earth only in local churches. The only "place" where the universal church exists on earth is the local church. There is no organized, political institution on earth called "the universal church."[41] Thus God intends for universal church membership to be realized in local church membership—that's the whole point of the keys of the kingdom.

This explains why Paul can slide so casually between universal and local in 1 Corinthians 12. Remember that in verse 13 Paul says, "For in one Spirit we were all baptized into one body." Assuming there's at least a secondary

---

[40] Note carefully that baptism's "effectiveness" is ecclesial, not soteriolgical. Baptism neither creates faith nor confers forgiveness. Baptism is prompted by faith and is an act of faith. Thus, faith must precede baptism, even though baptism should be the first formal, public act faith performs. Certainly baptism has a "vertical" component in that it is the way a believer formally ratifies the terms of the new covenant. As we've seen, it is a Godward appeal and pledge (1 Pet 3:21). But when I describe baptism as an effective sign, I have in mind the new *social*, *ecclesial* reality which baptism creates. Though I wouldn't agree with all of his conclusions, James McClendon is on-point when he calls baptism a "performative sign" in this context: "It is a prayer, but an acted prayer rather than just a spoken one. Like every petition, it is performative. It is also a 'word' from the church to the candidate—a 'word' in which the church says something like: 'We receive you as our brother in Christ.' And it is a 'word' from the candidate to the church, a 'word' in which the candidate says something like: 'Brethren, I take my place in your midst. Receive me!'" (James W. McClendon, "Baptism as a Performative Sign," *Theology Today* 23 [1966]: 410).

[41] For a theological defense of this stance see Volf, *After Our Likeness*, 154–58. Of course, Presbyterians and others holding to a connectional polity will disagree. Yet that disagreement would not endanger the main thrust of my argument since all Protestants see the local church as a necessary manifestation of the universal.

reference to water baptism here, exactly what body were we baptized into? Verse 12 would seem to indicate the universal church: "For just as the body is one and has many members, and all the members of the body, though many, are one body, so it is with Christ." Yet the following discussion makes sense only in terms of a local church. That's where feet and ears can be tempted to discouragement (vv. 14–20). It's where eyes and heads can be tempted to pride and self-sufficiency (v. 21). It's where we can give honor to the members who lack it (vv. 22–24), where we can care for one another, suffer together, rejoice together (vv. 25–26). And then Paul makes an even more specific reference to the local church, telling the church in Corinth: "Now you are the body of Christ and individually members of it" (v. 27). So which is it, Paul, universal or local? Yes. Both. Paul can flit back and forth between the two because of the inseparable relation-in-distinction between them.

Minimally, then, under normal circumstances baptism into the universal church necessarily entails membership in a local church. But we must go further. Where a local church exists, to be baptized is to be added to that church, as in Acts 2:41. Baptism is not just inseparable from local church membership but coincident with it. Membership is the house, baptism the front door. Since a church on earth represents the kingdom of heaven, it is authorized to affirm only those who submit to its authority, which is God's appointed means of having people submit to his authority. That is, a church may baptize only those who are coming out of the world *and into the church* through their baptismal profession of faith. There should be no affirmed but unattached Christians.[42] If a modern, autonomy-loving American happened to be living in Jerusalem at Pentecost and told the apostles, "I want to be baptized, but I don't want to join the church here in Jerusalem just yet," they would have sent him packing.

You cannot be a citizen without belonging to a body politic, and the kingdom of heaven's sole institutional manifestation on earth is the local church. Therefore, to be an authorized citizen of the kingdom is to be a local church member. By the authority of the keys of the kingdom, the official status of "kingdom citizen" is the local church's alone to confer, and it exists on earth only in

---

[42] Again, the Ethiopian eunuch is not "unattached" plain and simple but instead carries with him the seeds of the church that will spring to life as soon as others believe the gospel he brings to them. We'll return to the Ethiopian eunuch in chaps. 7, 9, and 11.

the membership of a local church. You don't get the jersey without joining the team. Therefore baptism not only necessitates church membership; it confers it.

Today, of course, we separate baptism from church membership in all kinds of ways. Most commonly we simply baptize people without any thought of church membership. That comes later if at all. And that's a problem. We'll address some practical issues surrounding baptism and membership in the book's final chapter. For now I simply want to reiterate that when you look at baptism, what you should see is someone walking through the door of church membership.

My church occasionally has the joy of welcoming a new believer into membership "pending" their baptism. This new believer will be interviewed by an elder. Then, at our monthly members' meeting, the congregation will vote to extend membership pending baptism. A week or two later, this new Christian will share his or her testimony at the close of our Sunday morning service and will then be baptized. Our senior pastor is usually the one who does the baptizing. Before heading back to the baptismal, he'll often say something like, "Members of Third Avenue, when Joe rises from the water, he will be a full-fledged member of this church. So welcome him with open arms and open hearts." That little word of encouragement has its pockets stuffed full of the cash value of this chapter. True, the congregation had already decided to extend membership to Joe prior to his baptism. But the new relationship between Joe and the church takes effect in and through baptism.

Baptism and Politics

Methodist bishop Will Willimon has written that "baptism has no qualms about the church being an utterly 'political' phenomenon. Baptism is a sign of the creation of a new kingdom, a visible, political reality called the church."[43] While I might dispute some of the territory Willimon claims on the basis of this insight, the point itself is dead-on. I'd even take it a step further: baptism isn't a mere sign of the creation of a new kingdom in the sense that it gestures at an independently existing reality. Instead, it plays a role in constituting the

---

[43] Cited in Anthony R. Cross, *Recovering the Evangelical Sacrament: Baptisma Semper Reformandum* (Eugene, OR: Pickwick, 2013), 300.

church as a visible, "political" body.[44] Ecclesially, baptism is an effective sign: it creates the reality to which it points.

Again, as Hubmaier rightly discerned: no baptism, no church. Baptism constitutes Christians as publicly authorized, passport-carrying kingdom citizens—the same kingdom citizens whose mutual covenant constitutes a church. As a social reality created by the kingdom of God, the local church is a visible, political institution, and baptism defines its shape by marking its entrance.

We've seen in this chapter that the keys of the kingdom are the institutional charter which gives a church this visible, political existence. The keys of the kingdom give a church the authority to hear a confession, consider the confessor, test both against Jesus' infallible word, and declare to the world, "This person belongs to the Triune God." And when the confessor in question is a new believer, the means by which the church pronounces its positive verdict is baptism. When someone legitimately claims to have become a child of God through faith in Christ and by the power of the Spirit, the church unites that person to itself, publicly endorses his confession, and hands him a passport with "Kingdom of Heaven" stamped on the cover. How? By baptizing him in the name of the Father, the Son, and the Holy Spirit.

Headlines
The keys of the kingdom (Matt 16:18–19; 18:18) function as a church-constituting charter which grants the local church the authority to publicly affirm those who credibly profess faith in Christ.
The church's initial and initiating exercise of the keys of the kingdom is baptism (Matt 28:19). In baptism the individual speaks to God and the church, and the church speaks for God to the individual.
Baptism, therefore, is both the passport of the kingdom and a kingdom citizen's swearing-in ceremony. It both identifies someone as a member of Christ's kingdom and inaugurates him into the public office of kingdom citizenship, that is, church membership.
Normally, then, baptism confers church membership. In ecclesial terms, baptism is an effective sign: it creates the reality to which it points. To baptize someone *is* to add him to the church (Acts 2:41). Baptism binds one to many.

---

[44] For an extensive biblical-theological account of the sense in which the church should be described as "political," see Leeman, *Political Church*, chap. 6.

Chapter 6

One Bread, One Body: The Lord's Supper and the Local Church

You are what you eat, or so they say. If people were machines, this would be strictly true: garbage in, garbage out. Of course, we're not machines, but we shouldn't ignore science or common sense. Some foods fuel you for hours, others give you a spike of energy followed by a crash, and others tie your stomach in a knot.

Yet food does more than feed us. It reminds us of our dependence on God and his fatherly care for us. We can use it to celebrate, feasting at weddings and holidays. We can use it by *not* using it, fasting in mourning or repentance. And food has nearly limitless social possibilities. Eating only organic, local, and whole can be an identity badge every bit as exclusive as a gated community. On the other hand, sharing a meal signals some intimacy, some openness to another. A meal can bring people together like few other things can.

Isn't it remarkable that Jesus gave the church a meal? The Lord's Supper is more than a meal, but it isn't less. Jesus broke bread and poured out wine. He said of the bread, "This is my body, which is given for you," and of the wine,

"This cup . . . is the new covenant in my blood." He told us to eat and drink in remembrance of him (Luke 22:19–20; Matt 26:26–28). Our ultimate meal is Jesus himself: his flesh is true food, his blood true drink (John 6:55). Yet Paul can write, "The cup of blessing that we bless, is it not a participation in the blood of Christ? The bread that we break, is it not a participation in the body of Christ?" (1 Cor 10:16).

In the Lord's Supper the gospel becomes not just something we hear, or even something we see, but something we eat. Therefore the Lord's Supper carries the demands of the gospel. It demands that we submit to Christ alone as Lord: "You cannot partake of the table of the Lord and the table of demons" (1 Cor 10:21). It calls us to love Christ's body like he does: Paul rebuked the Corinthians—and God killed some of them!—for despising the church's have-nots when they celebrated the Supper (1 Cor 11:17–34).

The Lord's Supper doesn't just picture the gospel; it proclaims it: "For as often as you eat this bread and drink the cup, you proclaim the Lord's death until he comes" (1 Cor 11:26). In the Lord's Supper we proclaim the gospel and participate in the gospel's benefits. Because of this, the Lord's Supper defines the church: what it is, who it is, and where it is. As Michael Bird puts it, "The meal tells a sacred story and creates a sacred community."[1] Tying together all these biblical threads, Michael Horton brings us full circle: "To put it somewhat crudely, the church *is* what it *eats*. The point at issue is covenantal identification: with which Lord and under which constitution and therefore to which communion does one belong? The sacred meal in which one shares not only reflects but also constitutes the kind of society of which one is a member."[2] This chapter is about just how the Lord's Supper constitutes the kind of society, a local church, of which we Christians are members.

The Why and What of This Chapter

More specifically, this chapter attempts to define the sense in which the Lord's Supper constitutes a local church. In 1 Corinthians 10:17 Paul writes, "Because

---

[1] Michael F. Bird, "Re-thinking a Sacramental View of Baptism and the Lord's Supper for the Post-Christendom Baptist Church," in *Baptist Sacramentalism 2*, ed. Anthony R. Cross and Philip E. Thompson, Studies in Baptist History and Thought 5 (Milton Keynes: Paternoster, 2008), 75.

[2] Michael S. Horton, *People and Place: A Covenant Ecclesiology* (Louisville: WJK, 2008), 123, emphasis original.

there is one bread, we who are many are one body, for we all partake of the one bread." On the face of it, Paul seems to be saying that participation in the Lord's Supper makes many into one, members into a body, Christians into a church. In fact, I think that's exactly what he's saying, though fitting that statement into a broader ecclesiology takes some work. That work is what this chapter, and to some degree the next, attempts.[3]

But why spend a whole chapter on the Lord's Supper? Is this a departure from the subject at hand? Hardly. You'll recall from chapter 1 that this debate has historically been conducted in terms of "open Communion" versus "closed Communion." There is a middle position, which I clunkily call the "open-closed" view. But for the most part both sides have maintained that the requirements for the Lord's Supper are the requirements for membership. There are good reasons for this, reasons I hope this chapter will strengthen. As we'll see, the Lord's Supper is the effective sign of the local church's unity. It's where you see church membership happen. It's also where exclusion from the church happens. Someone who claims to believe in Christ but whose life undermines that claim is excluded from the Lord's Supper and thereby excluded from the fellowship it entails.

We'll see that the Lord's Supper is a badge of belonging just as much as baptism is. Baptism is the front door into the house, and the Lord's Supper is the family meal. All who belong to the family identify themselves by "showing up" in baptism, and their unity as a family is both displayed and sealed as they sit down to eat together.

In other words, this chapter explores the ecclesial shape of the Lord's Supper. We'll start with four foundations of that ecclesial shape. (1) The Lord's Supper is a transformation of the Passover. (2) The Lord's Supper is a communal participation in the benefits of Jesus' death. (3) Analogous to what we discovered about baptism in chapter 4, the Lord's Supper is the renewing oath-sign of the new covenant. (4) The Lord's Supper is celebrated by the church, as a church, and it entails responsibility for the church.

Building on this foundation, I'll argue that the Lord's Supper plays a role in making a church a church. Analogous to what we saw about baptism in

---

[3] One could say this chapter outlines a Protestant, and specifically Baptist, account of how "the eucharist makes the church." For an influential Roman Catholic exposition of this slogan, see Henri de Lubac, *Corpus Mysticum: The Eucharist and the Church in the Middle Ages*, trans. Gemma Simmonds (Notre Dame, IN: University of Notre Dame Press, 2006), 88 and throughout.

chapter 5, the Lord's Supper is not just a sign, but an effective sign, in that it effects the unity of a local church. As a corporate, covenantal oath-sign, the Lord's Supper constitutes many Christians as one church. It embodies the church, making many one.

I'll conclude the chapter by drawing several theological and practical inferences from the Lord's Supper's church-constituting role. The most crucial for our purposes is this: baptism is a necessary prerequisite to the Lord's Supper. If the Lord's Supper is the renewing oath-sign of the new covenant, then only those who have undergone the initiating oath-sign may partake. If the Lord's Supper effects the unity of the church, then only those who have united themselves to the church in baptism should be admitted.[4] If the Lord's Supper is the church's family meal, the only entrance to that meal is the front door of baptism.

Four Foundations of the Ecclesial Shape of the Lord's Supper

In this section we'll survey four features of the Lord's Supper that contribute to its ecclesial shape. I'm not trying to comprehensively address the theological meaning of the Lord's Supper. Certainly the main lines of the ordinance's significance will be sketched in as we go. But my main interest is in the Lord's Supper's relationship to the local church's existence, membership, and other constitutive rite—baptism.

1. The Lord's Supper Is a Transformation of the Passover

First, the Lord's Supper is a transformation of the Passover. The Lord's Supper, of course, was instituted by Jesus at the Last Supper (Matt 26:26–29; Mark 14:22–25; Luke 22:14–20; cf. 1 Cor 11:23). And the Last Supper was a Passover meal: Jesus himself said, "I have earnestly desired to eat this Passover with you before I suffer" (Luke 22:15).[5]

---

[4] I don't think this rules out "visiting" or "transient" Communion, the practice of allowing baptized members of other evangelical churches to participate in the Lord's Supper. I'll explain why in due time.

[5] For a detailed defense of the view that the Last Supper was a Passover meal, see Anthony C. Thiselton, *The First Epistle to the Corinthians: A Commentary on the Greek Text*, New International Greek Testament Commentary (Grand Rapids: Eerdmans, 2000),

But this wasn't just any Passover meal. Remember that the Passover itself was different from every other meal: the Israelites ate bitter herbs and unleavened bread along with the Passover lamb. (A typical Passover dinner in the first century also included sharing cups of wine at different stages of the meal.) So a child would ask, "Why is this night different from any other night?" And the host would reply, "It is because of what the Lord did for me when I came out of Egypt" (Exod 13:8). These words proclaimed the significance of the meal. So also when Jesus hosted this Passover for his disciples, he explained the significance of the meal. But when he did so, he made it into a new meal with a new meaning: "And he took bread, and when he had given thanks, he broke it and gave it to them, saying, 'This is my body, which is given for you. Do this in remembrance of me.' And likewise the cup after they had eaten, saying, 'This cup that is poured out for you is the new covenant in my blood'" (Luke 22:19–20). By reinterpreting the bread and cup in light of his coming death, Jesus transformed the Passover into a new ritual, one commemorating his new covenant-inaugurating sacrifice.

Did you notice what the host of the Passover was supposed to say? "It is because of what the Lord did for *me* when *I* came out of Egypt" (emphasis added).[6] In Exodus 13 God established the Passover as a standing ordinance for Israel. These words are what each generation afterward was to say at the Passover (cf. Exod 12:14–20). The Passover plotted the lives of those present in God's past act of deliverance. It made God's past salvation present. Horton explains, "As part of the same covenant community, those who were removed from the original events by epochs could nevertheless be included federally in the founding generation."[7] Because later generations belonged to the same covenant, they were covenantally included in the same saving events.

Like the Passover, the Lord's Supper brings the past into the present. The acts of breaking and eating bread, and pouring out and drinking the cup, dramatically present the gospel events to our sight and taste. But the Lord's Supper also makes the future present, at least as a foretaste. Jesus said to his disciples, "I tell you I will not drink again of this fruit of the vine until that day when I drink it new with you in my Father's kingdom" (Matt 26:29). As Paul would

---

871–74; and I. Howard Marshall, *Last Supper and Lord's Supper* (Grand Rapids: Eerdmans, 1980), 57–75.

[6] See also Deut 26:5–7 and the discussion of that passage in Grant Macaskill, *Union with Christ in the New Testament* (Oxford: Oxford University Press, 2013), 203–4.

[7] Horton, *People and Place*, 104.

later say, "For as often as you eat this bread and drink the cup, you proclaim the Lord's death until he comes" (1 Cor 11:26). Both of these texts treat the Lord's Supper as a foretaste of the messianic banquet, what Revelation calls the marriage supper of the Lamb, where Christ's people will feast with him in the new creation (Rev 19:7, 9; Isa 25:6–10).[8] Tom Wright's vivid summary is on-point: "As we are travelling the line that leads from the Upper Room to the great feast in God's new world, from the victory of Calvary and Easter to the final victory over death itself (1 Corinthians 15:26), *we find at every station*—in other words, at every celebration of the Jesus-meal—*that God's past catches up with us again, and God's future comes to meet us once more*."[9]

Understanding the Lord's Supper as a transformation of the Passover enables us to see that it is a meal of covenantal remembrance which brings the past and future into the present. It enables each of us to say, "I eat this bread and drink this cup because of what the Lord did for me when he freed me from my sin on the cross."[10] And because of this past salvation experienced in the present, we look to our future feast with Jesus with eager expectation and sure hope.

2. The Lord's Supper Is a Communal Participation in the Benefits of Jesus' Death

Second, the Lord's Supper is a communal participation in the benefits of Jesus' death. Again recall Paul's words in 1 Corinthians 10:16: "The cup of blessing that we bless, is it not a participation in the blood of Christ? The bread that we break, is it not a participation in the body of Christ?"

The Greek word translated "participation" is *koinōnia*, which means "sharing in something with someone."[11] Who are we sharing with? One another. As

---

[8] I. Howard Marshall writes, "The Lord's Supper is linked to the Passover in that the Passover is a type of the heavenly banquet while the Lord's Supper is the anticipation of the heavenly banquet. The middle term of comparison between the Passover and the Lord's Supper is the heavenly banquet" (*Last Supper and Lord's Supper*, 80).

[9] Tom Wright, *The Meal Jesus Gave Us* (London: SPCK, 1999), 47, emphasis original. See also Brian J. Vickers, "The Lord's Supper: Celebrating the Past and Future in the Present," in *The Lord's Supper: Remembering and Proclaiming Christ Until He Comes*, ed. Thomas R. Schreiner and Matthew R. Crawford (Nashville: B&H, 2010), 313–40.

[10] So Vickers, "Celebrating the Past and Future in the Present," in Schreiner and Crawford, *The Lord's Supper*, 339.

[11] See J. Y. Campbell, "Κοινωνία and Its Cognates in the New Testament," *Journal of Biblical Literature* 51 (1932): 353; Michelle V. Lee, *Paul, the Stoics, and the Body of Christ*,

we'll consider below, we participate in the Lord's Supper as a church (1 Cor 11:17–18, 20, 33–34). And what are we sharing in? Fellowship with Christ, which includes all the benefits of his saving death. In the Lord's Supper we participate in what Christ's broken body and shed blood obtained for us: forgiveness, reconciliation, adoption, and all the other blessings of the new covenant. As C. K. Barrett puts it, "Paul is thinking of the share all Christians enjoy, and enjoy together, in the benefits secured for them through the blood of Christ."[12] Gordon Fee's comments are also helpful:

> The "fellowship," therefore, was most likely a celebration of their
> common life in Christ, based on the new covenant in his blood that
> had previously bound them together in union with Christ by his Spirit.
> But while their "fellowship" was with one another, its basis and focus
> were in Christ, his death and resurrection; they were thus together in
> his presence, where as host at his table he shared anew with them the
> benefits of the atonement. It is this unique relationship *between believers*
> *and with their Lord*, celebrated at this meal, that makes impossible
> similar associations with other "believers" at the tables of demons.[13]

For those who partake in faith, the Lord's Supper is a communal participation in the benefits of Jesus' death. As we feed on the bread with our mouths, so we feed on Christ in our hearts by faith. And the "we" is crucial.

3. The Lord's Supper Is the Renewing Oath-Sign of the New Covenant

Third, the Lord's Supper is the renewing oath-sign of the new covenant. In the last chapter we discovered that baptism is the initiating oath-sign of the new covenant. The Lord's Supper is similar, except that it is repeated frequently whereas baptism is a one-time event.

Society for New Testament Studies Monograph Series 137 (Cambridge: Cambridge University Press, 2006), 127. Cf. Jonathan Edwards: "The word 'communion,' as it is used in Scripture, signifies a common partaking of some good" (*Sermons on the Lord's Supper* [Orlando, FL: The Northampton Press, 2007], 120).

[12] C. K. Barrett, *The First Epistle to the Corinthians* (London: A&C Black, 1971), 232.

[13] Gordon Fee, *The First Epistle to the Corinthians*, New International Commentary on the New Testament (Grand Rapids: Eerdmans, 1974), 467. So also Jonathan Edwards: "True believers hence see communion as a joint participation by receiving Christ's sacrifice by faith" (*Sermons on the Lord's Supper*, 81).

Several lines of evidence demonstrate that the Lord's Supper is a sign of the new covenant. First, Jesus says, "This cup that is poured out for you is the new covenant in my blood" (Luke 22:20). Here Jesus identifies the sign with the covenant it signifies, just as God previously did with circumcision in Genesis 17:10. The Lord's Supper also draws on the broader precedent of covenant-ratifying meals in the Old Testament (e.g., Gen 26:30; 31:44–46), especially the covenant meal of Exodus 24:9–11. Consider Mark 14:24: "This is my blood of the covenant, which is poured out for many." Mark's version makes clear that Jesus' cup saying evoked not just the new covenant promise but also the ratification of the old covenant in Exodus 24:8: "Behold the blood of the covenant that the LORD has made with you." After this statement, Moses and Aaron and the elders of Israel went up into the presence of God on Sinai, where "they beheld God, and ate and drank" (Exod 24:11). The old covenant was ratified not just by blood but by a meal God himself hosted. Likewise the new covenant was inaugurated by Jesus' blood and is repeatedly ratified in a meal that Jesus hosts.[14]

This is why many Christians speak of the Lord's Supper as a seal of the covenant, on both God's part and ours.[15] As a seal ratifies a document, so the Lord's Supper ratifies the new covenant. Jonathan Edwards, for example, said that "God in this ordinance seals His covenant to us."[16] How? "The actions of breaking the bread and pouring out the wine, and giving them to the people are, as it were, a visible promise that upon our accepting the things signified by them at the hands of Christ we shall enjoy them; and the actions and signs signify the same to the eye as the promises do to the ear."[17]

The Lord's Supper is a sign and seal of the new covenant on God's part in that it visibly extends and confirms his saving promises to us. But the Lord's Supper is also a sign and seal of the covenant on our part. As Edwards put it:

> 'Tis the most solemn confirmation that can be conceived of, that so far
> as they know their hearts they make this union their own free act and
> deed. It is more solemn than a mere oath. 'Tis just in this ordinance as

---

[14] After surveying these textual connections, Grant Macaskill concludes that "in the New Testament the symbolism of [the Lord's Supper] is understood to include covenant ratification" (*Union with Christ*, 211).

[15] Reformed authors typically speak of it as a seal of the "covenant of grace," though I'd prefer "new covenant."

[16] *Sermons on the Lord's Supper*, 16.

[17] Ibid., 15.

it is in the mutual tokens of consent and acceptance in marriage. So in this ordinance the people of Christ solemnly confirm this union, and Christian love one to another.[18]

By taking the elements, we solemnly signify our faith in Christ and commitment to him, confirming our union with Christ and with one another. Edwards also identifies the Lord's Supper as an oath, or more specifically an oath-sign, when he writes, "'Tis with significant signs as it is with words: words are a profession of the thing signified by those words; so significant actions are a profession of the thing signified by those actions."[19] In other words, in the Lord's Supper we profess our faith in Christ by partaking of the "sensible signs" of his body and blood.[20] We thereby communicate our commitment to his covenant as surely as if we spoke a verbal oath.[21]

Edwards is exactly right here because participating in the Lord's Supper is a self-involving act.[22] When we eat the bread, we are saying, "Jesus' body was given for me." When we drink the cup we are saying, "Jesus' blood was shed to forgive my sins." When we do this, we plot our lives in God's drama of redemption. Like an Israelite celebrating the Passover, we confess, "It is because of what the Lord did *for me*." And while this is an act of faith, it's also an act of commitment because faith itself demands whole-souled commitment to Christ's commands (Matt 28:19; John 14:15). When we take the Lord's Supper, we pledge ourselves anew to be Jesus' disciples, to hold fast to his teaching, to follow the Lamb wherever he goes (John 8:32; Rev 14:4). This is precisely the dynamic we observed with baptism, in which we publicly

---

[18] Ibid., 76.

[19] Ibid., 77.

[20] Ibid., 17.

[21] This could well be the reason the Latin word *sacramentum*, which means "oath," first came to refer to the Christian "sacraments" of baptism and the Lord's Supper. A close association between an oath and the Lord's Supper may be attested in Pliny the Younger's letter to Trajan (*Epistle* 10.96; AD 112). He describes Christians gathering together to sing hymns to Christ and "to bind themselves by oath" to live upright lives, and afterward partaking of a meal together. See Pliny the Younger, *Letters, Volume II: Books 8–10. Panegyricus*, trans. Betty Radice, Loeb Classical Library (Cambridge, MA: Harvard University Press, 1969), 289. Many scholars have discerned a connection between 1 Cor 11:17–34 and Pliny's letter. See, e.g., C. F. D. Moule, "The Judgement Theme in the Sacraments," in *The Background of the New Testament and its Eschatology*, ed. W. Daube and W. D. Davies (Cambridge: Cambridge University Press, 1956), 471n1.

[22] See Anthony Thiselton, *The Hermeneutics of Doctrine* (Grand Rapids: Eerdmans, 2007), 510, for literature on the "self-involving" nature of baptism and the Lord's Supper.

commit to Christ through identifying with his death and resurrection. When we partake of the bread and the cup, we commit ourselves again to Christ and his covenant.

Hence the Lord's Supper is the renewing oath-sign of the new covenant. As the Puritan Thomas Manton said, "Now our answer to this demand of God, and to this interrogatory he puts to us in the covenant, it is sealed by us in baptism, and it is renewed in the Lord's Supper."[23] In the Lord's Supper we pledge ourselves to God according to his new covenant, even as—and because—he pledges himself to us.

As with baptism, the meaning of the Lord's Supper as the renewing oath-sign of the new covenant is determined by the newness of the new covenant. "Christ redeemed us from the curse of the law by becoming a curse for us," Paul writes in Galatians 3:13. The curse Christ became for us is *the curse*: cutting off, rejection, condemnation. Christ satisfied the ultimate covenant sanctions—the wrath of God—so that we would receive the new covenant blessings of justification (Gal 2:16), the indwelling Spirit (Gal 3:14), and adoption (Gal 4:4–6). The Lord's Supper does entail judgment for one whose life undermines their profession; yet the oath-sign itself is not a conditional self-malediction.[24] Eating

---

[23] *The Complete Works of Thomas Manton*, vol. 6 (repr., Homewood, AL: Solid Ground Christian Books, 2008), 72; cited in William Kiffin, *A Sober Discourse of Right to Church Communion* (London, 1681; repr., Paris, AR: Baptist Standard Bearer, 2006), 67. Cf. Roy Ciampa and Brian Rosner: "The Lord's Supper is best understood as a covenant-ratifying meal in which the whole community was to participate" (*The First Letter to the Corinthians*, Pillar New Testament Commentary [Grand Rapids: Eerdmans, 2010], 474). Thiselton also asserts that the Lord's Supper is a "solemn covenant pledge of involvement in all that is proclaimed in the death of Christ" (*The First Epistle to the Corinthians*, 896).

[24] A number of scholars rightly identify the Lord's Supper as a covenantal oath, yet wrongly perceive self-maledictory symbolism in it, in continuity with the Mosaic covenant. See, e.g., A. R. Millard, "Covenant and Communion in First Corinthians," in *Apostolic History and the Gospel: In Honour of F. F. Bruce*, ed. Ward Gasque and Ralph P. Martin (Exeter: Paternoster, 1970), 243–45; George E. Mendenhall, "Covenant," in *Interpreter's Dictionary of the Bible* 1 (Nashville: Abingdon, 1962), 722. The difference between the judgment implicit in the Lord's Supper and the conditional self-malediction implied in, say, circumcision is that threatened judgment is not an intrinsic part of the meal's symbolism. Instead, the meal symbolizes salvation accomplished through Christ's broken body and shed blood. Paul's language of *koinōnia* confirms this: in the Lord's Supper believers participate in the benefits of Christ's death (1 Cor 10:16). Yes, if you spurn the grace of God and partake hypocritically, the meal becomes a means of judgment (11:29). But note that Paul tells the Corinthians that when they do this, it is not the Lord's Supper they celebrate (11:20). To profane the ordinance is to invert the ordinance, making it something it isn't.

the bread and drinking the cup has no element of "May God do so to me if I forsake him." Why? Because God already did so to Christ. Like baptism, the Lord's Supper pictures sanctions satisfied, since satisfied sanctions are the ground of the new covenant these rites ratify. Christ drained the cup of wrath so we could drink the cup of blessing.

To treat the Lord's Supper as the renewing oath-sign of the new covenant does not turn the Lord's Supper into a "work." Nor does it distort the gospel by inserting our moral effort into the basis of our standing with God.[25] Instead, the Lord's Supper pictures the priority, sufficiency, and efficacy of God's grace by presenting to us a salvation that Christ has unilaterally accomplished. Yet that salvation is always and only appropriated by faith, which we picture and profess as we partake.

4. The Lord's Supper Is Celebrated by the Church, as a Church, and It Entails Responsibility for the Church

A fourth foundation of the Lord's Supper's ecclesial shape is that it is celebrated by the church, as a church, and it entails responsibility for the church. First, the Lord's Supper is celebrated by the church, a local church. Consider what Paul says in 1 Corinthians 11:

- "When you come together it is not for the better but for the worse" (v. 17);
- "When you come together as a church, I hear that there are divisions among you" (v. 18);
- "When you come together, it is not the Lord's supper that you eat" (v. 20);
- "When you come together to eat, wait for one another" (v. 33);
- "So that when you come together it will not be for judgment" (v. 34).

Whereas circumcision threatens wrath by the action of cutting off, the Lord's Supper only entails judgment if it is perverted and thereby inverted.

[25] Michael Horton seems to imply this when he writes, "It makes literally all of the difference in the world whether baptism and Communion are the believer's expression of an inner experience and commitment or God's official ratification of his promise" ("The Church After Evangelicalism," in *Renewing the Evangelical Mission*, ed. Richard Lints [Grand Rapids: Eerdmans, 2013], 151). This is a false disjunction.

It's clear that in Corinth the Lord's Supper was celebrated by the whole body in one gathering. It wasn't something individuals or families or small groups did; it was something the church as a whole did. And there's no solid evidence that any other New Testament church did otherwise.[26]

Second, the Lord's Supper is celebrated by the church, *as a church*. What I mean is that the Lord's Supper is an act of the church, not just the aggregate activity of its individual members coincidentally happening in the same place.[27] Again, notice that in 1 Corinthians 11:18 Paul describes the Corinthians coming together "as a church." As Anthony Thiselton explains, the Greek verb translated "come together" is "repeated in vv. 18, 20, 33, and 34, and this specific Eucharistic context denotes not simply *assembling together* but the meeting you hold as a church. In v. 18 this becomes explicit. It is as one believing community that they meet, not as a group of friends meeting for a private meal."[28]

As we saw in chapter 5, a church is more than the sum of its parts. It has a distinct churchness, an institutional dimension. More precisely, it is grounded in an institutional authorization from Jesus himself. And as this authorized, corporate body the church celebrates the Lord's Supper. As a body the church participates in the benefits of Christ's death and renews their commitment to Christ and his covenant. The Lord's Supper, therefore, is an exercise of the church's

---

[26] Acts 2:46 does say, "And day by day, attending the temple together and breaking bread in their homes," but the very next line is, "they received their food with glad and generous hearts." This seems to distinguish "the breaking of bread" in v. 42 from the similar phrase here. In v. 42, "the breaking of bread" (τῇ κλάσει τοῦ ἄρτου) is a slightly more formal-sounding articular noun phrase. This may suggest that "the breaking of bread" functions here as a technical term for the Lord's Supper. Yet in v. 46, "breaking bread in their homes" (κλῶντές τε κατ' οἶκον ἄρτον) is an adverbial participle modifying the finite verb μετελάμβανον, "they received [their food]." That "breaking bread" is grammatically subordinate to "they received their food" suggests the main idea is simply that the church ate together, not that the Lord's Supper is in view.

[27] This doesn't mean every single member must be present in order for a church to celebrate the Lord's Supper. A corporate body can act as a unified whole even if some of its members are absent. Think of the US Senate, for example.

[28] Thiselton, *First Epistle to the Corinthians*, 856, emphasis original. So also Gordon Fee: "The verb 'gather together,' repeated five times in vv. 17–22 and 33–34, is one of the key words that holds the argument together. Given its similar usage in 14:23 and 26, it had probably become a semitechnical term for the 'gathering together' of the people of God for worship. Thus the concern is with what goes on when they 'come together *as* the church'" (*First Epistle to the Corinthians*, 536).

authority to affirm and oversee its members' professions of faith in Jesus. It is not a private meal among friends but the church's public enaction of its fellowship.

Finally, participating in the Lord's Supper entails responsibility for the church. Paul's instructions in 1 Corinthians 11:17–34 were prompted by reports of division at the Lord's Supper: "For, in the first place, when you come together as a church, I hear that there are divisions among you" (v. 18). In the New Testament, churches typically celebrated the Lord's Supper in conjunction with a meal. So Paul goes on to rebuke wealthier members for having their own private meals and even getting drunk while poorer members, presumably slaves who had to work later, went hungry (vv. 20–22). Then Paul repeats and explains Jesus' words which instituted the Lord's Supper (vv. 23–25), concluding: "For as often as you eat this bread and drink the cup, you proclaim the Lord's death until he comes" (v. 26). From this Paul draws a bracing conclusion: "Whoever, therefore, eats the bread or drinks the cup of the Lord in an unworthy manner will be guilty concerning the body and blood of the Lord" (v. 27). In context, what Paul means by "unworthy manner" is partaking in a way that divides the church and despises its poorer members. So the Corinthians' disregard for the body means "it is not the Lord's Supper" they eat, exposing them to God's judgment (vv. 20, 29).

The flow of this passage teaches us that partaking of the Lord's Supper entails responsibility to love the body. Failure to love the body turns a celebration of the Lord's Supper into "not the Lord's Supper." One who fails to love the body "eats and drinks judgment on himself" (v. 29). If you eat without loving the body, then rather than participating in the body and blood of Christ, you become guilty of profaning that body and blood (v. 27).[29]

What holds this whole passage together is that the Lord's Supper proclaims the Lord's death. Therefore it proclaims life and blessing for all who trust in the Lord Jesus. But if by our selfishness we exclude or degrade poorer brothers and sisters, we're lying about the Lord's death. We're acting as if Christ died only for us, not them. As one scholar put it, "Love for this Christ can be shown only when the neighbors chosen by Christ are gladly accepted."[30] Paul's argument here finds an echo in 1 John 4:20: "If anyone says, 'I love God,' and hates his brother, he is a liar; for he who does not love his brother whom he has seen

---

[29] Consider Edwards's provocative claim that those who profane the Lord's Supper are equivalent to those who murdered Christ (*Sermons on the Lord's Supper*, 94–95).

[30] Markus Barth, *Rediscovering the Lord's Supper* (Louisville: WJK, 1988), 74.

cannot love God whom he has not seen." If you don't love the brothers, you don't love Christ. If you celebrate the Lord's Supper to the harm of the brothers, it's not the Lord's Supper you're celebrating.

Paul's argument presupposes that participating in the Lord's Supper entails responsibility for the church. This responsibility is so crucial that to neglect it vitiates the Lord's Supper itself and incurs the Lord's judgment. Paul draws a straight line from proclaiming Jesus' death to loving the brothers. If you aren't doing the latter, you aren't doing the former. According to Paul, participating in the Lord's Supper entails responsibility to love the church and preserve its unity.

We've just considered four foundations of the ecclesial shape of the Lord's Supper: the Lord's Supper is a transformation of the Passover, a communal participation in the benefits of Jesus' death, the renewing oath-sign of the new covenant, and a celebration by the church, as a church, entailing responsibility for the church. Taken together, these points paint a thoroughly corporate, ecclesial picture. The Lord's Supper isn't a private devotional act that a couple hundred other people happen to perform at the same time. Instead, the Lord's Supper is something we do not just with the church but as a church. Because of this, participating in the Lord's Supper not only professes faith and pledges obedience; it also entails responsibility for the body.

How the Lord's Supper Makes Many One

In the Lord's Supper we repeatedly ratify the new covenant, renewing our trust in and commitment to Christ. Therefore, the Lord's Supper is also the ongoing, repeated means by which the church's existence as a church is ratified. The Lord's Supper is therefore an effective sign of the local church's existence as a church. It both represents and effects the unity of the body. It embodies the church, making many one.

The crucial verse here is 1 Corinthians 10:17: "Because there is one bread, we who are many are one body, for we all partake of the one bread." Paul's central assertion in this verse is that we who are many are one body. And he twice grounds this assertion in our common participation in the Lord's Supper: "Because there is one bread, . . . for we all partake of the one bread." This double grounding weighs against seeing the one bread as merely representing the local church's unity. Instead, Paul is asserting that the Lord's Supper in some sense constitutes the local church as one body.[31] Oliver O'Donovan comments:

> The effectiveness of this sign should not be looked for in a "sacramental grace" which affects the believer in a different way from other kinds of grace; but in the *formation of the church*. The "one loaf" binds "many" into "one body" (1 Cor. 10:17). It determines the identity of this society by reference to the Passion: it is the community of those who have not only gathered to God's Christ, but have died with him.[32]

How exactly does the Lord's Supper bind many into one body? We can put the previous section's points together and say that our "vertical" fellowship with Christ necessarily and inseparably creates a "horizontal" fellowship in the church.[33] Because we have fellowship with Christ in the Lord's Supper, we also have fellowship with one another. And because the Lord's Supper is a covenant pledge to Christ, it is also, implicitly, a covenant pledge to one another. Remember Paul's straight line from the Lord's death to loving the brothers: to bind ourselves to Christ is to be bound to one another.

Understanding the Lord's Supper as the renewing oath-sign of the new covenant is crucial to understanding its role in binding many into one. The only way to "participate" in the body and blood of Christ at the Supper is to be a member of the new covenant by faith. Yet because the Lord's Supper enacts

---

[31] So, e.g., Ciampa and Rosner, *The First Letter to the Corinthians*, 476; Hans Conzelmann, *1 Corinthians: A Commentary on the First Epistle to the Corinthians*, Hermeneia (Minneapolis: Fortress, 1975), 172; David E. Garland, *1 Corinthians*, Baker Exegetical Commentary on the New Testament (Grand Rapids: Baker, 2003), 473; Richard B. Hays, *First Corinthians*, Interpretation (Louisville, KY: WJK, 1997), 167. After a detailed exegetical study of vv. 16–17, Wendell Lee Willis concludes, "This messianic community, established in and on Jesus's death, is both exemplified by and embodied in its memorial meal, the Lord's Supper" (*Idol Meat in Corinth: The Pauline Argument in 1 Corinthians 8 and 10*, SBL Dissertation Series 68 [Chico, CA: Scholars Press, 1985], 220). Thiselton's clarifying comment is helpful as well: "The causal force, however, applies not to the mechanics of bread and eating, but to the principle as an exposition of the previous explanation in v. 16 about the entailments of communal participation. The ground of unity is *Christ*, not the oneness of the bread or loaf (ἄρτος) as if to imply that the church would be fragmented if more than one loaf were shared at the one Eucharist" (*First Epistle to the Corinthians*, 767).

[32] Oliver O'Donovan, *The Desire of the Nations: Rediscovering the Roots of Political Theology* (Cambridge: Cambridge University Press, 1996), 180, emphasis original.

[33] So Michael Bird: "The theological or vertical dimension of sharing in Christ creates the horizontal or social dimension of ecclesial unity" ("Re-thinking a Sacramental View," in Cross and Thompson, *Baptist Sacramentalism*, 72).

our commitment to the covenant, it also enacts our commitment to one another. As we see in 1 Corinthians 11:17–34, you can't commit to the covenant without committing to the covenant community. And, as we saw in the previous chapter, our mutual commitment to one another constitutes the church as a church.

Of course, before we come to the table, we are already members of the "one body" into which we were baptized by the Spirit at conversion (1 Cor 12:13). Yet Paul argues in 1 Corinthians 10:17 that a local church derives its oneness from its participation in the Lord's Supper. Remember, in 1 Corinthians 12 Paul slides almost imperceptibly between universal church and local church. It's not surprising, then, that Paul can say we are baptized into one (universal) body at conversion; yet we become one (local) body through participating in the Lord's Supper.

In sum, the Lord's Supper is an effective sign of the local church's distinct, unified existence as a body. We've seen that baptism is an effective sign of an individual's inclusion in the church. The Lord's Supper, on the other hand, is an effective sign of the whole church's existence as a unity of one from many. Baptism binds one to many, and the Lord's Supper binds many into one.

The Lord's Supper's role as an effective sign of the "one body" unity of a local church is quite a bit like sexual intercourse's role as an effective sign of the "one flesh" union of marriage. I appealed to marriage in our discussion of baptism in relation to the new covenant, but here the analogy is even more precise. Marriage is the covenantal, lifelong, exclusive, comprehensive union of a man and a woman. This union is entered by solemn, public vows. It creates "one flesh" where previously there was only an individual man and woman (Gen 2:24). And this union is consummated by sexual intercourse. Until a couple consummates their marriage, they are not yet "fully" married. Sexual intercourse, therefore, is an effective sign of marriage. It is a covenant ratification and, after the first ratification, renewal—an oath-sign of marriage. Like the Lord's Supper, it should be done regularly (1 Cor 7:5; 11:25). And while the "one flesh" union of marriage transcends sexual intercourse, the union does not exist without it.[34]

Now consider the birth of a local church, the moment its members bind themselves to one another by "mutual covenant." This assembly is not "fully"

---

[34] For a response to the question of whether a heterosexual couple who are physically incapable of consummating a marriage may nevertheless be married, see Sherif Girgis, Ryan T. Anderson, and Robert P. George, *What Is Marriage? Man and Woman: A Defense* (New York: Encounter, 2012), 127n5.

a church until they take the Lord's Supper together. We can say this because if they never celebrate the Supper, they will never "consummate" their union as a church. They will never become one body by eating the one bread. In such a case, as with an unconsummated marriage, the failure to ratify covenantal vows by the covenant's effective sign undercuts the vows themselves, leaving the union in limbo.

However, when a church does "come together" to celebrate the Lord's Supper, they experience fellowship with Christ and with one another. This is similar—with appropriate differences, of course—to the fellowship a married couple enjoys with each other in sexual union. In both cases the fellowship the effective sign engenders both represents and seals the union it ratifies. Marriage is a comprehensive union of a man and woman, and sexual intercourse represents and seals that union in its consummation of sexual complementarity. Church fellowship is joint participation in the benefits of Christ and the life which flows from those benefits, and the Lord's Supper represents and seals fellowship with Christ and with one another.[35]

In both cases the effective sign is a kind of synecdoche and anchor for the whole relationship. A married couple bound together by sexual intimacy should also share the rest of their lives, from physical goods to the labor of raising children. A church bound together by communal participation in Christ's benefits should live a common life of love, sacrificial service, and colaboring for the progress of the gospel (Phil 1:27–2:4). Marriage and church fellowship transcend their effective signs, but the life lived within these unions is shaped by, and shaped like, these signs.

We've seen that the Lord's Supper is the renewing oath-sign of the new covenant. Not only that, but it is a corporate renewal of the new covenant. In the Lord's Supper we seal our fellowship with Christ and with one another. We pledge ourselves to Christ and also, implicitly yet necessarily, to one another.[36] Like sex within marriage, the Lord's Supper ratifies and renews a prior

---

[35] So Jonathan Edwards: "The Lord's Supper was instituted as a solemn representation and seal of the holy and spiritual union Christ's people have with Christ and one another" (*Sermons on the Lord's Supper*, 71–72).

[36] As Edwards put it, "By reason of the great obligations that are laid upon us by those things that are there exhibited evidently set forth crucified, and by reason of the solemn acts we there perform, the seal we set, the vows we there renew, and the oath we swear especially shows our obligation to these two things; purity and peace. Let me therefore earnestly warn all who have this day attended that holy ordinance of the Lord's Supper and partook of the sacred symbols to remember what they signify" (ibid., 94).

commitment, consummating the union that commitment inaugurated. The Lord's Supper is an effective sign of the church's unity. Because there is one bread of which we all partake, we, the members of a local church, are one body.

Five Conclusions

Let's consider five theological and practical conclusions which flow from this account of the Lord's Supper as the effective sign of local church unity. I'll start with the big one.

1. You Must Be Baptized in order to Participate in the Lord's Supper

First, you must be baptized in order to participate in the Lord's Supper.[37] You must perform the initiating oath-sign of the covenant before you can participate in the renewing oath-sign of the covenant. As Jonathan Edwards put it:

> The actions at the Lord's Supper thus implying in their nature and
> signification, a renewing and confirming of the covenant, there is a
> declarative explicit covenanting supposed to precede it; which is the
> profession of religion, before spoken of, that qualifies a person for
> admission to the Lord's Supper. And there doubtless is, or ought to be,
> as much explicitly professed in words, as is implicitly professed in these
> actions; for by these significant actions, the communicant sets his seal but
> to his profession.[38]

As a paedobaptist, Edwards separated "the profession of religion" from baptism. Yet we saw in chapter 3 that baptism is the New Testament way to profess faith. Filtered through credobaptist lenses, Edwards's argument perfectly summarizes why baptism is a prerequisite to the Lord's Supper. We must

---

[37] Open-Communion baptists excepted, this has been virtually the unanimous position of the church throughout history. For early statements in the *Didache*, Justin Martyr, and Cyprian, see Gregg R. Allison, *Sojourners and Strangers: The Doctrine of the Church*, Foundations of Evangelical Theology (Wheaton, IL: Crossway, 2012), 366–67.

[38] Jonathan Edwards, *An Humble Inquiry into the Rules of the Word of God Concerning the Qualifications Requisite to a Complete Standing and Full Communion in the Visible Christian Church*, in *The Works of Jonathan Edwards, Vol. 12: Ecclesiastical Writings*, ed. David D. Hall (New Haven, CT, and London: Yale University Press, 1994), 257.

make a profession before we can seal that profession. We must initiate a covenant before we can renew and confirm that covenant.[39]

The Lord's Supper publicly enacts the church's fellowship. Therefore those only may partake who have gone public as Christians in baptism. Theologically speaking, the Lord's Supper is an exercise of the keys of the kingdom by the local church. As we saw in the previous chapter, baptism is the initial and initiating exercise of the keys. In baptism a church affirms someone's profession of faith and therefore unites that person to itself. The Lord's Supper is also an exercise of the keys, but it is an ongoing, renewing one. Because the Lord's Supper is a participation in the benefits of Christ's death, the church should invite to the Table only those who profess faith in Christ, and have so professed in baptism.[40] In admitting persons to the Table, a church affirms their professions of faith—professions first made in baptism.

There's an analogy here between baptism and the Lord's Supper on one hand and circumcision and the Passover on the other. Consider Exodus 12:48: "If a stranger shall sojourn with you and would keep the Passover to the LORD, let all his males be circumcised. Then he may come near and keep it; he shall be as a native of the land. But no uncircumcised person shall eat of it." In ancient Israel, only those who had undergone the initiating oath-sign of the covenant could participate in the covenant meal.

And the parallels run even deeper. Numbers 9:13 says, "But if anyone who is clean and is not on a journey fails to keep the Passover, that person shall be cut off from his people because he did not bring the LORD's offering at its appointed time; that man shall bear his sin." In other words, all Israelites were not just permitted but required to participate in the Passover. Only the circumcised could participate, and all the circumcised (and their families) must participate, on pain of exclusion from the covenant. The Passover defined the shape of the covenant community of Israel. Circumcision initiated one's membership in the covenant, and the Passover marked one's ongoing participation in the covenant. So also with baptism and the Lord's Supper in the new covenant.

---

[39] Stanley Grenz writes, "Baptism properly precedes participation in the Lord's Supper. . . . The reaffirmation of our personal loyalty to Christ inherent in the Lord's Supper presupposes our initial declaration of loyalty made in baptism" (*Theology for the Community of God* [Nashville: B&H, 1994], 702).

[40] As John L. Dagg put it, "Profession is the substance, and baptism is the form; but Christ's command requires the form as well as the substance" (*Manual of Church Order* [repr., Harrisonburg, VA: Gano, 1990], 95).

This is the place to point out that the Lord's Supper's role as the renewing oath-sign of the new covenant, together with baptism's role as its initiating oath-sign, rules out the "open-closed" position on baptism and church membership. To hold that baptism is necessary for membership but not the Lord's Supper (the "open-closed" position) is to contradict the covenantal correspondence between the two ordinances. And on what biblical grounds could you bar someone from membership when you admit them to its effective sign?[41]

2. The Lord's Supper Is an Effective Sign of Church Membership

The second conclusion to highlight is just that: the Lord's Supper is an effective sign of church membership. I've called the Lord's Supper the effective sign of local church unity, of the local church's existence as one body. This means it is also the effective sign of an individual's membership in the body.

Why? Because the same relation which constitutes a church constitutes someone a member of a church. We've seen that a church is constituted by the mutual, covenant-like commitment of its members. This covenanting act at once makes many Christians into one church and makes each of them members of this new church. And any subsequent members will enter the church by making the same commitment to the church which, in the case of the founding members, constituted the church in the first place. Church membership is simply the church-constituting relation described from the standpoint of an individual's relationship to the whole. The relation which binds many into one also binds one to many.

To be sure, there are some internal tensions in this account of how a church is constituted. We'll let these tensions stand for now and address them head-on in the next chapter. For the time being, the important thing is that the Lord's Supper is an effective sign of church membership. It ratifies an individual's membership in *this local church*. It seals his fellowship with and responsibility for *these people* who partake of the same bread and drink from the same cup.

This is why the definitive privilege of church membership is participation in the Lord's Supper, and the definitive act of church discipline is exclusion from the Lord's Supper. The Lord's Supper is where the church on earth

---

[41] As noted in chap. 1, Dagg argued that whoever may be admitted to Communion once may be admitted to membership (John L. Dagg, *An Essay in Defense of Strict Communion* [Penfield, GA: Benj. Brantley, 1845], 45–46).

shows up most visibly. Therefore it is where inclusion in and exclusion from the church show up most tangibly. Exclusion from the Lord's Supper isn't merely a logical consequence of being excluded from the church's fellowship. Instead, exclusion from the Lord's Supper *is* exclusion from the church's fellowship, and the relational consequences of church discipline follow upon this exclusion.

Church membership isn't primarily a matter of having one's name on a list or having access to certain programs or perks. Instead, it consists first and foremost in a local church's formal, ongoing permission to participate in the Lord's Supper. All the other privileges and responsibilities of membership flow from this foundational act of inclusion.

3. The Lord's Supper Normally Entails Membership in That Local Church

Third, because the Lord's Supper is an effective sign of church membership, participating in the Lord's Supper normally entails membership in that local church. As we've seen in 1 Corinthians 11, participation in the Lord's Supper entails responsibility for the church. Paul rebuked the Corinthians, and God judged them, for partaking of the Lord's Supper in a loveless, divisive manner. What about someone who refuses to join a church in the first place? They're actually in a worse position. By keeping aloof from the body, they cut themselves off from even the possibility of fulfilling their responsibilities to the body. Cutting yourself off from a local body doesn't free you from responsibility, it only means you can't fulfill the responsibility Christ has already given you. Because the Lord's Supper entails responsibility for the church, it normally entails membership in the local church in which you partake of it. There's no way to be responsible for the church without being accountable to the church.

But what if you're visiting for just one Sunday or for a few weeks? Should you abstain from the Lord's Supper there? And should churches only welcome to the Table those who are members of their local congregation? I don't think so.[42] Think away modern, unattached, autonomous Christianity. Think away

---

[42] The position I'm arguing against here is sometimes referred to as "closed Communion" (members only) as over against "close Communion" (members and other baptized believers). I'll treat it in some depth because some view it as a necessary entailment of the view that baptism is required for membership and the Lord's Supper.

cities with dozens or even hundreds of churches. Think away denominational divides. Think away any lingering cultural favor toward Christianity that, in some places, can still incentivize false professions. In other words, think back to the New Testament. And then think with me through two scenarios.

Scenario one: Philippos, a Christian living in AD 62 is a member of the church in Smyrna, in what's now Turkey. He loses his job as a leatherworker and has to move a few dozen miles to Ephesus. On his first Sunday there he shows up at the Ephesian church's gathering. One of the elders of the church greets him warmly and asks him a few questions. "Are you a disciple of Jesus? Have you been baptized? Where did you come from? Oh, you're from the church in Smyrna. Great, great. How is pastor Stephanos doing? And the other elders? Glad to hear it. Well, let me introduce you to the rest of the church. I'm sure they will be glad to welcome you into our fellowship." And then Philippos joins the church for worship and participates with them in the Lord's Supper.

Scenario two: Philippos, now a member of the church in Ephesus, goes to visit his Christian mother-in-law in Miletus for a week. He's there on Sunday, so they gather with the church. One of the elders of the church greets him warmly and asks him a few questions. "Are you a disciple of Jesus? Have you been baptized? Oh, you're a member of the church in Ephesus. Great, great. How is pastor Gaius doing? And the other elders? Glad to hear it. Well, let me introduce you to the rest of the church. We're glad you'll be sharing in our fellowship this morning." And then Philippos joins the church for worship and participates with them in the Lord's Supper.

These scenarios are admittedly a bit contrived, but I think they preserve an important point that we see more easily from within the New Testament's context than from our own. Namely, an unknown Christian showing up for worship on Sunday morning can be a fit candidate for the Lord's Supper whether he'll be there one Sunday or indefinitely. In the New Testament there was no waiting period before church membership. At Pentecost 3,000 were baptized and added to the church that day (Acts 2:41). This means that in principle an unknown Christian does not need to prove his mettle by demonstrating "fruit" over time or undergoing a lengthy catechetical process before being admitted to church membership. If new believers at Pentecost could be added to the church on their first day as believers, then Philippos can be added to the Ephesian church on his first Sunday there.[43] And if Philippos can be added to the Ephesian church on his first Sunday there, then there's no reason the church in Miletus should bar him from the Table, even if he's only there one Sunday.

Thus, I would suggest that permanent residence is not a prerequisite for participating in the Lord's Supper. This is so not least because "permanent residence" is a relative term. Consider not just the uncertainties of life but the fact that we're called to *go* and make disciples (Matt 28:19). If membership in this local church is a prerequisite to the Lord's Supper, and residence is required for membership, what's the minimum term of residence required? And how can churches require something for membership and the Lord's Supper—a promise to reside there a certain length of time—which isn't in a Christian's power to fulfill?

Further, we might see a biblical instance of "visiting Communion" in Acts 20:7. Paul is traveling with a number of believers who go ahead of him to Troas. When he arrives at Troas, they all gather for worship with the church there: "On the first day of the week, when we were gathered together to break bread, Paul talked with them, intending to depart on the next day, and he prolonged his speech until midnight" (v. 7). Commentators are divided as to whether "to break bread" refers to the Lord's Supper. If it does, which I think is likely, there's no indication that Paul and his companions abstained, since Luke includes them in the "we" who gathered to break bread.[44]

But I don't think the practice of visiting Communion stands or falls with this example. Think back to our second scenario. Since Philippos is only staying in Miletus one week, the church there is only welcoming him into their fellowship for that week. He's not a "member" in the fullest sense. Yet there is a sense in which he's subject to that church's discipline for the one Sunday. He

---

[43] This is not to say that I think it's wrong for churches to require some sort of membership process that takes a few weeks or months. In fact, in areas with a long Christian history, different denominations, and the transience and anonymity that accompany urban life, I think some kind of membership process is at least prudent, and perhaps even necessary, in order for a church to responsibly affirm its members' professions of faith. We'll briefly return to this in chap. 11. For more, see chap. 6 of Jonathan Leeman, *The Church and the Surprising Offense of God's Love: Reintroducing the Doctrines of Church Membership and Discipline* (Wheaton, IL: Crossway, 2010).

[44] Similarly Thomas White, "A Baptist's Theology of the Lord's Supper," in *Restoring Integrity in Baptist Churches*, ed. Thomas White, Jason G. Duesing, and Malcolm B. Yarnell III (Grand Rapids: Kregel, 2008), 158.

has to make himself known to them in the first place in order to be welcomed to the Table. Further, imagine he had this conversation with an elder before the gathering and then during the gathering started spouting false teaching. The church would be right to bar him from their celebration of the Lord's Supper. In such a scenario Philippos is never really a "member" of the church in the way we typically use the term. But insofar as he is appealing to the church to participate in their fellowship for just one Sunday, he only does so by consent of the church and thereby submits to the authority of the church.

Church membership is a durable relation. Its duties of submission, accountability, mutual care, and so on can only be carried out over time. Elders leading and members following happen through time. If you're only at a church one Sunday, there's no time to be a member, so the theological category of "membership" doesn't obtain. But that doesn't mean its effective sign should be withheld. Instead, a baptized, in-good-standing member of another church should be welcomed to the Table precisely because he *would* be welcomed as a member if he were staying longer.

This is why I think it's a good idea for churches to admit to the Table not only their own members but also baptized members of other evangelical churches. That says you don't have to be a member here, but you have to be a member somewhere. If you're not submitting to a church where you live, you're not submitting to Jesus. But if you are submitting to Jesus by submitting to a local church, and if you have publicly identified with Christ in baptism, then you should be welcome to the Table.

Of course, "visiting Communion" is an exceptional circumstance. Normally, Sunday finds us in the place where we live and work. And because the Lord's Supper entails responsibility for the church, in order to participate you must be responsible for—that is, a committed member of—the church you attend.

4. The Lord's Supper Should Only Be Celebrated by Local Churches

A fourth implication is that the Lord's Supper should only be celebrated by local churches. Again, recall 1 Corinthians 11:18: "When you come together as a church, I hear that there are divisions among you." The Lord's Supper is celebrated by the church, as a church. Therefore, only a local church has the authority to administer the Lord's Supper, and it is only authorized to administer it to the whole church.

Recall our discussion of the keys of the kingdom in the previous chapter. The keys of the kingdom representatively identify an earthly people with the realities of the kingdom of heaven. And what is the Lord's Supper if not a tangible manifestation of those realities? Only the church is authorized to administer the renewing oath-sign of the new covenant. Only the church is authorized to preside over the renewing of our pledge to Christ and to one another.

Because the Lord's Supper effectively signifies a church's existence as a body, it shouldn't be celebrated by individuals or families or any other group. It shouldn't be celebrated by a part of the church separate from the whole, like a youth group or mission team or the bride and groom at a wedding. It shouldn't be celebrated by a campus ministry or other parachurch group. It shouldn't be celebrated by a military chaplain—unless, of course, his soldiers have constituted a church together. And it shouldn't be "taken" to those who are homebound or in the hospital, despite the commendable compassion that evidences.[45] To make the Lord's Supper something other than a communal, ecclesial meal is to make it something other than the Lord's Supper.

This is not to downplay the Lord's Supper but to put it on the pedestal Jesus gave us: the gathering of the whole church. The Lord's Supper defines our identity as a church, enriches our fellowship, and binds many into one because we do it *together*.

5. A Gathering that Regularly Celebrates the Lord's Supper Together Is a Church

Fifth, a gathering which regularly celebrates the Lord's Supper together *is* a church. According to Paul's logic that we've unpacked in this chapter, a local church is coextensive with that group of people who regularly celebrate the Lord's Supper together. This is a necessary inference from 1 Corinthians 10:17, and it slices in at least two different directions.

---

[45] See Robert Bruce, *The Mystery of the Lord's Supper*, ed. Thomas F. Torrance (Cambridge: James Clarke and Co. Ltd., 1958) 108: "If the Sacrament is administered to anyone privately, it is not a Sacrament, because the Apostle calls this Sacrament a *Communion*; therefore if you administer it to one person alone, you lose the Sacrament." So also Heinrich Heppe, *Reformed Dogmatics Set Out and Illustrated from the Sources*, ed. Ernst Bizer (Grand Rapids: Baker, 1984), 635.

First, think of a "ministry" that regularly celebrates the Lord's Supper but doesn't consider itself a church. That's a little bit like a cohabitating couple: they've got marriage minus the title and the commitment. If you're in this situation, you need to pick one side of the fence or the other. Either consider yourselves a church, with all the responsibility and structure that entails, or stop celebrating the Lord's Supper and more sharply distinguish your group from a church.

Second, this means that a number of "churches" that think they're one church are actually several churches. Yes, I mean multisite churches and even "multiservice" churches, where people have the choice of, say, a 9:00 a.m. or 11:00 a.m. service. Hear Paul again: "Because there is one bread, we who are many are one body, for we all partake of the one bread" (1 Cor 10:17). Paul has in mind one group of people, in one place, at one time, participating in one act together. He doesn't say, "Because we all have one vision statement, and leadership structure, and statement of faith, and budget, we who are many are one body." Instead, he points to concrete, in-the-same-place, communal participation in Christ as the effective sign of a church's existence. Where you have a regular, eucharistic assembly, you have a church. Where you have multiple such assemblies, you have multiple churches.[46]

The practical takeaway is similar to the first point: such churches should bring their labels and structures in line with reality, one way or the other. Either remain one and gather as one, or give the title and structure of "church" to each gathering. If what you've been accustomed to thinking of as one church is actually multiple churches, then wisely, patiently work to bring your language and polity in line with that reality. Some churches with multiple services have enough room to meet all together, though getting everyone into one room may be a tall order for other reasons. For multisite churches that transition to independent congregations, there's plenty you can still share together, just like the churches of the New Testament did.[47]

---

[46] Of course, the Lord's Supper without the gospel is no longer the Lord's Supper. So when I speak about a "eucharistic assembly" above, I am assuming that the gospel is believed and preached. If it isn't, that assembly isn't a church any more than a group of atheists who attempted to celebrate the Lord's Supper would be. Another note: I'm using the term *eucharistic* because it's the most convenient adjectival label for the Lord's Supper. The word itself has biblical roots: the "blessing" of 1 Cor 10:16 is most likely a thanksgiving, the Greek verb for which is εὐχαριστέω (*eucharisteō*).

[47] See Jonathan Leeman, "Independence and Interdependence," in *Baptist Foundations: Chruch Government for an Anti-Institutional Age*, ed. Mark Dever and Jonathan Leeman

The Greek word for church, *ekklēsia*, means "assembly." And an assembly has to assemble. But it's what we *do* when we assemble that defines the nature and identity of a church. This raises the question: must churches celebrate the Lord's Supper weekly? I'm honestly not sure. On the one hand, "as often as you drink it" (1 Cor 11:25) seems to suggest frequency without specifying weekly observance. On the other hand, Paul's references to the Corinthians celebrating the Lord's Supper when they "come together" as a church seems to imply that they celebrated it each time they came together. Further, when Acts 20:7 says, "On the first day of the week, when we were gathered together to break bread," this may indicate that the church in Troas celebrated the Lord's Supper every week. Further, Luke says they gathered *to* break bread, perhaps suggesting that the Lord's Supper was a constitutive element of the gathering, though again, it's not certain that "break bread" refers to the Lord's Supper.

Putting all this together, there may be a slim but consistent pattern of weekly observance in the New Testament. And the theological case we've made in this chapter could actually deepen the rationale for the practice. So I'm almost persuaded that weekly observance is normative. I certainly have no objection to weekly Communion, and I think there is much to commend it. Yet while "as often as you drink it" is compatible with weekly observance, it seems to imply a degree of flexibility. So, for now at least, I think the frequency of the Lord's Supper is a matter of prudence.

Regardless, my main point here is that a gathering which regularly celebrates the Lord's Supper is a church. And such assemblies, or assemblages of assemblies, would do well to bring their labels and structures in line with this reality.

Far from Incidental

In this chapter we've seen that the Lord's Supper's connection to the church is far from incidental. The Lord's Supper isn't something we just happen to do in church but can just as well do at camp or in a college classroom. Instead,

---

(Nashville, B&H, 2015). For a fuller engagement with multisite ecclesiology, see Jonathan Leeman, "Theological Critique of Multi-Site: What Exactly Is a 'Church'?" *9Marks Journal* 6, no. 3 (2009), available at http://www.9marks.org/journal/theological-critique -multi-site-what-exactly-%E2%80%9Cchurch%E2%80%9D; Darrell Grant Gaines, "One Church in One Location: Questioning the Biblical, Theological, and Historical Claims of the Multi-Site Church Movement" (PhD Diss., The Southern Baptist Theological Seminary, 2012), available at http://72.32.3.66/handle/10392/4113.

the Lord's Supper is done by the church, as a church, because it represents and ratifies the unity of the church.

In the Lord's Supper we rehearse the gospel events by plotting our lives in the gospel story, just as an Israelite declared in the Passover that God brought *him* up from Egypt. By taking the bread and cup, we say, "This Jesus is my Savior; his death delivers me from sin." And so we communally participate in the benefits of Jesus' death. Moreover, in the Lord's Supper we repeatedly renew our trust in and submission to Jesus according to the new covenant. Analogous to baptism, the Lord's Supper is the renewing oath-sign of the new covenant. As such, the Lord's Supper is celebrated by the church, as a church, and it entails responsibility for the church.

Therefore the Lord's Supper is the effective sign of the church's unity, its fellowship, its existence as one body. The Lord's Supper makes many one because by it we participate in the realities that unite us to Christ and therefore to one another. In the same act by which we renew our pledge to Christ, we renew our pledge to our fellow church members. The Lord's Supper is a corporate covenant renewal.[48]

After making this case, we considered five of its theological and pastoral consequences. The most important for our present argument is that baptism must precede the Lord's Supper. You must perform the initiating oath-sign of the covenant before you may participate in its renewing oath-sign. You must publicly pledge yourself to Christ and his people before you can publicly renew that pledge.

One final point is worth reiterating: because the Lord's Supper is the effective sign of church unity, it's also the effective sign of church membership. The same tie that binds many into one binds one to many. By enacting the reality which makes a church a church, the Lord's Supper also enacts each member's membership in the church. To be a member is to be admitted to the Lord's Supper. To be removed from membership is to be barred from the Lord's Supper.

---

[48] This is one reason why it is entirely appropriate for churches that have a formal church covenant to verbally renew this covenant with one another when they observe the Lord's Supper. Yet pastors of such churches should also be careful to instruct their people about the covenant-renewing nature of the Lord's Supper itself. At the Lord's Supper we renew our covenant with one another by our words precisely because in the meal itself, we do it by our actions. The explicit verbal covenant elaborates the implicit covenant of the Lord's Supper. I'll say more about this in the next chapter.

So we've seen that both baptism and the Lord's Supper are effective signs of church membership. Baptism confers membership; it constitutes someone a "church member." The Lord's Supper ratifies and enacts a believer's union with the church, like sexual union ratifies and enacts the "one flesh" union of marriage. And, as we'll see in the next chapter, the fact that baptism and the Lord's Supper are effective signs of church membership has decisive implications for how we think about membership itself.

Headlines
Like baptism, the Lord's Supper is intrinsically related to the church. This is seen in that it is a transformation of the Passover (Luke 22:7–20); it is a communal participation in the benefits of Jesus' death (1 Cor 10:16; 11:17ff.); it is the renewing oath-sign of the new covenant (Luke 22:20); and it is celebrated by the church, as a church, and it entails responsibility for the church (1 Cor 11:17ff.).
In the Lord's Supper we repeatedly ratify the new covenant, renewing our trust in Christ and commitment to his people. The Lord's Supper is therefore an effective sign of the local church's existence as a church. It binds many into one.
Therefore, you must be baptized in order to participate in the Lord's Supper. You must perform the initiating oath-sign of the covenant before you can participate in the renewing oath-sign of the covenant.
The Lord's Supper should only be celebrated by local churches as churches. It normally entails membership in a local church. And a gathering which regularly celebrates the Lord's Supper is a church. Why? Because the Lord's Supper, like baptism, is an effective sign of church membership.

Chapter 7

Badges of Belonging: Church Membership and Its Effective Signs

A few nights ago my wife and I watched one of our favorite shows. During the credits, this message appeared: "Promotional consideration furnished by Apple." I did a minor double-take. The words seemed to mean something different from what I knew they had to mean. The label didn't match the reality. Or if it did, it did so only after a detour, an attempt to throw you off the trail. It's easy to understand the rationale for such euphemism, since it's a little unseemly to say, "Apple paid this show's producers to ensure that every character uses a MacBook Air." In this case the distance between label and reality is the measure of a calculating corporate self-interest. I use a PC, by the way.

Sometimes we mislabel by simple mistake, as when I call my daughter Lucy "Rose," her big sister's name. The kid's two and a half years younger, but she looks just like her sister did yesterday. On the other hand, sometimes we mislabel things when we misunderstand them, as when I call the girls' leggings "tights" or tights "leggings." Despite my wife's repeated efforts, I have not yet attained to the secret, hidden knowledge of what differentiates the two.

In this chapter I'll argue that advocates of open membership unintentionally mislabel church membership itself when they argue that it can be extended

to those who have not been baptized.[1] More precisely: they extend the label to
something that lacks the reality.

Putting the Last Piece on the Table

This chapter puts on the table the last piece of our case for baptism as a prerequisite of church membership. I've argued that in order to relate baptism to
membership rightly, we need to discern the ecclesial shape of baptism. And
we've seen that baptism is where faith goes public. It's the initiating oath-sign
of the new covenant. It's the passport of the kingdom and the kingdom citizen's swearing-in ceremony. Because baptism is where faith goes public, and
the "public" you enter through baptism is the local church, baptism is an effective sign of church membership. Therefore, baptism is necessary for church
membership. You can't get your passport stamped if you don't have a passport
in the first place.

But in order to come full circle, we need to discern not just the ecclesial
shape of baptism but the baptismal shape of membership. That is, we need
to describe more accurately *what church membership is* in light of the fact that
baptism is one of its effective signs. Of course, membership has a eucharistic
shape too. The Lord's Supper is the renewing oath-sign of the new covenant
and the effective sign of the church's existence as a unified body. Baptism and
the Lord's Supper, therefore, are both effective signs of church membership.
For a new convert baptism confers membership, and then the Lord's Supper
ratifies and enacts membership.

This chapter, then, attempts to theologically redescribe church membership in light of its effective signs. In this debate and in free church ecclesiology more broadly, we too often treat baptism, the Lord's Supper, and church
membership as three discrete entities that all stand on their own two feet. As
we've seen, some argue that baptism is an individual ordinance and implies
no consequent relation to any local church. And while the Lord's Supper may
be celebrated by a church, the fact that there isn't an inviolable, one-to-one
relationship between the Supper and church membership means that some are

---

[1] On the other hand, some essentially argue that the church should treat some persons as baptized on the ground that they think they've been baptized, perhaps limiting that
provision to those who give exegetical reasons for thinking so. In this case the mislabeling
is of another sort: the church is reckoning as baptism something that is not baptism.

content not to go any further in describing the relationship between the two. In response, I hope chapters 3–6 have demonstrated that the ties between the ordinances and membership are much stronger than we often think.

Yet there is still something of a gap between the ordinances and membership. You can be baptized without joining a church (if a church doesn't yet exist where you live), and you can take the Lord's Supper without thereby joining that church (if you're visiting and you belong to another). But some have widened this gap into a chasm, a chasm evident in the open membership position. John Piper, for example, has said that he wants to admit paedobaptists to membership *not* because membership is unimportant but precisely because membership is so important.[2] This statement assumes what it needs to prove: that there's no intrinsic link between baptism and membership, so they can be separated at will. Throughout the book I've argued that there is a deep-rooted link between baptism and church membership, and this link means baptism is required for church membership. In this chapter we conclude our case by exploring what this link means for how we understand church membership itself.

We'll do this in four steps. First I'll revisit some ground from chapter 5 and theologically describe the birth of a church, focusing especially on the role of the two ordinances. Second, I'll explore the tension between viewing the church as constituted by a covenant and as constituted by the ordinances. Specifically, I'll describe what the covenant of "membership" explicitly tells us that the ordinances don't. Third, I'll attempt to resolve this tension by offering a definition of church membership that takes account of its effective signs. Fourth, I'll close the loop by arguing that baptism is required for membership because without baptism membership doesn't actually exist.

The Ordinances and the Birth of a Church

First, how does a church come into existence? And what role do the two ordinances play in this? I'm exploring this question again because the answer to what makes a church is also the answer to what makes someone a church

---

[2] John Piper, "More Clarifications on the Baptism and Membership Issue: How Important Is Church Membership?" (October 12, 2005), available at http://www.desiring god.org/resource-library/taste-see-articles/more-clarifications-on-the-baptism-and-membership -issue.

member. In the previous chapter we saw that because the Lord's Supper is an effective sign of the church's existence as one body, it's also an effective sign of church membership. The same act that constitutes a church constitutes someone a church member. Church membership is the church-constituting relation described from the standpoint of the individual's relation to the church. The relation which binds many into one is also what binds one to many.

To answer our question, let's engage in a thought experiment not unlike the one we undertook with our friend Philippos last chapter. Think back to the first century AD. Remember that where the gospel has spread, there's only one church in each town. There are no competing denominations, no conflicting understandings and practices of baptism. And there's no social incentive to become a Christian—just the opposite.

Say you're a member of the church in Pisidian Antioch in what's now southern Turkey. It's the late AD 40s. A famine devastates the city, and you hear conditions are better up north in Ancyra, so you travel there in search of food and work. When you get there, you discover that the gospel hasn't yet made its way to Ancyra. You're the only believer in Jesus in the whole city. So you befriend some local Jews. You go to their synagogue meetings and reason with them about how Jesus fulfills the Old Testament promises of a Messiah. You encounter plenty of devout pagans in the marketplace, and you talk to them about how there's one true God, the Creator and Ruler and Sustainer of all. And this one true God came to earth as the man Jesus, to rescue us from idolatry and condemnation.

After a few months of this, a handful of Jews and Greeks are ready to become Christians. What do you do? You're not an apostle or anything, but you know they need to be baptized, so you baptize them in the river. Now what? You know that Jesus gave his people a meal to celebrate together, so you start meeting together every Sunday to celebrate this meal in the home of Fortunatus, the one well-off believer in your group. Even though you're working all the time just to eke out a living, you know Jesus' teachings better than any of these new believers, so you start teaching them at these weekly meetings. You teach them to love God, to love one another, and to love their neighbors. You teach them to forgive one another, to share with one another, to bear one another's burdens.

A few weeks later Julia, the mother of one of the believers, comes to faith and asks to be baptized. The following Sunday, instead of meeting at Fortunatus's house, you meet at the river, baptize her, and then she joins in as you celebrate the Lord's Supper together. Over time a few more believers from other churches in cities like Iconium and Lystra move up to Ancyra and hear about your assembly. These believers have been baptized, and they boldly confess that Jesus is Lord. So at your gathering you introduce them to the other believers, who gladly welcome them into your fellowship. Once in a while one of the new members from down south will travel back, spend a week or two with the believers there, participate in their weekly gathering, and then come back with a message from the church. On one of those trips, they even came back with a copy of a letter from the apostle Paul to the churches of Galatia.

What do you have there in Ancyra? A church. All these believers, from the first converts to Julia to those from Iconium and Lystra, are members of your church. How did this church come into existence? We could describe it in two steps. In the first step you preached the gospel (Rom 10:14–17), and the Holy Spirit enabled the gospel to take root in people's hearts, causing faith to spring up (John 3:1–8; Acts 16:14; 2 Cor 4:6). In the second step these new believers' faith manifested itself in baptism, the initiating, public act of witness to their faith in Christ (Matt 28:19). And their faith manifested itself in a common life: gathering together, sharing their possessions, caring for one another, and especially partaking of the Lord's Supper together (1 Cor 11:17–34).

A church is born when gospel people form a gospel polity. These believers in Ancyra are gospel people in that they have been re-created by the good news of Christ in the power of the Spirit. And they have come together in a gospel polity in that they have declared a new allegiance in baptism, thereby entering a new body politic, and they eat together as a new family in the Lord's Supper.[3] God constitutes people as Christians through the Holy Spirit's application of the gospel, and then, in response, those people gather to constitute a church. The divine and human actions are tightly linked. As John Webster puts it, the church's human act of assembly "follows, signifies, and mediates a divine act of gathering; it is a moved movement of congregation."[4]

God creates Christians through the gospel. In that sense the gospel creates the church. Therefore, as Christoph Schwöbel says, "As the creature of

---

[3] Note that I'm using "polity" here not in the sense of a form or process of government but simply of an organized society.

[4] John Webster, "'In the Society of God': Some Principles of Ecclesiology," in *Perspectives on Ecclesiology and Ethnography*, ed. Pete Ward (Grand Rapids: Eerdmans, 2012), 216.

the divine Word the Church is constituted by divine action."[5] God's Word has always created God's people. The same power that called the stars into being calls each new believer into new being. We can no more create the church than we can create a galaxy. God speaks the church into life.[6]

Yet Webster points out that this "invisible" moment in which God constitutes someone a Christian is not the "only constitutive moment for ecclesiology."[7] Yes, God creates his people through the gospel. But if faith stayed invisible, there would be no church on earth, only individual Christians, or at best vague, indistinct associations of believers.[8] Instead, God's people have a visible, corporate, political existence on earth. We are a public polis. And, as we've seen in the last four chapters, God has appointed public, self-involving acts of witness to the gospel—baptism and the Lord's Supper—to craft this body's corporate existence. God constitutes the church not just by creating gospel persons but by ordaining and enabling their social, institutional response to the gospel.[9]

In other words, baptism and the Lord's Supper make the church visible. They are the hinge between the "invisible" universal church and the "visible" local church. They draw a line around the church by drawing the church together.[10] They gather many into one: baptism by adding one to many, the Lord's Supper by making many one. Oliver O'Donovan writes:

---

[5] Christoph Schwöbel, "The Creature of the Word: Recovering the Ecclesiology of the Reformers," in *On Being the Church. Essays on the Christian Community*, ed. Colin E. Gunton and Daniel W. Hardy (Edinburgh: T&T Clark, 1989), 122.

[6] For more on this, see Jonathan Leeman, *Reverberation: How God's Word Brings Light, Freedom, and Action to His People* (Chicago: Moody, 2011), especially chaps. 1–4; Timothy Ward, *Words of Life: Scripture as the Living and Active Word of God* (Downers Grove, IL: InterVarsity, 2009), especially chap. 2.

[7] John Webster, "The Self-Organizing Power of the Gospel: Episcopacy and Community Formation," in *International Journal of Systematic Theology* 3, no. 1 (2001): 73.

[8] As Webster puts it: if we attend only to the "invisible" constitutive moment, "a picture of the church is promoted in which the human Christian community is unstable, liminal, and so incapable of sustaining a coherent historical and social trajectory" (ibid.).

[9] Thus Webster writes elsewhere, "What *kind* of society is the church? The answer ecclesiology returns is this: the church is the human assembly that is the creaturely social coefficient of the outer work in which God restores creatures to fellowship with himself" ("In the Society of God," 201).

[10] Grant Macaskill writes that the two sacraments "have an important social dimension, marking the community of faith as distinct, circumscribing its boundaries. That social function is governed by their covenantal character" (*Union with Christ in the New Testament* [Oxford: Oxford University Press, 2013], 301).

> The sacraments provide the primary way in which the church is "knit together," that is, given institutional form and order. Without them the church could be a "visible" society, without doubt, but only a rather intangible one, melting indeterminately like a delicate mist as we stretched out our arms to embrace it. In these forms we know where the church is and can attach ourselves to it. They are at once "signs" of the mystery of redemption wrought in Christ, and "effective signs" which give it a palpable presence in the participating church.[11]

Notice all that O'Donovan draws together. The sacraments, baptism and the Lord's Supper, are what "knit" the church together, giving it "institutional form and order." They make the church visible; they tell us where the church is and how we can join it. Because the sacraments make the church visible, they are effective signs. They give the gospel a "palpable presence in the participating church" and thereby make the church itself something palpable.

Baptism and the Lord's Supper inscribe the gospel into the shape and structure of the church. The joints that hold the church together are made of gospel wood. Webster writes, "Church order is the social shape of the converting power and activity of Christ present as Spirit."[12] As church-ordering rites, baptism and the Lord's Supper craft the social shape of our response to the gospel. They define the shape of the church by marking the space it fills. As Balthasar Hubmaier puts it, that which baptism and the Lord's Supper "seek to achieve," the end toward which these ordinances "should finally be directed," is "to gather a church."[13]

---

[11] *The Desire of the Nations: Rediscovering the Roots of Political Theology* (Cambridge: Cambridge University Press, 1996), 172. Recall that O'Donovan locates the Lord's Supper's efficacy as a sign "not . . . in a 'sacramental grace' which affects the believer in a different way from other kinds of grace; but in the *formation of the church*" (ibid., 180; emphasis original).

[12] Webster, "Self-Organizing Power," 73. Further: "The church is a political society; that is to say, it is a sphere of human fellowship, though one created not by natural affinity or association but by the gathering power of the gospel" (ibid., 77).

[13] Balthasar Hubmaier, "On Fraternal Admonition," in *Balthasar Hubmaier: Theologian of Anabaptism*, ed. H. Wayne Pipkin and John Howard Yoder, Classics of the Radical Reformation, vol. 5 (Scottdale, PA: Herald, 1989), 384. Hubmaier's full statement repays—and requires—careful reading: "So all of those who cry: 'Well, what about water baptism? Why, all the fuss about the Lord's Supper? They are after all just outward signs! They're nothing but water, bread, and wine! Why fight about that?' They have not in their whole life learned enough to know why the signs were instituted by Christ, what they seek to achieve or toward what they should finally be directed, namely to gather a church, to

Another way to get at this is to say that the ordinances themselves give a church its "churchness." By gathering many into one, the ordinances make the church into something more than the sum of its parts. By drawing a line between the church and the world, the ordinances make it possible to point to something and say "church" rather than only pointing to many somethings and saying "Christians." A church is born when gospel people form a gospel polity, and the ordinances are the effective signs of that polity. They give the church visible, institutional form and order. They knit many into one.

What About the "Mutual Covenant" of Membership?

But what about the classical free-church account, which I endorsed in chapter 5, in which a church is constituted by the "mutual covenant" of its members? Are "ordinances" and "mutual covenant" contradictory accounts of how a church is constituted?

In the account of the birth of a church I've just sketched, an explicit covenant is conspicuous by its absence. I never mentioned a meeting in which the members drafted up a written covenant or made verbal vows to one another. I never mentioned new members making a verbal pledge to the church and the church pledging themselves in return. The reason for this is simple: the New Testament doesn't mention anything like this.

On the basis of this conspicuous absence, some have argued against the practice of formal church membership. One traditional reply has been to assert that, in fact, the New Testament *does* attest a practice of covenanting as local churches.[14] For instance, 2 Corinthians 8:5 says, "They gave themselves first

---

commit oneself publicly to live according to the Word of Christ in faith and brotherly love, and because of sin to subject oneself to fraternal admonition and the Christian ban, and to do all of this with a sacramental oath before the Christian church and all her members, assembled partly in body and completely in spirit, testifying publicly, in the power of God, Father and Holy Spirit, or in the power of our Lord Jesus Christ (which is all the same power), and yielding oneself to her in hand-pledged fidelity. Look to this, dear brethren, and not to water, bread or wine, lest our water baptism and breaking bread might also be only an appearance and a sleight of hand, nothing better than what the stupid child baptism and baby feeding have been before, if fraternal admonition and the Christian ban do not constantly accompany them."

[14] For one historic example see, e.g., Richard Mather, *An Apologie of the Churches in New-England for Church-Covenant . . .* (London, 1643), in *Church Covenant: Two Tracts*, Research Library of Colonial America (New York: Arno, 1972).

to the Lord and then by the will of God to us." One might argue from the lesser to the greater: if in this passage the Macedonian believers "covenanted" in a sense to relieve the poor saints in Jerusalem, how much more would they have solemnly bound themselves to God and to one another when they first came together as a church? While there may be some merit in this, it remains speculative. The New Testament simply doesn't provide any detailed narratives of the birth of local churches. And in what little we do have, we don't see anything that looks like a formal act of covenanting.

Remember what we saw in Acts 2:41 back in chapter 5: for new converts at least, baptism is the New Testament way to join a church. And we simply don't have a record of what transpired when baptized Christians moved to churches in other cities. Therefore, since a verbal "church covenant" seems absent from the pages of the New Testament, I'm hesitant to see it as absolutely essential for the existence or right ordering of a local church.

However, the reality of membership—that some people are in the church and others are out—is everywhere present in the New Testament.[15] For example, Paul writes, "For what have I to do with judging outsiders? Is it not those inside the church whom you are to judge? God judges those outside" (1 Cor 5:12–13). Provisionally, we can define church membership as a relation between a local church and a Christian in which the Christian belongs and submits to the church and the church affirms and oversees the Christian's profession of faith in Christ. We'll work toward a more precise definition soon. For now, though, we need to ask: How does this concept of membership relate to the ordinances? More specifically, what territory does membership gain us beyond the ground claimed by the ordinances? I'll answer in three parts.

First, "membership" makes explicit what is implicit in the two ordinances. We've seen that both baptism and the Lord's Supper are oath-signs—nonverbal acts that perform the same function as a verbal oath. Both ordinances have vertical and horizontal elements: they commit us to God and to one another. And in ecclesial terms both ordinances are effective signs. They knit the body together: baptism adds one to many, and the Lord's Supper makes many one. So we can say that both ordinances imply a covenant not just between an individual and God but also between an individual and the church. Or, to use an older term, each ordinance is an "implicit covenant": they implicitly enact a

---

[15] See Jonathan Leeman, *Church Membership: How the World Knows Who Represents Jesus* (Wheaton, IL: Crossway, 2012), chap. 2.

pledge between believer and church and between church and believer. Baptism initiates this covenant, and the Lord's Supper renews it.

Seen from this angle, "membership" names the relation the ordinances imply and normally create. To call someone a "member" is to say that they have been baptized, they partake of the Lord's Supper, and they are welcomed into, and responsible for, the ecclesial life these effective signs entail. Consider further that the two ordinances extend through time: baptism initiates a relation, and the Lord's Supper regularly renews it. The term *member*, then, describes a person whose ecclesial identity is determined by their ongoing participation in a particular local body. The ordinances create an ecclesial reality, and membership names that reality.

Second, the concept of "membership" distinguishes the ordinances from the relation they normally imply when, in legitimate though exceptional circumstances, the two are separated. As we've seen, the Ethiopian eunuch did not become a member of a church upon baptism because no church yet existed where he lived (Acts 8:26–40). And those visitors who may have celebrated the Lord's Supper in Troas (Acts 20:7) were presumably not considered "members" of the church there since they lived elsewhere. The relationship between the ordinances and membership is not automatic; it is not just theoretically possible but occasionally legitimate to have one without the other. "Membership," therefore, is a valid and necessary theological concept because it describes the durable relation between a church and a Christian which is normally, though not invariably, sealed in the effective signs of baptism and the Lord's Supper.

A third feature of membership is not attested directly in the New Testament but is nevertheless a valid inference from its teaching. This feature kicks in when a professing believer attempts to participate in the ordinances while evading the responsibility of membership. Again, think back to a first-century, one-church-in-one-city frame of reference. Say someone shows up at the church's gathering, claims to have become a Christian, and wants to be baptized but also indicates that he has no intention of gathering with the church week by week or submitting to its leaders. Such a person should be denied baptism because he is refusing the relation that baptism entails. Or consider a baptized Christian who moves to a new city, attends church a few times, but then stops showing up. Is this person in the church or out? He had been in the habit of participating in the Lord's Supper, but now he is forsaking the assembly (Heb 10:24–25). The person's status needs to be clarified one way or the other: either he repents and resumes regular attendance, or the church should bar him from the Lord's Supper.

Church membership thus fulfills the crucial role of protecting the ordinances as practices *of the church*. Membership ensures that the ordinances retain the relational character the Bible gives them: baptism creates a relationship to the church, and the Lord's Supper renews that relationship. Membership is the shape into which the ordinances build the church. Without membership the ordinances are in danger of becoming the spiritual accessories of autonomous consumers rather than the church's authoritative seals of a credible profession. Membership helps preserve the shape and significance of the ordinances like a truss supports a roof.

Note that in all this "membership" is a second-order description, a theological account of the relation the ordinances normally create. This relation is clearly present in the New Testament but is not named or defined. In this way *membership* is like any other theological term. For instance, all the components of classical trinitarian doctrine are stated or implied in the New Testament, but the doctrine as such is never explicitly articulated.[16] So too with membership.

This section has taken us a long way toward reconciling these two conflicting accounts of what constitutes a church and church membership. We've clarified that the relation we call "membership" is found in the New Testament. We've seen that the language and practice of membership makes explicit what is implicit in the ordinances. It names the relation the ordinances normally create. It distinguishes that relation from the ordinances in the exceptional circumstances in which they may legitimately be separated. And it protects the ordinances when a professing believer sinfully attempts to participate in them while refusing to enter the relationship of submission and oversight they entail.

But what we haven't yet resolved is this: what is essential in order to constitute this relationship? Must there be an explicit, verbal declaration of commitment in order for a Christian to become a church member and in order for multiple Christians to become a church?

---

[16] See, e.g., David Yeago's article "The New Testament and the Nicene Dogma: A Contribution to the Recovery of Theological Exegesis," in *Sewanee Theological Review* 45, no. 4 (2002): 371–84.

What Is This Thing Called Membership?

To answer this question, we must define church membership more precisely.
I'll start with Jonathan Leeman's definition, add a phrase, then burrow into a
key term. This should help untangle the knotty question of how a membership covenant relates to the ordinances as effective signs. Here's Leeman's definition: "Church membership is (1) a covenant of union between a particular
church and a Christian, a covenant that consists of (2) the church's affirmation
of the Christian's gospel profession, (3) the church's promise to give oversight
to the Christian, and (4) the Christian's promise to gather with the church and
submit to its oversight."[17]

The first thing we need to do is add the following italicized words: "Church
membership is (1) a covenant of union between a particular church and a
Christian, a covenant *whose effective signs are baptism and the Lord's Supper*, and
that consists of . . ."[18] For our purposes it's important to make membership's
connection to the ordinances explicit. Membership names the relation the ordinances imply and normally create. In order to understand this relation, we
need to understand that the ordinances create it.

Next, the key term we need to burrow into is "covenant." Leeman says that
membership *is* a covenant. This makes sense in light of the mutually binding
promises which his points three and four describe: the church promises to give
oversight to the Christian's discipleship, and the Christian promises to gather
with and submit to the church. Thus, to call membership a covenant is simply
to say that it is a formal relationship defined by mutual promises. Unlike some
of the covenants described in Scripture, such as marriage or God's covenant
with Abraham, the covenant of membership is not permanent. Christians can
change churches for a number of legitimate reasons, like moving to another
city. Leaving a church is not necessarily equivalent to divorce. Yet the covenant of membership is like certain biblical covenants in that the subordinate

---

[17] Jonathan Leeman, *The Church and the Surprising Offense of God's Love: Reintroducing
the Doctrines of Church Membership and Discipline* (Wheaton, IL: Crossway, 2010), 217.
When Leeman says the Christian promises "to gather with the church and submit to its oversight," this implies not merely passive presence but loving, serving, and building up the body.

[18] This addition is consonant with Leeman's own exposition. See the discussion of
baptism and the Lord's Supper in ibid., 165, 191, 193, 199, 268; and, with formulations
that are closer to and have influenced mine, in *A Political Assembly: How Jesus Establishes
Local Churches as Embassies of His International Rule* (Downers Grove, IL: InterVarsity,
forthcoming), chap. 6.

party—the Christian—may not unilaterally terminate the covenant. One may join or leave a church only with the consent of the church.[19] So this definition of membership uses the term *covenant* somewhat analogically or metaphorically, yet with substantial parallels to biblical uses of the word.

Further, this use of the term *covenant* to describe membership actually provides the key to resolving our conflict between the church as constituted by "mutual covenant" and the church as constituted by the ordinances. As Leeman uses the term here, "covenant" describes the relation of membership, a durable bond between church and individual. As we've seen, baptism and the Lord's Supper are covenantal oath-signs, initiating and renewing a believer's participation in the new covenant. Yet they also ratify and renew the "covenant" of local church membership. In baptism, in the same act by which you pledge yourself to Christ, you pledge yourself to and are received by his people. And in the Lord's Supper, in the same act in which you renew your commitment to Christ, you renew your commitment to those seated next to you.

For the same reason that the ordinances are the hinge between the universal and the local church, they are also the hinge between the new covenant and the covenant of local church membership. In the gospel we receive God as our Father and Christians as our brothers and sisters in one act. Congregationalist theologian P. T. Forsyth wrote: *"The same act which sets us in Christ sets us also in the society of Christ. It does so ipso facto, and not by a mere consequence or sequel, more or less optional. To be in Christ is in the same act to be in the Church. . . . It puts us into a relation with all saints which we may neglect to our bane but which we cannot destroy."*[20] And both of the gospel's ordinances enact this simultaneous vertical and horizontal reception. Normally the same act ratifies your covenant with both Christ and the local church.

---

[19] See Leeman, *The Church and the Surprising Offense*, 317–18. This was widely recognized by previous generations of Baptists. For instance, the Charleston Association wrote in 1774, "As consent is necessary to a person's coming into the church, so none can go out of it without its consent" (*A Summary of Church Discipline* [Charleston: David Bruce, 1774] in *Polity: Biblical Arguments on How to Conduct Church Life*, ed. Mark Dever [Washington, DC: Center for Church Reform, 2001], 129).

[20] P. T. Forsyth, *The Church, the Gospel, and Society* (London: Independent Press, 1962), 61–62, emphasis original. Miroslav Volf similarly writes, "Communion with this God is at once also communion with those others who have entrusted themselves in faith to the same God. Hence one and the same act of faith places a person into a new relationship both with God and with all others who stand in communion with God" (*After Our Likeness: The Church as the Image of the Trinity* [Grand Rapids: Eerdmans, 1999], 173).

We've been considering whether church membership, and therefore a church itself, is constituted by a "covenant" or by the ordinances. It should now be clear that this is a false dichotomy. A church and church membership aren't constituted by a covenant as opposed to the two ordinances, or vice versa, but *by the two ordinances which ratify a covenant*. The relation that binds one to many and many into one *is* a covenant, a set of mutually binding promises. And this relation is initiated and ratified by the two ordinances, oath-signs of the new covenant. Just as these ritual acts ratify the new covenant, so they also constitute the new covenant's corporate correlate on earth: the local church. The ordinances initiate and confirm the covenantal relation between Christians we call church membership. Together they build Christians into the shape we call a church.[21]

Let's return once more to this book's favorite analogy. Imagine a society whose marriage ceremony contains no words but only symbolic oath-signs. For instance: the groom's father rings a bell in the town square to summon the public. When the people have gathered, a town elder pours a cup of wine. The bride's father hands her to the groom, who takes her right hand in his left. With his right hand he takes the chalice, drinks from it, and then holds it to his bride's lips. She drinks, the groom's father rings the bell again, and the crowd erupts in a cheer to celebrate the new union.

If everyone in the culture understands this set of symbolic acts to enact both parties' intent to marry, then verbal vows are not necessary. The act says what the words would have. This is how the ordinances constitute a church: they are acts that speak. They effect a new, mutual relation between the Christians who participate in them together. In baptism a believer submits to the church, and the church affirms the believer's profession, creating the relation we call "membership." In the Lord's Supper the church is constituted as one body by participating in Christ's salvation together. Baptism binds one to many, and the Lord's Supper binds many into one. This means a group of believers need not perform a distinct, formal *act* in addition to and separate

---

[21] On baptism compare John Smyth, "The true forme [sic] of the Church is a covenant betwixt God & the Faithful made in baptisme [sic] in which Christ is visibly put on" (*The Works of John Smyth, Fellow of Christ's College, 1594–1598*, 2 vols., ed. William Thomas Whitley [London: Cambridge University Press, 1915], 2:645). Note that Smyth calls this church-constituting "forme" a covenant and further affirms that this covenant is made in baptism. See discussion in Jason K. Lee, *The Theology of John Smyth: Puritan, Separatist, Baptist, Mennonite* (Macon, GA: Mercer University Press, 2003), 151–52.

from their participation in the ordinances in order to constitute themselves as a body.[22]

Remember what we saw in chapter 5: those who were baptized in Acts 2:41 were added to the church in and by that very action. There was no two-step process of being baptized and then, by a later act, being added to the church. Similarly, every time a church celebrates the Lord's Supper, they renew their commitment to one another by that act. To partake of the Lord's Supper is to undertake responsibility for the body.

However, these "speaking acts" must always be preceded and surrounded by actual words that explain and confirm their significance. There is no gospel people without the preaching of the gospel. So the church must always preach the gospel and call people to repent and believe. Further, a church can't identify a gospel person without hearing a gospel confession. So in order for someone to become a fit subject for baptism and therefore a qualified participant in the Lord's Supper, that person must, in some form or other, verbally confess his faith in Christ to the church (Rom 10:9–10).

In addition, a church must always be explaining the whole counsel of God (Acts 20:27) and exhorting believers to obey everything Jesus commanded (Matt 28:19). It also must instruct candidates for baptism that to be baptized is to submit to Jesus' authority and commit to Jesus' people. A church must teach that baptism is not merely professing faith but pledging obedience. And only those who hear this instruction and freely embrace it should be baptized.

Without this prior instruction and assent, baptism would be like blindfolding a couple, taking them down to the justice of the peace, and having them sign on the dotted line of a marriage certificate without ever knowing that's what they were doing. In such a case the couple really has made a vow, but they have no idea they made a vow. Their subjective stance is completely at odds with and divorced from the objective reality they participated in. Similarly, a church must instruct its members and prospective members that to participate in the Lord's Supper is to sign your name under the solemn vow, "I undertake

---

[22] Though, as historic Congregationalist and Baptist precedent testifies, I think a formal "covenanting" or "constituting" service is eminently advisable. It clarifies who will be part of the church and what it means to form a church, calls forth explicit commitment to the church from each founding member, and demarcates a clear beginning to the church's existence as a body. Fittingly, such services have often culminated in the new church's celebration of the Lord's Supper. See, for example, the Baptist Association in Charleston, South Carolina, *A Summary of Church Discipline*, 118–19.

to love this body of believers as Christ loves them." Churches must teach believers both *that* the ordinances are vows and *what* vows the ordinances enact.

This instruction regarding the ordinances is necessary, in part, because the relation between the sign and what it signifies is ordained by Jesus, not intrinsic to the act itself. You are not eating the Lord's Supper every time you happen to eat bread and drink wine. You are not baptizing your friend if you happen to dunk him in a pool as payback for splashing you. These signs signify what they do because Jesus has linked them to his gospel. To borrow a useful older term, as "positive ordinances" appointed solely by the command of Christ, baptism and the Lord's Supper need to be explained in order to be performed with integrity.[23]

So the ordinances themselves constitute the church as a body. Yet in order for the exercise of the ordinances to have integrity, there must be something analogous to both a membership class and a church covenant, at least in seed form. Imagine a missionary is preaching to a group of unevangelized locals in the mountains of Peru, and eight of those locals tell the missionary they believe in Jesus and want to be baptized. In order for their baptism to have integrity—in order for their subjective intent to cohere with the objective reality being enacted—they must first be taught what baptism is, what baptism does, and what it calls them to do in response. So too with the Lord's Supper. The missionary must teach these believers that to be baptized and to take the Lord's Supper is to submit to Jesus and commit to his people. Fleshing out what that means for all of life is the lifelong task of discipleship. But the seed must be planted before baptism. Those who enroll as citizens in the kingdom of Christ must know what they're signing up for. A formal membership class simply develops what is already present in this seed of necessary prebaptismal instruction.

Now let's assume that these eight new believers all agree that they do want to follow Jesus and enter his people. As they do so, they are also at once identifying one another as those Christians to whom they are committing. In other

---

[23] In the historic Baptist lexicon, a "positive ordinance" is distinguished from other ethical obligations by the fact that it is only binding by virtue of God's command. For instance, God's revelation of himself in the created order is sufficient to convince us that parents must provide for their children, which is a universally binding obligation. But there is no universally binding obligation to be immersed in water or to eat bread and drink wine. Yet the special forms of these acts embedded in baptism and the Lord's Supper are binding on believers because of the command of Christ. This command, accordingly, is also what vests these "positive ordinances" with special significance.

words, their assent to enter the body includes their recognition and affirmation of one another as the other members of the body. In whatever form it takes—whether tacit or explicit, verbal or simply enacted—this prebaptismal assent is the seed of a church covenant since it conveys an individual's commitment to submit to and oversee this particular group of believers. Baptism signifies more than an individual's commitment to follow Christ and join his people but never less. And a formal church covenant simply makes that commitment explicit and specifies its terms.[24]

To return to the main point that the ordinances themselves constitute a local church, consider all this from the perspective of the keys of the kingdom (Matt 16:19; 18:18–19). The keys of the kingdom are the institutional charter of the local church. They authorize a group of Christians to act as one on behalf of Jesus as they representatively declare who on earth belongs to the kingdom of heaven. And the principal means by which the keys are enacted are baptism (initial affirmation) and the Lord's Supper (ongoing affirmation). Jesus has not prescribed any specific form or ritual by which a group of Christians is invested with the keys. There is no transfer of authority from a bishop or presbytery. There is no infinite regress of authorization. Instead, these keys which are exercised congregationally are assumed congregationally. Further, there's no prescribed church-constituting service in Scripture. Instead, a group of Christians assumes the responsibility of the keys when they gather regularly and celebrate the ordinances.

To say that the ordinances are the effective signs of church membership is to say that the ordinances ratify the covenant which is membership. And the Lord's Supper in particular corporately ratifies the covenant which constitutes a church as a church. Remember, the same relation which constitutes a church constitutes a church member. The relation which adds one to many also makes many one.

This clearing up of covenant confusion further illumines what we saw above: membership names the relation which the ordinances create. Baptism effects a new relation between one and many, and the Lord's Supper effects the

---

[24] Also present here is the seed form of a membership interview, insofar as the missionary, assessing the credibility of these confessions of faith, fulfills a role analogous to that of local church elders guarding the front door of the church. In principle the missionary would not baptize someone if he regarded their profession as insincere or otherwise incredible.

relation which makes many one. The ordinances mold the church into a shape called membership.

Closing the Loop

Now it's time to close the loop. We've seen that membership is not some third thing alongside baptism and the Lord's Supper. Instead, membership names the relation which the ordinances imply and normally create. In this section I'll show how this insight concludes our case for baptism and church membership.

The primary payoff is this: we can't remove baptism from membership because without baptism membership doesn't exist. Removing baptism from membership is like removing vows from marriage. As we've seen above, a marriage vow could be verbal or nonverbal, an oath or an oath-sign. But without the vow there is no union. If a man and woman who have not vowed themselves to one another engage in sexual union, the result is not marriage. Similarly, baptism is the vow that creates the union of membership. Because baptism is an oath-sign, an act which performs a vow, it may or may not be accompanied by a verbal vow. The analogy breaks down eventually because marriage is lifelong whereas church membership isn't necessarily. But the point is this: as a marriage does not exist without a vow, so membership does not exist without baptism.

Church membership is a public status, and baptism is the initial entrance into that status. Church membership is the church's endorsement of a profession, and baptism is the initial profession which the church's ongoing affirmation continues to endorse. This entire debate boils down to this: Jesus has appointed baptism to be a person's initial entry into the church. Baptism is the front door of the church; there's no other way in.

What this chapter has added to our case is that "membership" names the relation the ordinances create. Membership is how a church affirms that the vow you made to Jesus in baptism is valid, whether you made that vow five minutes ago in this church or five years ago in another country. Membership makes explicit what is implicit in baptism and the Lord's Supper. Therefore, there is simply no such thing as membership without baptism.

Of course, I'm not denying that a church has the *ability* to extend membership to unbaptized persons. But ability is not authority. If a church extends membership to an unbaptized person, the person really does become a member of that church with all the privileges and responsibilities that entails. But in doing so, the church departs from Jesus' authorizing warrant and operates outside its heavenly constitution. This is analogous to what would happen if a church appointed a woman elder. An elder is someone the Holy Spirit appoints to the office (Acts 20:28), and the Holy Spirit tells us that only men are to hold this office (1 Tim 2:12). So in this case the church appoints to the office someone whom the Holy Spirit hasn't and won't.[25] Similarly, when a church extends membership to someone who hasn't been baptized, they misunderstand what church membership is and grant the label to something which lacks the reality.

Sealing the Case

My central argument in this book has been that baptism and church membership are vitally and organically linked. Therefore, churches shouldn't give the latter to those who lack the former. In chapters 3–5 we set baptism in the foreground to examine its relationship to the church, and in chapter 6 we did the same with the Lord's Supper. In this chapter we've put the church itself in the foreground, revisiting the question of what constitutes a church and church membership in light of the fact that baptism and the Lord's Supper are its effective signs. We've shifted our focus from the ecclesial shape of baptism (and the Lord's Supper) to the baptismal (and eucharistic) shape of church membership.

And we've discovered that membership names the relation the ordinances imply and normally create. The ordinances ratify the covenant of union which is church membership. Therefore, there is no such thing as membership without baptism. To speak of membership without baptism is like speaking of marriage without vows. Marriage is a covenant relation constituted by vows; membership is a covenant relation constituted by the oath-signs of the ordinances.

Those who want to extend membership to paedobaptists intend to widen the fence surrounding the church, but what they're actually doing is dismantling that fence. Jesus established baptism as the line between the church and

---

[25] I'm assuming the vast majority of readers hold complementarian convictions regarding the Bible's teaching about men and women. I would encourage readers who are otherwise minded, or who simply haven't investigated the issue, to consult *Recovering Biblical Manhood and Womanhood: A Response to Evangelical Feminism*, ed. John Piper and Wayne Grudem (redesign ed., Wheaton, IL: Crossway, 2012).

the world. A church that includes unbaptized people is not rightly enlarging the household of God but taking apart its walls. Without baptism there is no local church.

Baptism promotes and protects the gospel by requiring those who believe the gospel to publicly confess the gospel. When a church removes baptism from the requirements for membership, it privatizes Christian profession. It undermines the authority of Christ's commands by allowing Christians to disobey one with impunity. It allows the individual conscience to trump the authority of the local church. In principle, however unintentionally, allowing unbaptized persons to join a church weakens that church's witness to the gospel. For the sake of freedom, that church compromises the true freedom found in keeping all of Christ's commands.[26]

Throughout the past five chapters I've built a case for understanding baptism as a requirement for church membership. Building on the general foundation of chapter 3, chapters 4–6 each presented decisive reasons baptism is necessary for church membership. Thus, this book's argument does not stand or fall with this chapter. However, this chapter takes the case a step further and, I would argue, seals it shut. Churches are not at liberty to extend membership absent baptism. To do so is to misidentify membership, as I sometimes misidentify my daughters or their clothes. Further, to extend membership without baptism is to confer the label where the reality does not in fact exist. Baptism isn't incidental to membership; instead, it initiates membership. Therefore baptism is necessary for church membership.

---

[26] For fuller discussion of the consequences of open membership, see chap. 10.

Headlines
A church is born when gospel people form a gospel polity, and the ordinances of baptism and the Lord's Supper are the effective signs of that polity.
Baptism and the Lord's Supper give the church visible, institutional form and order. They knit many into one.
"Church membership" names the relation which the ordinances create. The ordinances mold the church into a shape called "membership."
Therefore, we can't remove baptism from membership because without baptism, membership doesn't exist. That would be like speaking of a marriage with no vows. Marriage is a covenant relation constituted by vows; membership is a covenant relation constituted by the oath-signs of the ordinances.
When a church extends membership to someone who hasn't been baptized, they misunderstand what church membership is and grant the label to something which lacks the reality.
Jesus has appointed baptism to be a person's initial entry into the church. Baptism is the front door of the church; there's no other way in.

PART 3

The Case Stated, Defended, Applied

Chapter 8

Why Baptism Is Required for Church Membership: A Summary

I n the past five chapters I've carved out the pieces of a case for why baptism is required for church membership. Now it's time to put those pieces together. To switch metaphors, we've been swimming through some deep waters, and I've asked you to hold your breath for a long time. Now we surface, catch our breath, and take a look around.

I'm writing this chapter for two reasons. First, to put all the pieces of the puzzle together in the hope that a coherent, conclusive picture will emerge. If you think such a picture has already emerged, feel free to skip this chapter. Second, plenty of people won't read a book on this issue but will read a chapter. So go ahead and photocopy this chapter to give to people who are wrestling with why they need to be baptized in order to join your church. You have my permission. Not that you need it since photocopying this chapter falls within fair use copyright laws.

Keeping with the "two" theme, I'm going to do two things in this chapter. First, I'm going to fit together, one by one, all the pieces of the case we've carved out in the past five chapters. Second, I'm going to underscore one important implication of this case: Jesus has told the church how we are to recognize Christians. He hasn't left it up to us.

Seven Reasons Baptism Is Required for Church Membership

Here, then, are seven reasons why baptism is required for church membership. Five of these are basically summaries of the previous five chapters. The other two, numbers four and five, draw out conclusions from these chapters which we've already touched on. If these reasons raise questions, I trust the previous five chapters answer many of them. If you disagree with these reasons, hang in there until the next chapter, which is devoted to answering arguments against the case I summarize here.

1. Baptism Is Where Faith Goes Public

First, baptism is where faith goes public. The Christian life is a life of public witness to Christ (Matt 10:32–33), and that witness begins at baptism. At Pentecost those converted by Peter's preaching stepped out from the crowd, declaring allegiance to Christ as Lord and Savior by submitting to baptism (Acts 2:38–41). In baptism we out ourselves as Christians. We publicly identify with the crucified and resurrected Christ and with his people.

Jesus commanded his disciples to make disciples by preaching the gospel to them, baptizing them, and teaching them to obey everything he commanded (Matt 28:19). So it's no surprise that at Pentecost Peter commanded his hearers, "Repent and be baptized every one of you in the name of Jesus Christ for the forgiveness of your sins" (Acts 2:38). If you claim to follow Christ, this is the first of his commands you must obey. After trusting Christ, baptism is the first thing a believer does. If you haven't done it, you've not yet crossed off the first item on Jesus' discipleship to-do list.

Why is baptism required for church membership? Because baptism is where faith goes public. It's where invisible faith first becomes visible. It's how a new Christian shows up on the church and the world's radar. This is the seed from which the other reasons grow.

2. Baptism Is the Initiating Oath-Sign of the New Covenant

Baptism is also the initiating oath-sign of the new covenant. Through his death Jesus inaugurated the promised new covenant (Jer 31:31–34; Luke 22:19–20; Heb 8:1–13). All covenants are ratified by an oath—a solemn, self-obligating promise. Yet an oath can take nonverbal forms as well. When God made a covenant with Abraham, he passed between the halves of slaughtered animals (Gen 15:1–21). This oath-sign ratified his promise to Abraham and signified that if God proved unfaithful to his own covenant, he himself would bear judgment.

In the death of Jesus, God the Son did bear judgment—not for his unfaithfulness but for ours. The new covenant, therefore, was ratified when Jesus himself paid the ultimate price for our sins (Heb 9:15). The old covenant had circumcision, an oath-sign which marked an individual's entrance into the covenant. So also the new covenant comes with an oath-sign—actually two of them. The first, baptism, is its initiating oath-sign. It is a solemn, symbolic vow which ratifies one's entrance into the new covenant. In baptism we appeal to God to accept us on the terms of his new covenant (1 Pet 3:21), and we pledge ourselves to fulfill all that his new covenant requires of us (Matt 28:19). In baptism we own God as our God, and he owns us as his people.

So when the church asks, "Who belongs to the new covenant?" one part of the answer is, "Who has sworn the oath?" That is, who has been baptized? Just as a soldier can't take up arms until he has sworn allegiance to his country, you cannot enter the covenant community until you have sworn the covenant oath.

3. Baptism Is the Passport of the Kingdom and the Kingdom Citizen's Swearing-in Ceremony

Third, baptism is the passport of the kingdom and the kingdom citizen's swearing-in ceremony. When Jesus inaugurated the kingdom of heaven on earth, he established the church as an embassy of that kingdom. He gave the church the "keys of the kingdom" in order to identify its citizens before the world by affirming the professions of those who credibly confess faith in him (Matt 16:19; 18:18–19). And the initial and initiating means by which the church identifies individuals as kingdom citizens is baptism (Matt 28:19).

Baptism is the passport of the kingdom. We become kingdom citizens by faith in the king, but in baptism the church recognizes and affirms our citizenship. And baptism enables other embassies of the kingdom—that is, other local churches—to recognize us as kingdom citizens. From another angle baptism is a kingdom citizen's swearing-in ceremony. It's when we formally take up our new office of representing Christ and his kingdom on earth. Therefore, in order for a church to recognize someone as a kingdom citizen, that citizen needs to produce his or her passport. Baptism is necessary for church membership because it's the passport of the kingdom and the kingdom citizen's swearing-in ceremony.

4. Baptism Is a Necessary Criterion by Which a Church Recognizes Who Is a Christian

A fourth reason baptism is necessary for church membership is an inference from our first three points. Because baptism is how a church publicly identifies someone as a Christian, it's also a necessary criterion by which a church recognizes who is a Christian. Identification is for recognition. The Louisville Cardinals wear red so they can recognize one another on the court when they're trouncing the blue-jerseyed Kentucky Wildcats. And baptism is the team jersey of Christianity.

Baptism is therefore a necessary though not sufficient criterion by which the church is to recognize Christians. It's not enough for someone to claim to be a Christian or for everyone in the church to think someone is a Christian; Jesus has bound the church's judgment to baptism. Jesus gave us baptism, in part, so we can tell one another apart from the world. By publicly identifying people as Christians, baptism draws a line between the church and the world. Which means baptism is necessary for church membership.

5. Baptism Is an Effective Sign of Church Membership

Fifth, baptism is an effective sign of church membership. This is also an inference from our first three points. If baptism is where faith goes public, the initiating oath-sign of the new covenant, the passport of the kingdom, and a kingdom citizen's swearing in ceremony, then baptism is an effective sign of church membership. It creates the churchly reality to which it points: a Christian belonging to a local church, and that local church affirming a Christian's profession and uniting him or her to itself.

If membership is a house, baptism is the front door. By stepping through the front door you enter the house. Normally, therefore, baptism isn't just a precursor to church membership; it confers church membership. For a new convert baptism is the New Testament way to join a church. You cannot be affirmed as a citizen without thereby entering the body politic. You don't get the jersey without joining the team. And the flip side is, you can't play for the team without wearing the jersey. Because baptism is an effective sign of church membership, baptism is necessary for church membership.

6. The Lord's Supper Is the Other Effective Sign of Church Membership

In point two we saw that the new covenant comes with two signs. The first is baptism, its initiating oath-sign. The second is the Lord's Supper, which is the renewing oath-sign of the new covenant. When we partake of the bread and the cup, we commit ourselves anew to Christ and his covenant.

Yet this isn't something we do as individuals but as a church (1 Cor 11:17–18, 20, 33–34). And partaking of the Lord's Supper entails responsibility for the church. To eat and drink in a way that despises the body negates the Lord's Supper and incurs God's judgment (1 Cor 11:27, 29). Therefore, just as we pledge ourselves to Christ in the Lord's Supper, so we also pledge ourselves to one another. In the same act in which we again own him as our Savior, we own one another as brothers and sisters.

This means the Lord's Supper is the other effective sign of church membership. As Paul says, "Because there is one bread, we who are many are one body, for we all partake of the one bread" (1 Cor 10:17). The Lord's Supper doesn't just represent our unity; it ratifies and seals it. Because it enacts our fellowship with one another, the Lord's Supper makes many one. This is why church membership is first and foremost inclusion at the Table, and church discipline is first and foremost exclusion from the Table.

Baptism is required for church membership because you can't participate in the renewing oath-sign of the covenant until you've performed its initiating oath-sign. You can't participate in the family meal of the Lord's Supper until you've entered the house through the front door of baptism.

7. Without Baptism, Membership Doesn't Exist

What does all this add up to? Simply this: we can't remove baptism from what's required for church membership because without baptism membership doesn't actually exist.

"Membership" is a theological term for the relation between a Christian and a church which the ordinances imply and normally create. Baptism and the Lord's Supper ratify the covenant relation which is church membership. Therefore, there is no such thing as membership without baptism. To speak of membership without baptism is like speaking of a marriage without vows. Marriage is a covenant relation constituted by vows; membership is a covenant relation constituted by the oath-signs of baptism and the Lord's Supper. You can't have the relation without the oath that constitutes it. Therefore, you can't have membership without baptism.

A Public Statement

I want to underscore one more point, which is implicit in my whole case: church membership is a public statement. I don't mean this in the sense of something widely disseminated as opposed to kept under wraps, though there is an element of that. Instead, I mean "public" in a more theological sense, closer to "representative." Older theologians spoke of Adam as a "public person" because his actions represented all his progeny. In a similar vein it's important to distinguish a church's public decisions from the private judgments of individual Christians.

Why? Because the church represents Jesus. Jesus has delegated authority to the local church as a body that he hasn't given to you or me as individual Christians. In its membership and discipline, a church speaks for heaven on earth. This is what Jesus meant when he granted the church "the keys of the kingdom" (Matt 16:19; 18:18–19; see chap. 5). After commanding the church to exclude a professing believer who refuses to repent of sin, Jesus said, "Truly, I say to you, whatever you bind on earth shall be bound in heaven, and whatever you loose on earth shall be loosed in heaven" (Matt 18:18). When the church admits a member, it makes a heaven-sanctioned statement that the person is a Christian. When a church excludes a member, it revokes that heaven-backed affirmation.

When a church admits a member, they're not saying, "The pastor thinks this person is a Christian," or "Steve Smith thinks this person is a Christian," or "This person claims to be a Christian, which is good enough for us." Instead, they're saying, "We as a church, on behalf of Jesus and according to the criteria he's given us, solemnly affirm this person's claim to be a Christian." They're making a public statement that's bound to a public standard. Because church membership is a public affirmation of someone's profession, that affirmation is bound to Jesus' own criteria, and baptism is on that list. Jesus appointed baptism, in part, to be the church's formal, public means of marking someone off as a Christian. Which means baptism is among the criteria he's given the church for formally recognizing Christians.

Two points are tied together in this idea of membership as a public statement. The first is that membership is a statement by *the church*, not by an individual Christian. No individual Christian has the right to extend church membership to someone. That's a prerogative of the church as a church. Second, because membership is a prerogative of the church, and the church speaks for Jesus, the church may only extend membership to those to whom Jesus has authorized to be members. Because Jesus has delegated authority to the church, the church must exercise that authority on the terms he sets. And Jesus has set baptism as the front door of the church.

Of course baptism isn't a sufficient criterion for recognizing someone as a Christian. Peter told Simon the magician that despite his baptism, he was on his way to hell (Acts 8:20–23). A church needs to consider the content of a person's confession and whether anything in his life calls the credibility of his confession into question. But that's not all they need to do. They also need to ask: "Have you gone public as a follower of Christ in baptism?" If not, a church has no authority to extend the public affirmation which is church membership.

This does *not* mean a church should consider everyone who isn't baptized to be a non-Christian. Many Christians simply haven't been taught that baptism is a biblical mandate. Or if they have, they may just need a loving, pointed challenge to obey. Other Christians consider themselves to have been "baptized" as infants. Many such brothers and sisters can provide a sophisticated, time-honored rationale for this based on their understanding of the biblical covenants. In no case is a refusal to admit such persons to membership equivalent to saying, "We think you're not a Christian." Instead, it's simply withholding a public affirmation because a criterion for that affirmation has not been met. It's not that the embassy thinks the person isn't a citizen; it's just that they have no authority to issue a visa to someone without a passport. We'll think about this in much more detail in the next chapter.

From Offense to Defense

Throughout these six chapters I've built a positive case for why baptism is required for church membership. I've deliberately steered clear of opposing arguments simply because you can't say everything at once. Before answering objections, I've first built a case from the ground up, synthesizing the Bible's teaching on baptism, the Lord's Supper, and church membership.

Now it's time to switch from offense to defense. Many serious objections have been raised against the position this book argues. The next chapter is devoted to answering them.

Headlines
Because baptism is how a church publicly identifies someone as a Christian, it's also a necessary criterion by which a church recognizes who is a Christian.
Baptism is like the team jersey of Christianity: it identifies Christians so the church can recognize them.
It's not enough for someone to claim to be a Christian, or for everyone in the church to think someone is a Christian; Jesus has bound the church's judgment to baptism. Jesus gave us baptism, in part, so we can tell one another apart from the world.
Church membership is a statement by the church, not by an individual Christian.
Because membership is a prerogative of the church, and the church speaks for Jesus, the church may extend membership only to those whom Jesus has authorized to be members. And baptism is among the criteria Jesus has given the church for recognizing and affirming Christians.

Chapter 9

Answering Objections

Y ou've been patient. I'm sure that in the minds of many readers, counter-arguments have been stamping their feet and kicking against the starting gates since chapter 1. Now I'm finally going to let those arguments out on the track and try to outrun them one by one.

In this chapter I'll engage the seven strongest arguments I've encountered against requiring baptism for membership. I'm going to present these arguments in the most sympathetic, most compelling light I can. In many cases these arguments have found their way into print, so I'll let their exponents speak for themselves before answering. And in each case I'll do my best to offer a satisfying response.

A Response to Seven Opposing Arguments

Here's a preview of the seven arguments this chapter will address, then we'll jump right into the first, which is the most significant.

1. It's wrong for a church to exclude anyone from membership whom they're confident is a Christian.
2. This is an issue that should be left to individuals' consciences rather than being a standard of fellowship.
3. It's wrong to give baptism membership-defining status when agreement about other, weightier doctrines isn't required for membership.

4. The New Testament simply doesn't address this situation, so we can't appeal to it as a normative model.
5. We're the only evangelical church in our area! There's nowhere else for them to go.
6. It's inconsistent to exclude paedobaptists from membership while inviting them to preach in your church and working together in other gospel efforts.
7. It's wrong to exclude people from our churches who wouldn't exclude us from theirs.

1. It's Wrong for a Church to Exclude Anyone from Membership Whom They're Confident Is a Christian

The first and weightiest argument we need to answer is that it's wrong for a church to exclude anyone from membership whom they're confident is a Christian. This has been the central claim of open membership advocates from the seventeenth century to today. John Bunyan, for instance, wrote, "All I say is, that the church of Christ hath not warrant to keep out of their communion the Christian that is discovered to be a visible saint by the word, the Christian that walketh according to his light with God."[1] That is, a church is obligated to extend membership to every applicant they regard as a Christian.[2] In recent years John Piper has written:

> When I weigh the kind of imperfection involved in tolerating an invalid baptism because some of our members are deeply persuaded that it is biblically valid, over against the kind of imperfection involved in saying

---

[1] John Bunyan, *Differences in Judgment About Water-Baptism, No Bar to Communion*, in *The Miscellaneous Works of John Bunyan*, vol. 4, ed. T. L. Underwood (Oxford: Clarendon Press, 1989), 193.

[2] In the nineteenth century Robert Hall similarly argued that it is illegitimate for a church to enact anything as a requirement for membership that is not a requirement for salvation. "If it be once admitted that a body of men associating for christian [sic] worship have a right to enact as terms of communion, something more than is included in the terms of salvation, the question suggested by St. Paul—"Is Christ divided" is utterly futile: what he considered as a solecism is reduced to practice, and established by law" (*On Terms of Communion; with a Particular View to the Case of the Baptists and Paedobaptists* [1st American ed., from the 3rd English ed., Philadelphia, 1816; repr., London: Forgotten Books, 2012], 135).

to a son or daughter of the living God, "You are excluded from the local church," my biblical sense is that the latter is more unthinkable than the former. The local church is a visible expression of the invisible, universal, body of Christ. To exclude from it is virtually the same as excommunication. . . . Very few, it seems to me, have really come to terms with the seriousness of excluding believers from membership in the local church. It is preemptive excommunication.[3]

To say that excluding an unbaptized Christian from membership is "preemptive excommunication" is a powerful charge, and I'll answer it at length. But first I want to survey three responses other baptists have offered and show why I find them somewhat lacking.

First, William Kiffin appeals to Paul's command in 2 Thessalonians 3:6 to "withdraw yourselves from every brother that walketh disorderly" (KJV). He reasons that paedobaptists are brothers whose "walk" is out of accord with the divine command regarding baptism; therefore we are justified in withdrawing fellowship from them.[4] Yet the word the KJV renders "disorderly" (*ataktōs*) seems in context to refer to disorderly or irresponsible behavior, specifically idleness, not to a departure from ecclesiastical order. Thus the ESV renders the word as "in idleness," the NIV has "is idle," and the HCSB says "irresponsibly." Verse 7 clarifies, "For you yourselves know how you ought to imitate us, because we were not idle when we were with you." And then again in verse 11, *ataktōs* is defined as idleness: "For we hear that some among you walk *ataktōs*, not busy at work, but busybodies."

Therefore it seems somewhat of a stretch to apply this passage to those who refuse believer's baptism because they are convinced of the validity of paedobaptism. The issue at the heart of 2 Thessalonians 3 is that some believers' idle lives were sharply out of accord with a Christian profession. Addressing the same issue elsewhere, Paul says, "But if anyone does not provide for his relatives, and especially for members of his household, he has denied the faith and is worse than an unbeliever" (1 Tim 5:8). By contrast, many paedobaptists' lives

---

[3] John Piper, "Response to Grudem on Baptism and Church Membership" (August 9, 2007), available at http://www.desiringgod.org/resource-library/taste-see-articles /response-to-grudem-on-baptism-and-church-membership.

[4] William Kiffin, *A Sober Discourse of Right to Church Communion* (London, 1681; repr., Paris, AR: Baptist Standard Bearer, 2006), 32–33.

are above reproach, and their failure to be baptized does not render their profession incredible.[5]

Second, appealing to 1 Corinthians 5, Abraham Booth argues that sometimes churches are duty-bound to sever fellowship from those whom they nevertheless regard as true Christians:

> Besides, gospel churches are sometimes obliged, by the laws of Christ, to exclude from their communion those whom he has received; as appears from the case of the incestuous person in the church at Corinth. And have those churches that practice free communion never excluded any for scandalous backslidings; whom, notwithstanding, they could not but consider as received of Christ?

And Booth reasons from the legitimacy of excommunicating a true brother to the legitimacy of refusing Communion to a true brother in the first place.[6] Yet I think Booth is reasoning from a faulty premise.

First, Paul does not regard the immoral man in 1 Corinthians 5 as a true believer. Instead, Paul says he needs to undergo a radical transformation in order to be saved on the last day (1 Cor 5:5). Further, when Paul applies his teaching on discipline more broadly, he instructs the Corinthians "not to associate with anyone *who bears the name of brother* if he is guilty of sexual immorality or greed, or is an idolater, reviler, drunkard, or swindler" (1 Cor 5:11, italics added). Such persons claim to believe in Christ, but their lives contradict that claim. Paul doesn't say they're "brothers," but that they bear that name, implying that their lives undermine the label. As Jonathan Leeman writes:

> A church cannot responsibly believe the words of a member who has been willfully living in a habitual sin. It's almost as if the nature of some sins "disables" a church's ability to continue affirming the person's overall posture of repentance, and so the church has no choice but to

---

[5] While I am critical of Kiffin on this point, many of his arguments are more persuasive; so also the other two authors I engage here. For a concise overview of Kiffin's *Sober Discourse*, see Michael A. G. Haykin and C. Jeffrey Robinson, "Particular Baptist Debates About Communion and Hymn-Singing," in *Drawn into Controversie: Reformed Theological Diversity and Debates Within Seventeenth-Century British Puritanism*, ed. Michael A. G. Haykin and Mark Jones (Göttingen: Vandenhoek & Ruprecht, 2012), 292–95.

[6] Abraham Booth, *An Apology for the Baptists* (London, 1778), in *A Defense of the Baptists* (Paris, AR: The Baptist Standard Bearer, 2006), 81.

remove its affirmation for the time being. The sin pushes its side of the balance straight down and the evidence of repentance side straight up.[7]

A church's exclusion from fellowship is the removal of its affirmation of someone's profession of faith. Therefore, a church should not remove anyone from its fellowship whom they are convinced is genuinely repentant.[8] As such, Booth's appeal to the broader principles of church discipline doesn't furnish a satisfying answer to Piper's charge of preemptive excommunication.

Third, John Dagg responds to the preemptive excommunication charge as follows: "The church which excludes a Pedobaptist from the Lord's table, does not design to inflict a punishment on him, but merely to do its own duty, as a body to which the Lord has intrusted [sic] one of his ordinances. The simple aim is, to regulate the observance according to the will of the Lord."[9]

Dagg makes some good points here, and his assertion that such a church is only doing its duty is both true and important, yet it is insufficient. To refuse membership is to refuse to affirm someone's profession of faith in Christ. Therefore, requiring baptism for membership lands us in a serious dilemma. Churches that require baptism for membership will, in principle, be forced to withhold their affirmation from people whom they are convinced are genuine followers of Christ, leaving an acute tension between our private judgment and the church's public judgment. This is no light matter.

But is it a decisive objection against requiring baptism for membership? I don't think so. The first thing to note is that Piper himself does not hold his "no preemptive excommunication" view consistently. Note that he regularly says things like, "The local church, it seems to us, should have a front door about as wide as the door Christ has built for his own invisible church."[10] But the word "about" acknowledges some slip between the categories, and Bethlehem's Member Affirmation of Faith includes statements that Piper himself would acknowledge someone could disagree with and still be a Christian. Therefore, in principle, Piper could find himself in the position of "preemptively excommunicating" someone who disagrees with one of his church's

---

[7] Jonathan Leeman, *Church Discipline: How the Church Protects the Name of Jesus* (Wheaton, IL: Crossway, 2012), 62.

[8] Ibid., 63.

[9] John L. Dagg, *Manual of Church Order* (repr., Harrisonburg, VA: Gano, 1990), 219.

[10] John Piper with Alex Chediak and Tom Steller, "Baptism and Church Membership at Bethlehem Baptist Church: Eight Recommendations for Constitutional Revision," 19, available at http://cdn.desiringgod.org/pdf/baptism_and_membership.pdf.

doctrinal affirmations—such as, for instance, the inerrancy of the Bible's original manuscripts—whom Piper nevertheless regards a true Christian. So Piper
is not exempt from his own charge.

Further, as I've argued throughout the book, baptism fits within the box
marked "how a church knows someone is a Christian." Baptism is not a separate requirement from "credible profession of faith" but is how someone professes faith. Therefore, it is a necessary but not sufficient factor in how a church
is to know who is a Christian in the first place. All the members of a church
might be convinced that a certain unbaptized person is a Christian, but Jesus
has bound the church's judgment—and therefore its formal, public affirmation—to baptism. Even if all the members of a church are convinced that a
person's faith in Christ is genuine, Jesus has given the church no authority to
affirm that faith until it is publicly professed in baptism.

Recall John Bunyan's claim that a church "hath not warrant to keep out of
their communion the Christian that is discovered to be a visible saint by the word,
the Christian that walketh according to his light with God."[11] But how is someone "discovered to be a visible saint by the word"? By being baptized! Therefore
William Kiffin is exactly right to say that in baptism the first believers "became
visible professors of the Gospel of Truth," and so do we.[12] John Dagg is also on
point: "As profession is necessary to church-membership, so is baptism, which is
the appointed ceremony of profession. Profession is the substance, and baptism
is the form; but Christ's command requires the form as well as the substance."[13]

Remember that baptism is where faith goes public. It is what causes someone to show up on the church's radar as a Christian. It is the initiating oath-sign
of the new covenant. It is the passport of the kingdom and a kingdom citizen's
swearing-in ceremony. It is an effective sign of church membership. Because
of all that baptism is and does, a church is simply not authorized to extend the
relation of membership to those who have not performed its effective sign. A
church may not admit to the renewing oath-sign of the new covenant anyone
who has not performed its initiating oath-sign. To do so would be to depart
from Jesus' own appointed means for marking off his people from the world
and binding them to one another. Baptism draws the line between the church
and the world. We are not at liberty to draw it elsewhere.

---

[11] Bunyan, *Differences in Judgment*, 193.
[12] Kiffin, *Sober Discourse*, 29.
[13] Dagg, *Manual of Church Order*, 95.

Imagine I go to the airport to catch a plane. When I get to the front of the security line, I hand my boarding pass to the TSA agent. Instead of taking it back, I leave it with him and head through the X-Ray machine. Why? Because I am convinced by my reading of airline policy that boarding passes are to be deposited with security agents. In due time I make my way to the gate, my boarding group is called, and I attempt to walk past the gate agent to board the plane.

"Please present your boarding pass," she says.

"I've already handed it to the security agent."

Bypassing the exegetical debate, she cuts to the chase: "I'm sorry, sir, but you won't be able to board the plane without a boarding pass."

"Seriously? But I've paid for a seat on this flight."

"I'm sorry, sir, but that's the rule."

I unfold a sheet of paper. "No, really. Look—here's my credit card statement showing when I bought the ticket."

"Sorry, sir, I need a boarding pass."

I pull out a smartphone. "But here's the e-mail confirmation. Look, it even has my name and everything."

"I believe you! But unless you have a boarding pass, we simply can't let you onto the plane. If you'll just see my colleague at the desk here, we can print a new one for you right now."

"I'm afraid I can't do that. I'm convinced that boarding passes are meant to be handed to security agents. If I get another boarding pass, I'd be saying the first one wasn't valid."

"Then I'm sorry, sir, but you'll not be able to board the plane today. Please step aside to allow other passengers to board."

I think the parallels here are instructive. If baptism is a public profession of faith, then infant baptism isn't baptism. I mean paedobaptists no disrespect whatsoever when I say this. Nor do I accuse them of any willful neglect of the Lord's ordinances. I trust that a sincere paedobaptist brother or sister intends to obey Jesus' commands, including the command to be baptized, every bit as much as I do.

The problem is, intention isn't enough. As I've argued throughout the book, baptism marks Christians off from the world. It identifies someone as a Christian much like a boarding pass identifies someone as an airline passenger. As Dagg put it, Jesus' command requires a form of profession as well as the substance, and the form is baptism. Thinking you've been baptized—even on the basis of a sophisticated, widely held, time-honored interpretation of Scripture—does not mean you've been baptized. And a church is no more free to admit an unbaptized person to membership than a gate agent is to admit someone onto a plane without a boarding pass.

Church membership is defined by the ritual privilege of participating in the Lord's Supper, and Jesus has appointed baptism as its ritual prerequisite.[14] Paedobaptists are denied membership because they lack not the substance of a credible profession but its form. As we saw in chapter 7, baptism and the Lord's Supper give the church its "institutional form and order."[15] Without the ordinances the church is formless.[16] The local church simply *is* the shape into which the gospel and the ordinances form us. Therefore, in order to become a church member, someone must fill out the form by which we inscribe our faith in the church's public record.

Say you went to buy groceries, swiped your debit card, and then refused to enter your PIN number when prompted. Why would the cashier halt the transaction? Not because you don't have the money in the bank—the reality of which the debit card is a sign, so to speak. Instead, you would be unable to purchase the groceries because of a failure to fulfill a necessary, formal step in the transaction: authenticating your identity as the cardholder. The baptism and membership issue is similar. It's not that a paedobaptist's failure to be baptized undermines the credibility of their faith in Christ. Instead, however unintentionally, a paedobaptist is refusing to authenticate his or her faith through baptism, the means Jesus appointed for that end. And without that authentication, a church is not authorized to conclude the "transaction" of membership.

Yes, refusing membership to paedobaptists allows a major tension between our private judgment as individuals and the church's public judgment. We are convinced someone is a Christian, but the church is forced, as it were, to withhold its affirmation. However, the only way for that tension to be truly resolved is for every person who credibly claims to follow Christ to be baptized. Of course, evangelical paedobaptists are not unbaptized due to rebellion,

---

[14] "To enjoy ceremonial privileges, there must be ceremonial qualifications" (Augustus H. Strong, *Systematic Theology* [repr., Valley Forge, PA: Judson, 1977], 972).

[15] Oliver O'Donovan's phrase, from *The Desire of the Nations: Rediscovering the Roots of Political Theology* (Cambridge: Cambridge University Press, 1996), 172.

[16] Strong writes, "For no visible church is possible, unless some sign of membership be required, in addition to the signs of membership in the invisible church" (*Systematic Theology*, 979).

which would undermine their claim to follow Christ. Nor is it due to mere ignorance which, being remedied, would resolve into obedience. Instead, they are unbaptized because they are theologically committed to viewing infant "baptism" as true, biblical baptism. As long as they hold that conviction, they remain unintentionally in tension with Scripture.

And because paedobaptists are failing to perform a church-forming ordinance, this tension manifests itself acutely in the gap between our private judgment and the church's public judgment of membership. We believe our paedobaptist brothers paid for a plane ticket, but we can't let them on the plane without a boarding pass. We believe they have the "money in the bank" of a credible claim to follow Christ, yet we can't extend membership without their authentication of that claim in baptism.

While it may appear to ease the tension between our judgment and the church's, accepting paedobaptists to membership doesn't resolve the root tension; it only transfers it into the membership of a local church. I'll say more about how this tension can and can't be resolved in the next chapter. For now my point is simply that we have no authority to resolve this tension by decoupling baptism from membership. The church is to confer membership on those who credibly profess faith in Jesus, and baptism is the form that profession must take.

Piper is right: it is troubling to exclude from membership a faithful, godly, paedobaptist Christian. But it should be more troubling to revise the role Christ has assigned to baptism, to make one of his commands optional, to undermine his authority in the church. It should be more troubling to allow a Christian—however sincere in his or her error—to continue in disobedience to Christ, and to add the church's approval to that disobedience. It should be more troubling to allow the public profession of the gospel to be privatized. It should be more troubling to try to gather the church by setting aside the ordinance Jesus appointed for that purpose. It should be more troubling to dismantle the church walls which Jesus himself has framed.

Extending membership to a paedobaptist Christian may seem like the more compassionate thing to do, but that only takes the short view. A longer-term view recognizes that by granting membership only to those to whom Jesus has authorized us to grant membership, we deepen the grooves of the church's obedience to Christ, we promote its witness to Christ, and we strengthen its ministry not just to one paedobaptist but to everyone who comes through the doors.

In a sense the entire argument of chapters 3–8 is my answer to the charge of preemptive excommunication. Baptism can't be opposed to a credible profession of faith; it *is* faith's profession. It is deeply saddening to refuse membership to anyone who is evidently a Christian. Yet membership is not a matter of private opinion but public judgment, and Jesus has bound the church's judgment to baptism.

2. This Is an Issue That Should Be Left to Individuals' Consciences Rather than Being a Standard of Fellowship

A second argument against requiring baptism for membership is that this issue should be left to individuals' consciences rather than being a standard of fellowship. Orthodox, evangelical Christians continue to disagree over whether baptism is for believers only or their infant children as well. We're no nearer to settling this issue than we were 500 years ago. Shouldn't we leave this up to individual Christians' consciences rather than requiring agreement for church membership?

Most historic exponents of open membership have argued along these lines, and this is a popular appeal today. John Brown advanced a version of this argument when he wrote:

> The apostolic practice was to allow liberty of conscience, and to exercise great forbearance towards brethren who, through weakness and education-principles, were mistaken in things of as great moment as the outward mode of Water-Baptism, not refusing fellowship with those who were zealously attached to some of the abolished rites of the ceremonial law.[17]

Many make Brown's implicit appeal to Romans 14–15 explicit, arguing that we baptists should receive our paedobaptist brothers just as Paul exhorted the Romans to receive those who had weak consciences regarding meat and other issues. Arguing from Romans 15:7, Bunyan writes, "God hath received him, Christ hath received him, therefore do you receive him."[18]

---

[17] John Brown, *The House of God Opened and His Table Free for Baptists and Paedobaptists* (London, 1777; repr., Hampshire, UK: ECCO), 5.

[18] John Bunyan, *A Confession of My Faith, and A Reason of My Practice*, in Underwood *The Miscellaneous Works of John Bunyan*, 173.

This is an appealing argument. Paul recognizes that some issues in the church cannot be resolved to the satisfaction of everyone's conscience. So he exhorts us not to pass judgment on another's servant (Rom 14:4) but instead to "welcome" those who differ (Rom 14:1). We are to allow each to be "fully convinced in his own mind" (Rom 14:5), to refrain from passing judgment (Rom 14:10), to bear with the weak (Rom 15:1), and to welcome one another as Christ has welcomed us (Rom 15:7). The issue in the Roman church was that some regarded certain foods as off-limits for Christians. Some Jewish believers continued to observe the dietary restrictions of the Mosaic law, and some Gentile converts may have regarded all food sacrificed to idols as unclean (cf. 1 Cor 8:1–13; 10:14–22). In both cases Paul makes room in the church for those with weaker consciences, refuses to allow their scruples to bind others, and urges others to bear with them and avoid giving offense.

But the parallels with baptism are more apparent than real. The decisive difference between baptism and the cases of conscience in Romans 14–15 is this: a sensitive conscience regarding food imagines a divine command where none exists, whereas infant baptism results in disobedience to a divine command. In this respect the two situations are exact opposites. Paul refuses to allow food to divide fellowship because God has not commanded Christians to abstain from idol meat or from foods labeled unclean by the Old Testament. Yet all Christians are positively commanded to be baptized. Joseph Kinghorn writes, "Weakness of faith leading men to do what was *not enjoined*, or to avoid what was *not forbidden*, is very different from opposition to the least of those things which *were enjoined:* and the cases differ not merely in degree, but in their nature."[19]

The bottom line here is that baptism is a divine command that a believer either obeys or disobeys. There's a yawning gap between a convictional paedobaptist and someone who simply refuses to be baptized, yet despite the gap both remain unbaptized. Both have yet to ratify the new covenant. Both have yet to be sworn in as kingdom citizens. Both have yet to go public as Christians by the means Jesus appointed.

---

[19] Joseph Kinghorn, *Baptism, A Term of Communion* (Norwich, 1816; repr., Paris, AR: Baptist Standard Bearer, 2006), 44, emphasis original. See also Booth, *Apology for the Baptists*, 86–90; William Buttfield, *Free Communion an Innovation: or, an Answer to Mr. John Brown's Pamphlet* (London, 1778; repr., Hampshire, UK: ECCO), 18–19; and R. B. C. Howell, *The Terms of Communion at the Lord's Table* (Philadelphia: American Baptist Publication Society, 1846; repr., Paris, AR: Baptist Standard Bearer, 2006), 85–88.

Further, baptism is a means by which the church exercises the keys of the kingdom, as is the Lord's Supper. This means that the church may not defer to an individual conscience regarding the proper definition and practice of baptism.[20] To do so would transfer the keys of the kingdom from church to individual, which Jesus has nowhere authorized. The church's responsibility for its ordinances is nondelegable. As John Dagg writes: "But may not each individual be left to his own conscience, and his own responsibility? He may be, and ought to be, so far as it can be done without implicating the consciences and responsibilities of others. If each were left wholly to himself, the discipline of the church would be nothing, and the power to exercise it would be attended with no responsibility."[21]

Baptism is how a church affirms a believer's profession of faith and unites that believer to itself. This means baptism is something Jesus requires the church to do, not just individual Christians: an individual gets baptized, but the church baptizes. Therefore, a church is not at liberty to allow individual Christians to determine what baptism means and whether they have been baptized. Do we do this in other areas of doctrine and practice? Do we allow Christians the individual liberty to decide what the gospel is? Or what constitutes fidelity in marriage?

What then does love require of us baptists toward our paedobaptist brethren? Again Dagg is helpful:

> Towards such an one, how can we be otherwise than tolerant and forbearing? Shall we persecute him? God forbid. We would rather lay down our lives for him. Shall we indulge in any bitterness, or uncharitableness towards him? We will love him with pure heart fervently. Shall we, in any manner, prevent him from worshipping and serving God according to the dictates of his conscience? The very thought be far from us. Even if he err, to his own Master he standeth or

---

[20] Joseph Kinghorn writes, "Matters of mere opinion or taste, and partialities to things which are not express duty, may consistently enough be gratified in private; but a command of Christ respecting the profession of his gospel, should be recognized *in* the church, and there placed on its proper footing; otherwise we practically lower the authority of the great lawgiver" (*Baptism, a Term of Communion*, 105).

[21] Dagg, *Manual of Church Order*, 221. Joseph Kinghorn adds that to require the church to defer to an individual's judgment regarding baptism "would practically annihilate all regulations for the admission of members into any society, either civil or religious" (*Baptism, a Term of Communion*, 80).

falleth. We, too, are fallible and erring; and we will fervently pray that
the grace which pardons our faults may pardon his also.[22]

We must love those with a different practice of baptism, cherish and pray for
them, and partner with them in gospel work to the fullest extent our unity
in the faith enables. All this God requires us to do when he commands us to
love one another (John 13:34–35). But God's commands do not contradict one
another.[23] The demands of conscience and mutual forbearance cannot require
a church to sever what Christ has joined together.

3. It's Wrong to Give Baptism Membership-Defining Status when Agreement About Other, Weightier Doctrines Isn't Required for Membership

A third argument against my case is that it's wrong to give baptism
membership-defining status when agreement about other, weightier doctrines
isn't required for membership. Many argue that only agreement about "essential" doctrines should be required for membership in a local church. And the
fact that there are many evangelical paedobaptists shows that believing in
credobaptism is not essential to salvation or to the preservation of orthodoxy.
Further, many churches whose leaders are wholly committed to the doctrines
of grace—sometimes nicknamed "Calvinism"—will nevertheless not require
full agreement on those doctrines in order to join. (Nor would many Arminian
churches refuse to admit Calvinist members.) Given all this, why should we
allow baptism to be a barrier to membership when the gospel-supporting,
sanctification-fueling doctrines of grace don't even play that role?[24]

In response, the first thing to point out is that baptism differs sharply
from other so-called "secondary" issues in that it involves obedience to a command. There's no divine command you leave undone if your eschatology is

---

[22] Ibid.

[23] Abraham Booth applies this point to the present issue in *Apology for the Baptists*, 93.
See also Dagg, *Manual of Church Order*, 96: "We owe nothing to a weak brother which can
render it necessary for us to disobey God."

[24] John Piper says this is the driving force behind his position on baptism and church
membership in an interview titled, "Can You Update Us on the Baptism and Church
Membership Issue from 2005?" (December 4, 2006), available at http://www.desiring
god.org/resource-library/ask-pastor-john/can-you-update-us-on-the-baptism-and-church
-membership-issue-from-2005.

amillennial instead of premillennial or vice versa. Even one's understanding of the doctrines of grace, which radically influence the entire Christian life, does not entail the fulfillment or neglect of a specific duty. Baptism, on the other hand, is an obligation Jesus lays on everyone who trusts in him.[25]

Further, baptism is in a different category from other doctrines because, as we saw in chapter 7, it is one of the two ordinances which give the church its institutional form and order. Baptism orders the church in two senses. First, it identifies someone as a public professor of faith in Christ. It thereby makes an individual fit "matter" for a church, to use a classic category. Second, baptism unites an individual to the body. To borrow another classic term, baptism is therefore an aspect of the "form" of a church: that which unites the church into a distinct body.[26] Baptism and the Lord's Supper are the mortar that binds individual Christians together into one building. Baptism binds one to many, and the Lord's Supper binds many into one. Remember, a church is more than the sum of its parts. In order to have a church, you need not just a gospel people but a gospel polity: an institutional form and order. And baptism and the Lord's Supper are the foundations of that polity.

---

[25] Comparing baptism to the millennium, John Hammett writes, "But baptism is more than a doctrine; it involves obedience to Christ's command. On such an issue I am hesitant to act contrary to my conscientious understanding of that command or to encourage others to disregard and mistakenly disobey a biblical command" ("Membership, Discipline, and the Nature of the Church," in *Those Who Must Give an Account: A Study of Church Membership and Church Discipline*, ed. John S. Hammett and Benjamin L. Merkle [Nashville: B&H, 2012], 20).

[26] John Owen writes: "The church may be considered either as unto its *essence*, constitution, and being, or as unto its *power* and *order*, when it is organized. As unto its essence and being, its constituent parts are its *matter* and *form*. . . . By the matter of the church, we understand the persons whereof the church doth consist, with their qualifications; and by its form, the reason, cause, and way of that kind of relation among them which gives them the being of a church, and therewithal an interest in all that belongs unto a church, either privilege or power, as such" (*Of the True Nature of a Gospel Church*, in *The Works of John Owen*, ed. William H. Goold, vol. 16 [repr., Edinburgh: Banner of Truth Trust, 1965], 11, emphasis original). Seventeenth-century Baptist Benjamin Keach wrote, "The matter of Churches are godly persons, or true believers; the true form is the order or constitution of the Gospel Church, viz. The Adult upon the profession of Faith and Repentance, Baptized; and so with joint consent give themselves up to the Lord, and one to another, to walk in fellowship and communion in all the Ordinances of the Gospel" (*The Golden Mine Opened* [London, 1694], 9, accessed online at http://www.unz.org/Pub /KeachBenjamin-1694).

It's reductionistic and self-defeating to say a church should only require agreement on essentials and then set what's essential to the church outside the category of essentials. To do this is to undermine the theological foundations of a local church's existence as a church. If we treat what's essential to the existence of a local church as "nonessential" for membership, then the church begins sawing off the branch it sits on. As Joseph Kinghorn puts it, "That may be essential to the *scriptural existence of a church*, which is *not* essential to the salvation of the Christian."[27]

Baptism should be required for membership not because it carries more doctrinal "weight" than, say, the doctrines of grace—as if we could weigh up the Bible's teaching and commands and then decide which bits we want to insist on. Instead, baptism should be required for membership because it sits in a class by itself, or rather a class with only one other item, the Lord's Supper. As an effective sign of church membership, baptism is essential to the constitution of a local church. You can't make "Christians" into "church" without baptism and the Lord's Supper. Therefore, in order to have a church together, you need to agree not just about the gospel and essential doctrines entailed by the gospel; you need to agree about baptism as well.

4. The New Testament Simply Doesn't Address This Situation so We Can't Appeal to It as a Normative Model

Some argue that the New Testament simply doesn't address this situation so we can't appeal to it as a normative model. Robert Hall, for instance, freely grants that all who came to faith in the earliest post-Pentecost church were baptized and that no one would have been admitted to church membership who refused to be baptized.[28] Yet, "We live in a mutable world, and the diversity of sentiment which has arisen in the christian [sic] church on the subject of baptism, has placed things in a new situation." It has "given birth to a case which can be determined only by an appeal to the general principles of the gospel, and to those injunctions in particular, which are designed to regulate the conduct of Christians, whose judgment in points of secondary moment differ."[29]

---

[27] Kinghorn, *Baptism, A Term of Communion*, 162, emphasis original.
[28] Hall, *On Terms of Communion*, 68–70.
[29] Ibid., 75.

In other words, in the New Testament only baptized persons were church members, but that was simply the way it was, not the way it must be for us. As yet there were no genuine Christians whose practice of baptism differed from the apostles'. Once such a practice arose, it placed the church into a genuinely new situation, out of the reach of apostolic precedent.

This argument regards the fact that all members of New Testament churches were baptized as mere happenstance. It assumes that while the apostles would have regarded anyone who simply refused baptism as a false professor, if anyone presented a good enough reason for refusing baptism, the apostles would have admitted them to fellowship. But this makes "a good reason for refusing baptism" a legitimate substitute for baptism. What biblical warrant do we have for that? Further, this stance asserts that there is no link whatsoever between baptism and church membership, an assertion my entire argument has sought to overturn.

Therefore, instead of treating apostolic precedent regarding baptism and membership as arbitrary, I'd regard it as corroborating evidence of the theological links we've discerned between baptism and membership. This precedent may not be decisive in and of itself.[30] But in light of baptism's role as an effective sign of church membership, apostolic precedent takes on the character of a normative example to be followed, not a contingent circumstance to be transcended.

While the persistent presence of paedobaptism does create certain challenges for credobaptist churches, it does not put us in a radically new theological situation. If some people have come to understand marriage to be something other than the permanent, exclusive union of a man and a woman, that doesn't change what marriage is. Similarly, if some Christians have come to understand baptism to apply to infants as well as believers, that doesn't change what baptism is. Nor does it sever the biblical tie binding together baptism and membership.

There's also a burden-of-proof issue lurking here. Many open membership advocates have demanded an explicit biblical command to justify requiring baptism for membership.[31] But that's an assertion planted firmly in midair.

---

[30] Though I'd argue the burden of proof is on those who say it isn't.

[31] E.g., Bunyan, *Differences in Judgment*, 218; Hall, *On Terms of Communion*, 78, 137; John Piper, "Should We Require Agreement of All Members on the Doctrine and Practice of Baptism?" Appendix A in "Baptism and Church Membership at Bethlehem Baptist Church," 21n12.

Does it take an explicit biblical command to say that viewing Internet pornography is a sin? Of course not. Why? Because it clearly falls within the territory specified by broader biblical teachings on sexual purity. Similarly, baptism is required for membership because of the theological territory it occupies—territory that overlaps with church membership to such an extent that you can't rightly understand one without implying the other. Prooftexting alone won't settle the issue either way.[32]

5. We're the Only Evangelical Church in Our Area! There's Nowhere Else for Them to Go

A fifth argument against requiring baptism for membership is this: We're the only evangelical church in our area! There's nowhere else for them to go. This is a powerful objection and is clearly motivated by Jesus-like compassion. No Christian pastor should want to leave sheep without a shepherd.

This objection is often put forward by those in a "missionary context": another country that, to American eyes at least, has little evangelical witness and is dominated by other religions. Similarly, one pastor friend of mine in New England voiced this concern because the nearest evangelical paedobaptist church is more than a forty-minute drive away. The assumption seems to be that under normal circumstances churches should require baptism for membership, but in a missionary context where there are no other churches around, churches should allow paedobaptists to join. Otherwise, they argue, the paedobaptist brothers and sisters would be excluded from church fellowship altogether.[33]

---

[32] Abraham Booth puts the shoe on the other foot: because of the consensus throughout church history that baptism is required for membership, the burden is on open-membership advocates to prove their position from Scripture (*Apology for the Baptists*, 27). And Joseph Kinghorn's response to the burden-of-proof charge is on target: "The New Testament does not prohibit the unbaptized from receiving the Lord's supper, because no circumstance arose which rendered such prohibition necessary. It is acknowledged, that the law of baptism was clearly understood, and that the unbaptized could not be received into the church. There was, therefore, no reason why a prohibitory declaration should exist" (*Baptism, A Term of Communion*, 32).

[33] John Piper writes: "Would we, if there were no other churches for people to be a part of, exclude true Christians from membership over disagreements about baptism? This would be tantamount to excluding them from the visible church on earth. It would be the same as a church excommunication that left them to be treated 'as a Gentile and a tax collector' (Matthew 18:17). This is troubling" ("Should We Require Agreement," 18–19).

The first thing we have to point out in response is that the New Testament itself is a missionary document. The Epistles, for example, were written by apostles engaged in bringing the gospel to places where it had not yet been heard (Rom 15:20). Many of these letters were written to young churches which were the first groups of Christians to emerge in their area. And those churches were likely each the only church in their city. So, if requiring baptism for membership is truly a biblical principle, then it applies just as much in a "missionary context," since the New Testament itself was written from and to a missionary context.

Further, if you're planting a church in a missionary context, why are there already paedobaptist Christians in your city? If they're not missionaries, what are they doing there? And who taught them to be paedobaptists? Questions like these reveal a certain slipperiness in our idea of what constitutes a "missionary context." In countless ways a place like, say, Sri Lanka feels like the far side of the moon to an American. And when we engage in cross-cultural ministry, we absolutely need to reckon with the radically different context. That's the only way to ensure that we enjoin biblical principles rather than cultural customs and allow a truly indigenous Christianity to take root.[34] Yet from an ecclesial angle, I'd argue that there's only one truly missionary context: a place where a local church does not yet exist. It's when we're moving on the frontier of the gospel's church-creating progress that we encounter exceptions to ecclesial norms, like how the laws of physics break down as you approach the speed of light. The Ethiopian eunuch wasn't baptized into church membership only because no church in Ethiopia yet existed. That's a missionary context in the fullest sense, and that's why you see an exception to a biblical norm.[35]

But if you've already got a church up and running with members and leaders and all the rest, there's a technical, ecclesial sense in which your city is no

---

[34] For some reflections on how to do this, see "Contextualizing Ecclesiology," an interview with Ed Roberts, *9Marks Journal* 10, no. 4 (2013), available at http://www.9marks.org /journal/contexualizing-ecclesiology.

[35] I'm not saying we should reserve the title *missionary* for people who engage unreached people groups. Instead, I'm arguing that certain ecclesial norms flex only when the first church in an area is coming into existence, not when we simply pass from one cultural context into another. Further, even if you are in a "frontier" missionary context, with no church yet in existence, I'd argue that the biblical norm of requiring baptism for membership and the Lord's Supper still holds since baptism and the Lord's Supper are precisely how a local church comes into existence.

longer a "missionary context." Praise God, you've crossed the line from "no church" to "church." Now your church gets to carry on the work of evangelism, discipling believers, and planting new churches in your region. But if your "missionary context" means you're the only church in your area, with no paedobaptist churches around, well, that's precisely the situation we find in the New Testament.[36] And if the New Testament treats baptism as a requirement for membership, your church should too.

So yes, to be clear, I am saying that you should not accept unbaptized persons into membership even if you're the only church in your city, in a nation dominated by Islam or Hinduism, on the far side of the planet from where I write. Does this mean I'm telling you to cast paedobaptist sheep out into the ecclesial wilderness? Not exactly. Think again about our favorite Ethiopian eunuch. As a Christian heading back into his native Ethiopia, he's all alone, but he shouldn't remain so for long. If he obeys Jesus' command to spread the gospel (Matt 28:18–20), at some point he should find that one or two others are ready to confess faith in Christ. And once they do, they all should come together as a body to call on the name of their Lord and exercise the keys of the kingdom he gives to them (Matt 16:18–19; 18:18–20). Left to himself, no Christian should remain churchless for long. You don't need fifty people and a pulpit and a pianist. At bare minimum, all it takes is two or three gathered in Jesus' name.

So if you're the only church in your city, and you've got convinced paedobaptists coming to your church, and they remain so despite your best efforts to convince them otherwise, I'd suggest that your long-term goal should be to help them start a church. Something like a long-term incubation may be most likely to bear lasting fruit. Perhaps these folks attend your church's gatherings for a few months or a few years. You and your other elders can help raise up church leaders from within their number or connect them to other believers who might be able to help them find a pastor. When they're ready to begin meeting as a church, you can pray for them and send them off with your blessing. If your church has its own facilities, you can share them. And you can remain in the closest possible partnership as you proclaim the gospel throughout your city day by day.

---

[36] Further, if a "missionary context" means there are no paedobaptist churches, yet there are paedobaptist Christians, and this is grounds for having paedobaptist members, how will a paedobaptist church ever come into being?

John Piper challenges the reasoning undergirding this solution when he writes: "If we say, no, we are not turning people away to *no* church, but to *other* churches, then we are, in effect, justifying our standards by the very practice (in other churches) that we disagree with. We are glad others will do what we will not do so that we can feel okay about not doing it."[37] In response, I'd simply suggest that paedobaptist churches are a relative good. An absolute good would be every Christian being baptized. But if not every Christian is going to be baptized because some persist in viewing infant "baptism" as baptism, then it is better that there be paedobaptist churches than that paedobaptists have no church. Further, truly convictional paedobaptists will form their own church whether a baptist church likes it or not since that's the only way they can practice baptism according to their understanding of Scripture.

In sum, excluding paedobaptists from the only church in town isn't so much an absolute matter as a relative one. In a time-lapse view, the issue isn't necessarily being part of a church versus having no church but being part of a relatively thriving, more populous church versus starting a newer, smaller one. The result of excluding paedobaptists from membership isn't that they don't have a church but that they get to start one: one that embodies, rather than contradicts, their baptismal convictions. And, far from shooing these sheep out into the desert, you can help them construct their own sheepfold while they informally shelter around yours.

6. It's Inconsistent to Exclude Paedobaptists from Membership While Inviting Them to Preach in Your Church and Working Together in Other Gospel Efforts

A sixth objection: it's inconsistent to exclude paedobaptists from membership while inviting them to preach in your church and working together in other gospel efforts.[38] There's a broader and a narrower version of this argument. The broader version I referred to in chapter 2: if baptists and paedobaptists can worship together and enjoy fellowship through a conference like Together for the Gospel, they should be able to enjoy local church fellowship. Some put

---

[37] "Baptism and Church Membership," 19, available at http://cdn.desiringgod.org/pdf/baptism_and_membership.pdf.

[38] See, e.g., Brown, *The House of God Opened*, 21–22.

it more starkly, arguing that if such brothers can't share the Lord's Supper together, their "unity" is no unity at all. The narrower version of this argument refers specifically to pulpit fellowship: baptists and paedobaptists preaching in each other's churches. I'll address the broader version first.

My primary response to the "If T4G, then church membership" argument is that church membership isn't the only kind of fellowship Christians can have.[39] By definition Christians who are geographically distant can't be members of the same church. Yet we read of them enjoying fellowship in all kinds of ways: contributing together to the needs of the saints (2 Cor 8:6; 9:13), supporting an apostle's ministry (Phil 1:5), sending and receiving preachers and missionaries (2 Cor 8:18; 3 John 5–6a), and so on.[40] Fellowship between Christians isn't all-or-nothing. If distance keeps us from celebrating the Lord's Supper together, we can still pray for one another and give sacrificially for one another's needs. Likewise, if disagreement over baptism keeps us from being members of the same church, we can still enjoy fellowship and unity in Christ in all kinds of ways.

Preaching in each other's churches is one way. But is it inconsistent to invite a minister to break the bread of life to us and not allow him to break bread at the Lord's Table with us?[41] I'd suggest not. First, we see in 2 Corinthians 8:18 and 3 John 5–6a that the earliest Christians would occasionally hear trusted preachers from other churches. This means the New Testament doesn't require someone to be a member of a certain church in order to preach to that church. And if someone isn't required to be a member, I can't see why he would need to fulfill all of a church's requirements for membership. Obviously, a church should only listen to a visiting preacher who is sound in doctrine and life (Gal 1:8–9; 1 John 4:1; 2 John 7–8a). Yet it is entirely appropriate for churches to hear from guest preachers who agree extensively with their doctrine yet differ on

---

[39] Consider, for instance, the way Thomas Goodwin distinguishes between the "fixed, instituted, and political communion" which is church membership, and "simply mystical, and moral, and occasional" communion between Christians (*Of the Constitution, Right Order, and Government of the Churches of Christ*, in *The Works of Thomas Goodwin*, vol. 11 [repr., Eureka, CA: Tanski, 1996], 6–7).

[40] See further Jonathan Leeman, "Independence and Interdependence," in *Baptist Foundations: Chruch Government for an Anti-Institutional Age*, ed. Mark Dever and Jonathan Leeman (Nashville: B&H, 2015).

[41] This phrasing follows Abraham Booth's presentation of this objection, which he answers well (*Apology for the Baptists*, 117–19).

ecclesial distinctives and therefore couldn't join their church.[42] Unity between churches is made of different stuff than unity within churches.

7. It's Wrong to Exclude People from Our Churches Who Wouldn't Exclude Us from Theirs

A final argument to consider is that it's wrong to exclude people from our churches who wouldn't exclude us from theirs. This is a variation on the "odd man out" point I engaged briefly in chapter 2. The first thing to point out is that not all paedobaptist churches do accept baptists. Some Reformed denominations require subscription to a confession that contains paedobaptism in order to join the church or even participate in visiting communion.

Second, consider J. L. Reynolds's comments on the issue. He first points out that apart from open-membership baptists, all Christians have held baptism to be "an indispensable prerequisite to the Lord's Supper." Thus, "Had there remained one baptism, as well as one Lord, and one faith, there would have been but one communion." Yet baptists hold that baptism by definition is applied only to believers. Therefore:

> To receive unimmersed persons to their own communion, would
> amount not only to a virtual renunciation of their own views of baptism,
> but an abandonment of the fundamental law of communion, in the
> churches of Christ in general. And yet, because they refuse to do this,
> the cry of bigotry is raised against them. It would be well for those who
> are disposed to join this cry, to consider what respect they could have for
> persons who would thus betray, at once, their own principles and the
> common principles of the Christian world.[43]

---

[42] Booth writes, "When we ask a Paedobaptist minister to preach in any of our churches, we act on the same general principle, as when we request him to pray with any of us in a private family. And as no one considers *this* as an act of church communion, but as a testimony of our affection for him, so we consider *that*; and it is viewed by the public, as a branch of that general intercourse which it is not only lawful, but commendable and profitable to have, with all that preach the gospel" (*Apology for the Baptists*, 118–19, emphasis original).

[43] J. L. Reynolds, *Church Polity or the Kingdom of Christ, in Its Internal and External Development* (Richmond, VA: Harold & Murray, 1849), in *Polity: Biblical Arguments on How to Conduct Church Life*, ed. Mark Dever (Washington, DC: Center for Church Reform, 2001), 391–92.

The issue here is a common principle producing divergent results. We baptists shouldn't be charged with malice for treating the relationship between baptism and the Lord's Supper precisely the way our paedobaptist brothers do. As Abraham Booth puts it, if we're wrong, the error is in our judgment, not our temperament.[44] The stubborn fact remains that if credobaptists are right, paedobaptists are unbaptized. The resulting traffic between churches is asymmetrical because our practices of baptism are asymmetrical.

One Last Card to Play

I hope it is evident in this chapter and the whole book that I have great respect and affection not only for my paedobaptist brothers and sisters but also for open-membership baptists. And I don't think anyone in either baptismal debate intends to disobey or minimize any of the Lord's ordinances. Instead, open-membership advocates make serious, conscientious arguments that deserve serious answers, and I've attempted to answer them fully and fairly.

If you're still not persuaded that requiring baptism for membership is a biblical norm, I've got one last card to play. In the book so far, I've built a case and defended that case. In the next chapter I'm going to switch back to offense and lodge some objections of my own against the open-membership position.

Headlines
Baptism draws the line between the church and the world. We are not at liberty to draw it elsewhere.
Church membership is defined by the ritual privilege of participating in the Lord's Supper, and Jesus has appointed baptism as its ritual prerequisite. Paedobaptists are denied membership because they lack not the substance of a credible profession but its form.
You can't make Christians into a church without baptism and the Lord's Supper. Therefore, in order to have a church together, you need to agree not just about essential gospel doctrine but about the proper practice of the ordinances.

---

[44] Booth, *Apology for the Baptists*, 16.

Chapter 10

Turning the Tables

In the unlikely case that you're just tuning in, here's a recap. So far I've built a case for why baptism is required for church membership and have defended that case against the strongest objections I can find. Our final theological task is, as it were, to cross-examine the prosecution: to critically assess the open membership position itself.

In this chapter I'll mount seven objections to the open membership position. Some of our discussion will overlap with the previous chapter, but this is far from an exercise in dead-horse beating. In the previous chapter I defended an ecclesial structure that I think is biblical against the claims of critics. Now it's time for us to get out a clipboard, put on a hard-hat, and inspect open membership's ecclesial construction site.

Seven Arguments Against Open Membership

I'll list my seven arguments here to show where we're heading and to put all my cards on the table from the start. Then we'll jump right in.

1. Open membership builds on error.
2. Open membership requires churches to accommodate not just error but willful inconsistency.
3. Open membership privileges the individual conscience over the authority of the local church.

4. Open membership either creates unbiblical distinctions among a church's members or requires a church to pare down its convictions.
5. Open membership overreaches. It tries to resolve a tension that's beyond our power to resolve.
6. Open membership arbitrarily privileges the Lord's Supper over baptism.
7. Open membership effectively makes baptism optional.

1. Open Membership Builds on Error

My first argument is that open membership builds on error. It enters a faulty value into the ecclesiological equation. It takes paedobaptism, which baptists regard as error and therefore as non-baptism, and makes it a load-bearing theological structure.

Why is this a problem? Because our practical judgment regarding baptism and membership is inextricably theological. This is not merely an issue of wisdom. Either Jesus has made baptism a requirement for church membership or he hasn't. And both positions make a theological statement about what baptism and membership are.

Here we need to return to a crucial ambiguity in open membership reasoning. Many exponents of the position don't simply remove baptism from the requirements for membership and allow any unbaptized Christian to join. Instead, they only widen their membership borders to include those "baptized" in infancy. And in John Piper's view, the border is only widened to those who hold to a Reformed understanding of paedobaptism. But, as we've briefly touched on already, this accords paedobaptism a theological status it does not merit. In the right circumstances it allows paedobaptism to make the decisive difference between being included in or excluded from the church. It therefore makes paedobaptism part of the church's constitution, insofar as paedobaptism has become a potential qualification for membership.

In other words, this form of open membership gives paedobaptism a load-bearing role in ecclesiology. It effectively puts paedobaptism into the category of what marks off Christians from the world. This is like putting a misshapen slab of concrete into the foundation of a house: error in the foundation will skew the shape of the whole building.

I would argue that even open membership advocates who intend to erase baptism from membership requirements altogether similarly build on error. How? In that they would not extend membership to someone who simply rejects Jesus' command to be baptized. It's still the theological rationale they offer, however faulty, which gets them the ticket to membership. There must be some *reason* a Christian isn't baptized, or else we're dealing with rebellion and false profession. As we saw in the previous chapter, Robert Hall's entire argument for open membership depends on the rise of a different—that is, erroneous—understanding of baptism among genuine Christians.[1] Hall says churches should practice open membership *because* some Christians are in error regarding baptism. If these Christians were not in theological error, churches' membership would de facto be restricted to the baptized. Thus, even this more consistent open membership stance builds on error in a similar and similarly compromising way.

Certainly our ecclesiology must account for sin and error among church members—no argument there. The moral requirement for church membership is not perfection but repentance. And you should be able to have all kinds of wrong ideas about all kinds of things and still be a member of a church in good standing. Churches are right to actively tolerate diversity among their members regarding millennial positions, spiritual gifts, the finer points of soteriology, schooling practices, how we apply our faith to political policies, and more. Some of these issues have a theological right and wrong, and some are matters of wisdom. Of course, there are plenty of ways to be wrong about a "wisdom issue," such as considering your position the only Christian option. My point is simply that a church can easily accommodate error among its members on a wide range of subjects.[2] In saying we must not theologically build on error, I'm not arguing for some sort of perfectionist ecclesiology.

Yet you can't put error regarding baptism into the structure of the church. Why? Because baptism, along with the Lord's Supper, *is* what structures the church. Remember, baptism draws the church together by drawing a line between church and world. If you throw a baptismal wrench into the ecclesial

---

[1] Robert Hall, *On Terms of Communion; with a Particular View to the Case of the Baptists and Paedobaptists* (1st American ed., from the 3rd English ed., Philadelphia, 1816; repr., London: Forgotten Books, 2012), 68–70. Presumably Hall would open membership to someone who held the Quaker view that Spirit baptism at conversion is the only baptism required of Christians.

[2] Helpful in this regard is John Webster's distinction, borrowed from Aquinas, between "divergence of opinion" and "divergence of will" in the context of theological controversy ("Theology and the Peace of the Church," in *The Domain of the Word: Scripture and Theological Reason* [London: T&T Clark, 2012], 169).

machine, the gears will grind. Open membership doesn't merely tolerate error; it builds on it. And no ecclesiology can build on error in this way and remain faithful to Scripture's blueprint.

2. Open Membership Requires Churches to Accommodate Not Just Error but Willful Inconsistency

Second, open membership requires churches to accommodate not just error but willful inconsistency. In seeking to join a baptist church, a convictional paedobaptist necessarily compromises his conscience to some degree. Every time a church member's child is born and not baptized, the paedobaptist's conscience should jab him. Why are these members of the covenant being denied the sign of the covenant? Why are God's promises to his people being neglected, even distorted, by withholding baptism from those to whom it is due?

And what if the paedobaptist member gets married and starts a family? His choice to join a baptist church will then hinder him from obeying God according to his understanding of Scripture. If paedobaptism is biblical, then he is commanded by God to have his children baptized. Yet even if he has the boldness to ask, the church will refuse.

So why would a paedobaptist seek to join a baptist church? Most likely because there's something about the baptist church he values more than his paedobaptism. Likely candidates include preaching and community. But if a conviction is something you're willing to sacrifice for the sake of better preaching, is it really a conviction?

It's possible to be convinced of paedobaptism and still seek membership in a baptist church—as long as you're not currently adding to your family. If you are, your "conviction" goes kaput. But if you're not, you could potentially hold your conviction and stomach a baptist church's disobedience. Perhaps you could consider it a lesser evil than, say, attending a paedobaptist church that denies the gospel and endorses sin.[3]

Yet for many of those baptized in infancy who seek membership in baptist churches, the issue may not be conviction as much as convenience. Their

---

[3] Of course, if your only options in town are a faithful baptist church and a heretical paedobaptist church, we have to ask, how did you get to this town in the first place? If it was by choice, why did you decide to move somewhere without knowing there would be a church you could join?

consciences aren't bothered by the unbaptized infants all around them. If they have children, they're not seeking to have them baptized. Instead, their attachment to their own infant "baptism" may owe something to the awkwardness of being "re-baptized" as an adult after walking with Christ for many years. Or they may not want to distance themselves from their parents' beliefs and practices, implicitly critiquing their parents for having them baptized as infants.

Whatever the case, my sense is that many of those "baptized" in infancy who seek membership in baptist churches are attached to their infant "baptism" by something weaker than conviction. Indifference may be closer to the mark: we're nearing cake-and-eat-it-too territory. If you're not convinced enough to have your own children "baptized," what does that say about your own "baptism"? Was it necessary? If it wasn't necessary, was it valid?

Or maybe it's that you think your infant "baptism" wasn't ideal. But if it wasn't ideal, was it still a biblically valid baptism? How do you know? If it was valid, then all the infants of believers should be baptized, and you should seek a church where they will be. You can't treat your own infant "baptism" as right but others' as wrong. And if your infant "baptism" wasn't biblically valid, then you haven't been baptized and need to be. Often I fear that what seems to be humility—"Who am I to say what is and isn't baptism?"—is much closer to indifference. And indifference is right next door to disobedience. Jesus isn't indifferent to baptism; neither should we be.[4]

In principle, open membership requires churches to accommodate not just error but willful inconsistency. And in practice open membership often means accommodating not compromised convictions but indifference to one of Christ's commands. No church can be obligated to accommodate someone's attempt to compromise his own convictions. Nor can they be required to endorse indifference to a divine ordinance.

---

[4] Joseph Kinghorn similarly writes: "But the inquiry will *irresistibly* rise,—if they really and heartily believe, that infant baptism is an institution of Christ, why do they wish to unite with people by whom one of his institutions is, in their view, so manifestly opposed? How can they in justice to their families, unite with Baptists? How can they act as some of them do, if they believe that infant baptism is a command of Christ, and a matter of any importance? Is it the fact, that though they do not like our opinion, yet they do not think there is sufficient evidence to establish their own? Or is it, that in many of them there is a considerable degree of indifference concerning it; so that though they may oppose us . . . yet they do not think that it is a matter of much consequence?" (*Baptism, A Term of Communion* [Norwich, 1816; repr., Paris, AR: Baptist Standard Bearer, 2006], 104).

3. Open Membership Privileges the Individual Conscience over the Authority of the Local Church

Third, open membership privileges the individual conscience over the authority of the local church. Bunyan, for instance, argues:

> If baptism respect believers, as particular persons only; if it respects their own conscience only; if it make a man no visible believer to me, then it hath nothing to do with church-membership. Because, that which respects my own person only, my own conscience only: that which is no character of my visible saintship to the church, cannot be an argument unto them to receive me into fellowship with themselves. But this is true.[5]

Note especially Bunyan's claim that baptism "respects" an individual believer's "own conscience only." Bunyan earlier writes of baptism, "He therefore that doth it according to his light, doth well; and he that doth it not, for want of light, doth not ill; for he approveth his heart to be sincere with God."[6]

Bunyan's argument is that baptism is solely a matter between an individual believer's conscience and God. The church has no concern with it as long as a believer acts according to his own understanding. But this isn't how a church treats any other biblical command. We don't say, "He who assembles with the church does well, and he who forsakes the assembly, because he lacks understanding, does no ill." Even when disobedience is mitigated by misunderstanding, consequences still follow. And, as I've argued throughout the book, one consequence of paedobaptism is that many people consider themselves baptized but are not yet qualified for church membership.

On the open membership view, baptism, a command of Christ, is reduced to "indifferent" status because some Christians misunderstand it. Because of diverse Christian views, a church may not insist on obedience to this command of Christ's, since to insist on obedience would be to exclude paedobaptists from membership. This privileges the individual conscience over the authority of the local church.

---

[5] John Bunyan, *Differences in Judgment About Water-Baptism, No Bar to Communion*, in *The Miscellaneous Works of John Bunyan*, vol. 4, ed. T. L. Underwood (Oxford: Clarendon, 1989), 222.

[6] Ibid., 220.

Yet recall that the church has a nondelegable responsibility to practice the ordinances. The ordinances exercise the keys of the kingdom, which are given to the church as church, not to believers as individuals. Therefore, a church may not allow individuals' convictions to overrule its corporate obligation to obey Christ in the exercise of the ordinances. John Dagg is helpful here:

> When a church receives an unbaptized person, something more is done than merely to tolerate his error. There are two parties concerned. The acts of entering the church and partaking of its communion are his, and for them he is responsible. The church also acts when it admits him to membership, and authorizes his participation of the communion. The church, as an organized body, with power to receive and exclude members according to the rules which Christ has laid down, is responsible for the exercise of this power.[7]

As charitable as it may seem, for a church to defer to an individual's conscience is actually to abdicate the responsibility Jesus has given it. Again recall Dagg's words: "If each were left wholly to himself, the discipline of the church would be nothing, and the power to exercise it would be attended with no responsibility."[8]

If a church allows individual conscience to trump corporate judgment, conscience becomes a universal acid that can burn all the way through the authority of a local church. To say that a church must defer to an individual's understanding of baptism is to say that the church has no authority to declare and uphold the Lord's will on this point. Thus open membership unhinges baptism from the keys of the kingdom, undoes baptism's role as a badge of belonging, and undermines the church's authority as Jesus' representative.

If an individual's conviction trumps the church's confession, it's not the church that has authority but the individual. On this point the individual no longer submits to the church but the church to the individual. This reverses the relation which constitutes membership—and constitutes a church—in the first place. In principle, by privileging the individual conscience over the local church, open membership actually begins to unravel the theological fabric of a local church's existence as a church.

---

[7] John L. Dagg, *Manual of Church Order* (repr.; Harrisonburg, VA: Gano, 1990), 221.
[8] Ibid.

4. Open Membership Either Creates Unbiblical Distinctions Among a Church's Members or Requires a Church to Pare Down Its Convictions

A fourth argument against open membership is that it either creates unbiblical distinctions among a church's members or requires a church to pare down its convictions. Assume as our starting point a baptist church with an explicitly credobaptist statement of faith to which all members must subscribe.[9] If such a church is going to accept paedobaptist members, what will they do with the division in baptismal conviction and status this introduces into its membership?

As I see it, there are three basic options, the first two of which can coexist. Option one is to allow the paedobaptist applicants to take exception to the article on baptism in the statement of faith. Option two is to admit paedobaptists to the status of "non-voting" member because their beliefs on baptism differ from the church's.[10] Option one is necessary unless a church pursues option three: revise the article on baptism in their statement of faith so that both credobaptists and paedobaptists can assent.

Let's consider options one and two first. What biblical principles can warrant either? On what ground can we require all members to agree with the church's stance on baptism, except those who disagree? How can a church legitimately require subscription to the other articles of its statement of faith when it allows liberty to disagree with one?

Regarding option two, nonvoting members, on what grounds can a church parse out the privileges and responsibilities of church membership, conferring some while withholding others? If someone is granted a share in the church's fellowship—embodied in their participation in the Lord's Supper—on what basis can they be denied a share in the corporate responsibility that fellowship entails?[11] For these reasons and more, I don't find either of these options to be

---

[9] Such as, for example, the revised New Hampshire confession of 1853: "We believe that Christian Baptism is the immersion in water of a believer, into the name of the Father, and Son, and Holy Ghost; to show forth in a solemn and beautiful emblem, our faith in the crucified, buried, and risen Savior, with its effect, in our death to sin and resurrection to a new life." In William L. Lumpkin, *Baptist Confessions of Faith*, 2nd rev. ed., ed. Bill J. Leonard (Valley Forge, PA: Judson, 2011), 382.

[10] Some churches attempt to split the difference by calling such paedobaptists "adherents," which admits them to the Lord's Supper but not to voting privileges. In my view, if this is an attempt to preserve a baptized membership, it fails since it authorizes unbaptized persons to participate in the Lord's Supper, even though the term *member* is withheld.

[11] Along with virtually all Baptists through the centuries, I'd argue that final responsibility for matters of membership, discipline, and doctrine rests with the congregation

a biblically justifiable solution to the division open membership injects into a local church.

In option three, revising the statement of faith's article on baptism so that both credobaptists and paedobaptists can assent, a church formally retracts its credobaptist conviction. It henceforth leaves the proper subjects of baptism undefined. Certainly no one's individual beliefs have changed. And, in principle, this doesn't necessarily change what the elders will teach concerning baptism. Nevertheless, having been removed from its confession, credobaptism can no longer be considered a conviction *of the church*.

One historical consequence of this is that a number of open-membership baptist churches have turned into paedobaptist churches. After John Bunyan's death his own church hired a paedobaptist minister, and for the next hundred years the church's ministers were all paedobaptists.[12] Since baptist churches are characteristically congregational, all it takes for a church to lose its credobaptist practice is a paedobaptist majority.

Admitting paedobaptist members, and especially removing credobaptism from a statement of faith, will pressure both preachers and members to shy away from airing their full convictions about baptism. Credobaptism, and the need for paedo-"baptized" members to obey Jesus by being baptized, becomes something awkward to insist on. Now it's much harder to say to the person in the pew next to you, "You need to obey Jesus and get baptized." Why? Because the church has defanged Jesus' command. The church has deliberately become a safe zone in which a certain class of believers may remain unbaptized. To announce and apply credobaptist convictions threatens that church-sanctioned safety.

Therefore, the long-term result of removing credobaptism from a church's statement of faith is that it erodes their credobaptist convictions. Paedobaptists will count this no great loss, but I'm writing as a convinced credobaptist. Whether by formal removal or informal erosion, a church's loss of credobaptist convictions is the loss of a right interpretation of Scripture leading to a right practice. This makes way for error on both counts and implicates credobaptist members in a practice they disavow. This is not something we should simply

---

as a whole. For a defense of congregational polity, see section II.4 of my article, "Why New Testament Polity Is Prescriptive," *9Marks Journal* 10, no. 4 (2013), available at http://www.9marks.org/journal/why-new-testament-polity-prescriptive.

[12] Joseph Kinghorn, *A Defense of Baptism, A Term of Communion* (Norwich, 1816; repr., Paris, AR: Baptist Standard Bearer, 2006), xv.

chalk up to the cost of unity. Just the opposite: it is ceding the only ground on which true unity can stand.

Behind all three of these doors lie varying degrees of weakened unity and eroded convictions. However a church chooses to relieve the pressure, the presence of error among its members will inevitably introduce division and truncate conviction. The approval of paedobaptism intrinsically undermines a convictional confession of credobaptism. And disagreement on baptismal practice and status will necessarily disrupt a church's unity in some measure. Doctrinal division about a church-constituting ordinance cannot do otherwise.

5. Open Membership Overreaches. It Tries to Resolve a Tension That's Beyond Our Power to Resolve

Fifth, open membership overreaches. It tries to resolve a tension that's beyond our power to resolve. It tries to address an ecclesial symptom of paedobaptism, but the symptom can't be treated apart from the cause.

Error is the original schism. Why? Because it is a division from the truth. When Christians depart from a biblical understanding and practice of baptism, division is inevitable. Again, I say all this with nothing but respect and affection for my paedobaptist brothers and sisters. Jesus has given commands to baptize and to be baptized. Either those commands apply to believers' infant children or they don't. And if they don't, but some Christians believe they do, division has been introduced into the church.

Consider a baptist church a hundred miles from any other church. Ten families in that church develop paedobaptist convictions. All of these families have or are having young children. Their consciences now tell them that they must have these children baptized. Who will baptize them? Not the church. So what options do they have? One is to stay in the church at the expense of their convictions. But then, as we've seen, it's not really a conviction if you can just ignore it. So if they persist in this conviction, their only option is to start their own church. Where you previously had one church, now you have two, one of which some Christians can no longer happily attend.

But what has the first church done? Nothing. They haven't changed. They haven't adopted any new belief or practice. And they haven't even changed their requirements for membership. They certainly haven't "forced" anybody out. Instead, seen against a credobaptist background, it is the rise of paedobaptist convictions that has created the division. Therefore, the responsibility to heal the division rests with those who introduced it.[13] And, taking the root of division into account, not just its fruit, they're the only ones who can heal it. How? By returning to the truth. If this sounds crass, remember that paedobaptist brothers and sisters say the same thing about us baptists. If we hadn't abandoned infant baptism, we wouldn't have created this mess in the first place! It's just that we baptists think the shoe's on the other foot.

I'd submit that requiring baptism for membership is actually the most respectful, conscientious response to paedobaptism. If we respect the paedobaptist position, we should wish them freedom to practice according to their conscience, which is something they certainly can't do within our churches. This is why many paedobaptists through the centuries have actually applauded the closed-membership position. They recognize we're simply doing what they'd do in our shoes.

Open membership, on the other hand, tries to resolve a tension that's not within our power to resolve. It refuses to recognize that this is simply one of those problems we can't fix ourselves. In so doing, it hides the true source of division—namely, error—and the true solution: informed submission to the teaching of Scripture.

The only way to undo the division paedobaptism creates is to undo paedobaptism. As long as there are credobaptists and paedobaptists, the existence of credobaptist and paedobaptist churches is a tension we simply have to live with.[14] God has given us neither the authority nor the ability to fix this problem. One day he himself will fix it, on that great day when he fixes all our problems. And we baptists know we've got plenty.

---

[13] Although his rhetoric is a little overheated, R. B. C. Howell's articulation of this point is worth consulting. See *The Terms of Communion at the Lord's Table* (Philadelphia: American Baptist Publication Society, 1846; repr., Paris, AR: Baptist Standard Bearer, 2006), 247–49.

[14] Some readers may wonder how I can recognize a paedobaptist church as a true church since, in principle, all its members could be unbaptized persons and therefore unfit "matter" for a church. I would suggest that because a paedobaptist church preaches the gospel and practices the ordinances together, they are in fact a church. (Remember, it's not that paedobaptists *don't* baptize believers; it's just that they "baptize" infants too, thus preventing them from being baptized if they come to faith.) Not being baptized, did these individuals have the initial authority to form a church? Perhaps not. But once they're a church, they're a church. The situation is analogous to a couple who were each unbiblically divorced before marrying each other. They lacked the authorization to marry, but once they're married, they're married.

6. Open Membership Arbitrarily Privileges the Lord's Supper over Baptism

Sixth, open membership arbitrarily privileges the Lord's Supper over baptism. Remember that the Lord's Supper is an effective sign of church membership, and the chief privilege of membership is participation in the Lord's Supper. So why insist on the Lord's Supper at the expense of baptism? Why is one ordinance apparently more important, and more binding, than the other?

Open-membership advocates allow an individual's conscience, in certain circumstances, to settle the question of whether they need to be baptized. But why not allow the same liberty for the Lord's Supper? If you don't insist on baptism for membership, is someone free to join the church yet perpetually abstain from the Lord's Supper?[15] Open membership logic would seem to require this, provided a sufficient theological rationale was offered. Yet the Lord's Supper, like baptism, is a commanded observance: "Do this in remembrance of me" (Luke 22:19).

The point is, we're not free to dispense with either of the Lord's ordinances. And to dispense with one in order to extend the other is arbitrary.[16] Instead, we should uphold both in their proper place: baptism as the front door, the Lord's Supper as the family meal.

7. Open Membership Effectively Makes Baptism Optional

Finally, open membership effectively makes baptism optional. Certainly open membership advocates agree that baptism is a command of Christ, binding on all believers. Yet by extending membership to unbaptized believers, open-membership churches give them permission to remain unbaptized. When a church admits an unbaptized person to the Lord's Supper, "that person receives a commission from the church to omit a positive duty required by the word of God, which, in other words, is no other than a commission to live in a sin of omission."[17]

---

[15] Abraham Booth, *An Apology for the Baptists* (London, 1778), in *A Defense of the Baptists* (Paris, AR: The Baptist Standard Bearer, 2006), 50.

[16] Ibid., 131; also Kinghorn, *Baptism, A Term of Communion*, 165. Dagg asks, "Is [the Lord's Supper] more spiritual than baptism? If not, why should baptism be trodden under foot, to open the way of access to the eucharist?" (*Manual of Church Order*, 225).

[17] William Buttfield, *Free Communion an Innovation: or, an Answer to Mr. John Brown's Pamphlet* (London, 1778; repr., Hampshire, UK: ECCO), 26.

Abraham Booth illustrates this point with an important hypothetical: what if, after being admitted to membership, a paedobaptist becomes convinced that paedobaptism is invalid, yet still refuses to be baptized?[18] The person is unbaptized and knows it. Now they're willfully disobeying Christ's command; yet they're already a member of the church. Will they now be excluded from the Lord's Supper? If the answer is yes, then believing error regarding baptism has become a qualification for membership, at least for some. And now to cease believing that error is grounds for excommunication! Yet if the church doesn't exclude this unbaptized person, then it is tolerating outright disregard for baptism among its members. That is, it's making baptism optional.

Although he later warmed toward open membership, earlier George Beasley-Murray cogently argued against it on these grounds. "If it is not necessary for members coming over from Methodism to submit to baptism, on what grounds is it said to be necessary for adolescents growing up in a Baptist church to be baptized?" And again:

> In these circumstances baptism has been made a purely private option
> for the Christian who wants it; he does not have to be baptized, for he
> may just as well join the Church without it, and to press him would
> evidently be quite wrong, for this is a matter of individual judgment!
> Baptism is no longer the door of the Church; it's a pew in the front rows,
> which the minister would like you to occupy, but you can sit elsewhere if
> you wish.[19]

Commenting on the trajectory of British Baptists, Stephen Holmes points out that in the long term, open membership tends to erode baptism's normative status:

> British Baptists find themselves in a curious position as a result of this
> tradition of ecumenical openness: they are, in practice, less committed
> to the importance of baptism in ecclesiology than almost any other
> mainstream denomination. In most British Baptist churches a person
> may be in membership or even leadership, and may receive or even

---

[18] Booth, *Apology for the Baptists*, 48–49.
[19] G. R. Beasley-Murray, *Baptism Today and Tomorrow* (New York: St Martin's, 1966), 87–88.

celebrate the Eucharist, without being baptized, either as believer or infant.[20]

If something is optional for church membership, it's optional for the Christian life. A church may verbally insist that all believers must be baptized, but if they accept unbaptized persons to membership, they tear down with the left hand what they've built up with the right. Here actions do speak louder than words.

What Now?

And here ends the argument. Not just for the chapter, but for the book. I've built a case, defended that case, and done my best in this chapter to undermine the opposing case. The point of all this has not been to score points or win a fight. Instead, I've sought to discern the will of the Lord as revealed in his Word so that our churches might obey it.

If Jesus requires believers to be baptized, our churches should too. Yet from sincere and loving motives, some Christians have proposed that in certain circumstances our churches shouldn't require people to be baptized. I'm convinced that this fails to comply with one of Jesus' commands. It also weakens our ecclesiology and disconnects crucial church-building materials which Jesus has joined together: baptism, the Lord's Supper, and church membership.

The seven points covered in this chapter describe ways open membership weakens the church. To accommodate error and willful inconsistency, to privilege individual conscience over the authority of the church, to pare down baptismal convictions, to attempt to solve a problem that's beyond our power to solve, to arbitrarily privilege one ordinance over the other, and to effectively make baptism optional—all these are detrimental to the health and witness of a local church. However well-intentioned, all these consequences of the open-membership position erode a church's unity, submission to Christ's commands, and authority to mark off believers from the world. All these consequences tend toward the unraveling of the local church rather than its upbuilding. So I've sought not only to positively sketch the ecclesial shape of baptism and the baptismal shape of membership but also to answer and undermine arguments to the contrary.

---

[20] Stephen R. Holmes, *Baptist Theology* (London: T&T Clark, 2012), 93. In the present context Holmes does not commit himself to one side or the other of this debate.

The goal of argument is to persuade, so I hope you're convinced. For those who aren't, I hope you've found at least some things to agree with, and I hope those insights will enrich your understanding of Jesus' church and its ordinances. And I hope that understanding, in turn, will enrich your church's common life. But especially for those who are convinced, the next—and last—question is, What now? What does all this mean for how a church should practice baptism, the Lord's Supper, and church membership? In the final chapter we turn at last to a few practical suggestions.

Headlines
The open-membership position (1) builds on error; (2) requires churches to accommodate not just error but willful inconsistency; (3) privileges the individual conscience over the authority of the local church; (4) either creates unbiblical distinctions among a church's members or requires a church to pare down its convictions; (5) overreaches, that is, it tries to resolve a tension that's beyond our power to resolve; (6) arbitrarily privileges the Lord's Supper over baptism; and (7) effectively makes baptism optional.
You can't put error regarding baptism into the structure of the church. Why? Because baptism, along with the Lord's Supper, *is* what structures the church.
No church can be obligated to accommodate someone's attempt to compromise his own convictions. Nor can the church be required to endorse indifference to a divine ordinance.
If an individual's conviction trumps the church's confession, it's not the church that has authority but the individual.
The approval of paedobaptism intrinsically undermines a convictional confession of credobaptism.
If something is optional for church membership, it's optional for the Christian life. A church may verbally insist that all believers must be baptized, but if they accept unbaptized persons to membership, they permit those persons to persist in disobedience to Jesus.

Chapter 11

Practicing Baptism, the Lord's Supper, and Church Membership

This book is an effort to rethink the relationship between the ordinances and the local church for the purpose of discerning baptism's relation to church membership and the Lord's Supper. The central case about baptism and membership has important practical implications, and in this chapter we'll deal with some of those first. But requiring baptism for membership only makes sense within a broader ecclesial practice. So in this chapter I'm going to apply this book's entire theological argument to how churches should practice baptism, the Lord's Supper, and church membership. Fair warning: I won't address many practical issues related to the ordinances and membership. I'm just dipping into a few of the most pressing to help pastors answer the question, What now?

I'll start with how churches that have allowed paedobaptists into membership can transition to a more consistent practice. Next we'll examine a few practical issues related to the Lord's Supper, then baptism. Finally, we'll consider how to make membership meaningful since all this assumes membership is more than a name on a list.

A Transition Plan

Our first practical sketch is a transition plan for requiring baptism for membership. I have in mind churches that have deliberately allowed paedobaptist members and those who may not have paid consistent attention to whether applicants for membership have been baptized. In this section and throughout most of the chapter, I'm speaking directly to, for lack of a better term, "senior pastors." If you're an elder of a church but not the main preacher, you absolutely have a stake in this issue. But churchwide change will most likely need to go through—and even be spearheaded by—the man who most often fills the pulpit. With that in mind, here's a six-step transition plan.

First, pursue unity among your church's elders. Study the issue as a group. Work for like-mindedness, and if possible even unanimity. Be patient; grudging acceptance won't do. Tightening your church's standards for membership will almost certainly come with a pastoral cost, and you want every single elder to be willing to pay some of that cost. However, if you've given the issue plenty of time, and there's a strong majority consensus but not unanimity, it could be best to move forward still. If six elders are convinced baptism is required for membership but two aren't, the six aren't going to recommend anyone for membership who isn't baptized, making it a de facto policy even without formal change.

Second, teach publicly on the issue. Perhaps you could use this issue as an opportunity to teach more broadly about baptism, the Lord's Supper, and church membership. Take this chance to equip your people with a compelling biblical vision of Christ's plan for his church. If you think it would serve the church, hold question-and-answer sessions with your members. Again, be patient. The only true change in a church comes when God the Holy Spirit applies God's Word to the hearts of God's people. So pray and work and wait for a membership that understands and embraces the biblical ties between baptism, the Lord's Supper, and church membership.

Third, in the US at least, perhaps the best way to formalize the change is by amending your church's constitution or bylaws. Where those documents discuss the qualifications for membership, simply add a phrase specifying believer baptism. I'd argue that matters of membership—including oversight of its qualifications—are the nondelegable responsibility of the whole congregation (Matt 18:17; 1 Cor 5:4–5; 2 Cor 2:6). So the elders should lead by exploring this issue, teaching on it, drafting an amendment to the church's governing documents, and recommending it to the congregation, but the congregation as a whole should be asked to formally decide the change.

Fourth, if your church's statement of faith doesn't specify that baptism is an ordinance for believers, it could be a good idea to make that explicit. This process would parallel changing the constitution. (Most baptistic churches' statements of faith will already speak to this issue by default by naming believers as the subjects of baptism. This implicitly rules out paedobaptism.)

Fifth, if you currently have unbaptized paedobaptist members, I'd suggest they should be "grandfathered in"—that is, remain members. When they joined the church, this wasn't an issue, but now the ground has shifted underfoot. And I don't think their refusal to be baptized necessarily amounts to grounds for excommunication. This is a bit like the US Constitution's provision against *ex post facto* laws: the government can't prosecute you for doing something that wasn't a crime when you did it. In the long run, of course, there are two preferable solutions to the problem of unbaptized paedobaptist members: (1) they become convinced credobaptists and get baptized; (2) they find a paedobaptist church to join. But the first option can't be forced, and I don't think the second should be.

What if you have unbaptized members who aren't paedobaptists but simply haven't been and refuse to be baptized? That's tricky. On the one hand, their spiritual posture is clearly different—different to the point of potentially undermining the credibility of their claim to follow Christ. On the other hand, their baptismal status is the same as some who remain members, which would make it difficult to exclude them while including others. Given this dilemma, the issue might need to be handled on a case-by-case basis.

Sixth, ask each applicant for membership when, where, and how they were baptized. I think it's generally a good idea for a church elder to perform a membership interview in which he gets to know a person's testimony, asks them to articulate the gospel, sees if they have any questions about the church, and explains the church's expectations of members. The elders then consider these things together, and unless there are any red flags, they recommend the person to the congregation for membership. So, if you conduct an interview like this, simply ask a person when he or she was baptized, where, and by whom.

This transition plan is a sketch, not a decree. Your mileage may vary. But I hope it's enough to help you and your fellow elders start brainstorming about how to get from here to there.

The Lord's Supper: Fences and the Family Meal

The case I've built in this book also has significant implications for how we practice the Lord's Supper. We explored several in chapter 6, a couple of which we'll return to here. The first is that the church, and only the church, should celebrate the Lord's Supper. You shouldn't take the Lord's Supper with your family, or in a campus ministry, or at a school chapel service, or with your friends around a campfire. Instead, you should celebrate the Lord's Supper only with a gathered local church. And a church should only celebrate the Lord's Supper in the context of a whole-church meeting, not a smaller gathering of only some of its members. To do anything else is to rob the Lord's Supper of its role as an effective sign of church membership, the family meal of the body of Christ.

Second, how should churches "fence the Table"—that is, declare who is welcome to participate? I'd suggest they say something like this: "If you're a member of this church, or a member of another evangelical church, and you've been baptized as a believer, you're welcome to partake."[1] The two qualifications here are that someone is baptized and is a member of a gospel-preaching church, whether yours or another. Baptism and church membership are simply the public, institutional means Jesus has given us to identify ourselves as Christians. Baptism is required for participation in the Lord's Supper because the initiating oath-sign of the new covenant must come before its renewing oath-sign. Church membership is required because we enact our submission to Jesus by submitting to his church. We embrace our membership in the universal body by becoming members of a local body. Professing Christians who don't belong to any church are rejecting Jesus' authority by refusing to submit to his proxy. Allowing individuals who aren't members of any church to participate in the Lord's Supper gives them the benefits of fellowship without the commitment, the intimacy without the promise.

Another practical implication of our case is that the Lord's Supper is not a private devotional act that just happens to occur with a bunch of other people in the room. Just the opposite, it's a communal meal. So, pastor, teach your people this. Revel in the togetherness of the Lord's Supper. Don't just close

---

[1] This language is contextual. I'm speaking into a context where there is widespread confusion about membership and disagreement about baptism. I might fence the Table differently in, say, a house church in Central Asia, or if I were confident that all present understood baptism biblically.

your eyes and confess your sins; look around and marvel at who he's redeemed. Use the regular occurrence of the Lord's Supper as a chance to evaluate your life in the body and consider whether you have any sin to confess to others, any breaches to heal. And rejoice in the unity in diversity which the Lord's Supper signs and seals. As one modern hymnist put it: "Now the strong ones and the weak / are the same under his blood. / For empty-handed all must come / to receive his endless love."[2] Because there is one bread, Paul says, we who are many in Christ are one body (1 Cor 10:17). At the Lord's Supper, divisions disappear. Therefore, the Lord's Supper should plant a passionate pursuit of unity in the heart of every Christian.

If your church has a covenant, one way to highlight the corporate and covenantal nature of the Lord's Supper is to recite your covenant together before celebrating. This powerfully proclaims that the Lord's Supper is a meal of the church, not of a coincidental collection of Christians. It directs our attention both to the Lord and to one another, to what he's done for us and what we, in turn, pledge to him and to our brothers and sisters.

Baptism: Into the Church, by the Church

What does this book's theological framework say for how we should practice baptism? First, remember that baptism is an effective sign of church membership: it creates the ecclesial relation to which it points. Baptism normally confers church membership. Therefore, you should consistently baptize people *into church membership*.

This observation slices a few different ways. First, you should not baptize anyone who is not intending to join your church. With only one exception (addressed below), no one should be baptized who is not intending to come under Jesus' authority by submitting to his church. The affirmation given by a passport goes hand in hand with the responsibility and accountability of citizenship.

Second, churches should not insert a waiting period between baptism and membership. Some might do this out of a desire to emphasize baptism. They decouple baptism from membership in an attempt to draw more attention to it. But the biblical way to draw attention to baptism is to make it the

---

[2] Wesley Randolph Eader, "Victory in the Lamb," available at http://noisetrade.com /wesleyrandolpheader.

gateway into the church and therefore the entry into the Christian life. On the other hand, some might insert a lag between baptism and membership because membership brings serious responsibilities, and maybe a new believer isn't ready for those responsibilities. The problem with that is, every Christian is both required and enabled by God to take their place in the body. So if you're willing to affirm someone as a Christian, there's no reason to keep them out of the body. That's the only place they will thrive, responsibilities and all. And if you're hesitant about a person's willingness or ability to jump into the life of the body, perhaps that hesitancy should back you up into reconsidering whether you're ready to affirm their profession of faith.

Under normal circumstances baptism and church membership should be inseparable. Theologically, baptism confers church membership. So you shouldn't baptize people without bringing them into the church, and you should confer membership on all whom you baptize.[3] Normally a new believer's membership should be conditional upon baptism and should take effect at baptism.

The only legitimate exception I can see is when a new believer is immediately moving to an area where, as far as anyone knows, no church exists. For example, a brand-new Christian who serves in the Navy might be heading out to spend a year living on a ship. Or someone who works for an international consulting firm may be moving to the Middle East and have no idea whether a church exists in their future city. Such situations aren't ideal, but they're often unavoidable. These new believers find themselves in Ethiopian eunuch-like territory. So in these truly exceptional circumstances, a church should baptize them, pray for them, send them off, and encourage them to find whatever Christian fellowship they can during their sojourn abroad.

Another issue to address is how and when churches should baptize. Here Scripture seems to provide few firm prescriptions. Baptisms inside and outside normal "church services" seem allowable, and the only New Testament examples are the latter. It would seem prudent for an elder of the church to baptize since he formally represents the church, but that does not appear to be an absolute requirement.

The only two conditions that seem theologically normative are these: first, where a church exists, baptism is understood as an act of the church, not an

---

[3] For similar arguments, see Brandon C. Jones, *Waters of Promise: Finding Meaning in Believer Baptism* (Eugene, OR: Pickwick, 2012), 146–47; George R. Beasley-Murray, *Baptism Today and Tomorrow* (New York: St Martin's, 1966), 105.

individual acting on his own initiative. In other words, you can't just decide to baptize your cousin Tommy in the pool in his backyard. Second, where a church exists, that church should be the audience for a baptism. Because baptism is the church's affirmation of an individual's profession, baptism's most important "public" is the church itself. If baptism is a public profession of faith, the primary audience for that profession is the church. And baptizing in a gathering of the whole church—whether in a church building or down by the river—embodies the symbolism of the new Christian being added to, and received by, the whole body. Since baptism is an oath-sign by which one covenants with God's people, that aspect of baptism's meaning is highlighted if the whole church is present and obscured if it isn't.

However, a "public" beyond the baptizer is not absolutely necessary to the rite since the baptizer is himself a public witness to the profession of faith. Yet I would suggest that such "audience of one" baptisms are most fitting in a missionary context, where other witnesses are unavailable. If other Christians are around, there's no reason not to have witnesses and many reasons to have them.

One sticky issue this whole discussion raises is the age at which churches should baptize young people.[4] Historically, Baptists have tended to begin baptizing believers around age eighteen. But baptismal ages have plummeted in recent generations, especially in America, so that now it's common for churches to baptize children as young as six or even four. The most obvious problem this creates is a huge number of "re-baptisms." If you were "baptized" at six but are certain you were not converted at the time and only came to faith later, then you were never really baptized.[5] Further, baptizing young children can contribute to false assurance of faith. A decision made years ago to great parental

---

[4] For treatments of the issue with which I am in broad agreement, see Mark Dever, "Baptism in the Context of the Local Church," in, *Believer's Baptism: Sign of the New Covenant in Christ,* ed. Thomas R. Schreiner and Shawn D. Wright (Nashville: B&H, 2007), 344–50; Mike Gilbart-Smith, "'Let the Little Children Come to Me . . .' but Should We Baptise Them? Why Believers' Baptism Should Usually Be Adult Baptism," *Foundations* 63, no. 2 (2012): 90–110, available at http://www.affinity.org.uk/foundations-issues/issue -63-article-5---why-believers-baptism-should-usually--be-adult-baptism. For an insightful argument for baptizing and extending membership to children, see Ted Christman, "Forbid Them Not: Rethinking the Baptism and Church Membership of Children and Young People," available at http://www.hbcowensboro.org/forbid-them-not-free-pdf-download.

[5] For counsel to someone in this position, see my article, "You Asked: Should I Get 'Re-Baptized'? (Credobaptist Answer)," available at   http://thegospelcoalition.org/blogs/ tgc/2013/02/06/you-asked-should-i-get-re-baptized-credobaptist-answer.

pleasure can become the basis for considering yourself a Christian afterward, regardless of fruit.

But the most acute ecclesial problem this creates is that it often separates baptism from membership. Often churches that baptize young children wait until at least the teen years before bringing them into membership (though some extend membership to children while, for example, withholding voting responsibilities). Often, then, a child may be baptized, grow up, never join a church, and yet still consider himself a believer.

However, we have here not just a rock but a hard place. Recall that all the examples of baptism we have in the New Testament took place as soon as someone believed in Christ. And certainly there are many children who come to faith, sometimes at a young age. So it looks like we're on the horns of a genuine dilemma—or trilemma. We either have to sever baptism from membership, or introduce people into membership who are not yet ready for its responsibilities, or depart from the apparent New Testament pattern of immediate baptism.

How can we resolve this dilemma? The first thing to consider is the question of who decides what counts as a credible profession of faith. Functionally, the answer is often a child's parents. But theologically the answer should be the church. The church is vested with the keys of the kingdom. The church speaks for heaven on earth and declares who belongs to the kingdom of Christ. The issue is not simply whether a child claims to believe in Christ, or whether a child's parents think the child believes in Christ. The issue is that the keys of the kingdom require a church to assess whether that child's claim to believe in Christ is credible. And in the case of children generally, I'd suggest that churches are not in a strong position to do so.

Children innately desire to imitate and please their parents. God has made it so. It is natural and good for them to want to do what their parents do, say what they say, believe what they believe. And Christian parents should train their children to trust in Christ and walk in God's ways. Add all this up, and kids being raised in a Christian home should generally look and act like Christians. How then can a church tell if they really are? I'd suggest they can't, at least not in a consistent, principled, across-the-board kind of way. As long as children live at home under the nurture and authority of Christian parents, the pull to look and live like a Christian is strong, even if a child is unregenerate. Of course, that pull weakens as a child enters the teen years and grows somewhat more independent. But it remains in some measure as long as a child is dependent on his or her parents and lives under their direct authority.

Look at it this way: the persuasive power God has given parents and the pliable posture he has given children combine into a kind of static interference that prevents a church from getting an accurate read on a child's spiritual life. They effectively disable the church's "credible confession" radar. It's only when a child takes major steps toward adulthood—like starting college, or getting a job, especially if either involve moving out of the house—that the character of their faith becomes more objectively evident. Are they chaste? Do they go to church when no one's making them? Whom do they befriend? How do they spend their time? What goals do they chase?

Am I saying children can't be saved? Of course not. Am I saying children who grow up in Christian homes should have no assurance of salvation until they're adults? Not at all. All I am saying is that I don't think a congregation is in a position to confidently and consistently affirm the professions of faith of young people until they reach something like "functional adulthood." And therefore churches should only baptize young people when they reach functional adulthood. In our culture this tends to happen somewhere around eighteen at the youngest.

However, if a young person is coming from a non-Christian background, I think a church could baptize them a few years younger since they are swimming against the current of their home and their peers and taking initiative to participate in the life of the church. And in a culture that's increasingly hostile to Christianity, the age at which children in Christian homes' faith becomes more objectively apparent may well be dropping. One could argue that once these children reach high-school age and the issues it brings, if they're living openly as Christians among non-Christian peers, that's enough for a church to go on. Ultimately, what constitutes "functional adulthood" is something of a judgment call, but that doesn't empty the category of all meaning.

But what about the New Testament pattern of immediate baptism? First, it's important to point out that this "pattern" is never explicitly applied to children. As far as I can discern, the New Testament doesn't directly address this question one way or another, so I don't think a straightforward appeal to the precedent of immediate baptism can decide the issue.[6] Thus, I'd suggest that children are simply a special case by virtue of their being children. In addition to our discussion above about the church needing to affirm a credible

---

[6] To argue that young children were included in "household baptisms" (e.g., Acts 16:15, 32–34) is to argue from silence. And the argument could apply equally to infants!

profession, consider: what constitutes a profession in the first place? If we're bound by Scripture to baptize someone as soon as they profess faith, does a three-year-old repeating a confession after you count? What about a two-year-old saying yes when asked if she believes in Jesus? And if you wouldn't baptize a two- or three-year-old, why would you baptize a six-year-old? If you wouldn't baptize a six-year-old, why would you baptize a ten-year-old? My point is not that there's no difference between a two-year-old profession and a ten-year-old profession but that when it comes to baptizing young people, every credobaptist "delays" baptism for someone and has some reason for doing so. No one except paedobaptists can be perfectly consistent with the "immediate baptism" principle. I'd suggest that's because it's a principle we shouldn't apply to children in the first place.

So I think churches are justified in "delaying" baptism when it comes to children. And every credobaptist church will have to anyway; it's just a question of degree. Further, based on the entire theological structure I've sketched in this book, I don't think we can legitimately separate baptism from church membership. To do so is to undermine its role as an effective sign of church membership. It's to divorce "beginning the Christian life" from "entering the church," which we have no biblical warrant to do.

But what about the middle option, baptizing children and extending membership to them but withholding some of its privileges and responsibilities, such as voting on matters of discipline? Consider, for instance, an eight-year-old boy who's a member of a church. If it falls to the congregation to excommunicate a member for unrepentant adultery, this young boy is simply not ready to be part of that conversation, much less to responsibly exercise a share in the church's corporate judgment. So it might seem appealing to welcome children to membership while exempting them from some of its responsibilities. But at what point would the church flip the switch and confer "adult" responsibilities? Say, eighteen? But what if a fifteen-year-old fornicates unrepentantly? Should he be excommunicated? How could a church withhold responsibility on the one hand, yet demand accountability on the other?

I'd argue that to extend membership yet withhold its responsibilities—and possibly its accountability—vacates membership of its biblical meaning. It confers the label without the reality. You can't be a member of the body without sharing responsibility for the body and being accountable to the body. The goods and duties of membership are a package deal; we can't divvy them up as we see fit.

In sum, I'd suggest that churches should wait until young believers have at least one foot firmly planted in adulthood before baptizing them. If the link between baptism and membership is biblically normative, then we lack the authority to sever it. So, first and foremost, we should keep baptism and membership together. If we do, that necessarily precludes at least young children from baptism. Further, we lack the authority to admit persons to membership while denying them some of its responsibilities. Churches should only accept as members those who are ready to live as members.

I'm well aware that this stance raises its share of pastoral issues, but I don't think any of them are insurmountable. Further, I happily affirm that faithful, like-minded pastors differ on this and that churches can provide godly, effective care for their young people while taking a variety of stances on when to baptize them. Yet I've picked over the issue in some detail because in our context the baptism of children may be the practice that drives the hardest wedge between baptism and church membership. And if churches habitually separate baptism from church membership when it comes to our children, it can be tough to see why the two should go together in other circumstances or why baptism should be required for membership in the first place.

Membership: Making It Meaningful

Moving right along, on church membership I've got one point to assert and one question to answer. The point to assert is that membership has to mean something. Limiting the Lord's Supper to the members of churches and insisting that baptism be "into membership" only make sense if membership is more than a name on a list. Otherwise, what's the big deal?

Let's consider two necessary foundations of meaningful membership. The first is that the label should align with the reality. What reality? Well, what does it mean to be a member of a body? It means you depend on the body and the body depends on you. It means you're radically, inextricably attached to the body. It means you don't primarily define yourself as an individual but as part of a whole. Practically, church members should attend church consistently. They should pray with and for the church. They should give. They should serve. They should bear one another's burdens. They should knit their lives to one another so tightly that if you try to pull one member out of the body, another dozen come with him, pulling him back in.

The second aspect of making membership meaningful is that "membership" should draw a clear line between the church and the world. This means you shouldn't have members who live like non-Christians. For this, church discipline is crucial.[7] When Christians stop repenting of sin, the church should rebuke them, plead with them, pray for them, and, if they still don't repent, remove their affirmation by excluding them from membership. You also shouldn't have nonmembers who act like members. What I mean is that in the life of the church there should be a clear distinction between who is a member and who isn't. No nonmember should lead worship, teach Sunday school, serve in the nursery, or lead a small group. Why? Because all of these ministries represent the church. If you're not a member, you're not accountable to the church, so you should have no role in representing it. Of course, a church might have some "ministries" that anyone can participate in, like an evangelistic Bible study. But no nonmember should lead the effort.

In other words, meaningful membership means your church should be a tough place to be either a false Christian or a sovereign-consumer Christian. False Christians should find themselves frequently rebuked and exhorted to repent, trust in Christ, and bear spiritual fruit. And sovereign-consumer Christians should find that they can't just pop in, take all they want, and pop back out.[8]

Next the question to answer is this: if baptism and the Lord's Supper effect church membership, then what should we make of all the other steps in a typical church membership process, steps like a membership class, interview with an elder, signing a statement of faith and church covenant, and a congregational vote? Aren't these other steps superfluous at best and legalistic at worst?

My basic answer is that each of these practices simply elaborates what must necessarily be present in order for the practice of baptism and the Lord's Supper to have integrity.[9] This integrity has two components. First, the individual must have heard, embraced, and confessed the gospel and must intend

---

[7] See Jonathan Leeman, *Church Discipline: How the Church Protects the Name of Jesus* (Wheaton, IL: Crossway, 2012).

[8] For a practical strategy for reclaiming meaningful membership, see Mark Dever, "Regaining Meaningful Church Membership," in *Restoring Integrity in Baptist Churches*, ed. Thomas White, Jason G. Duesing, and Malcolm B. Yarnell III (Grand Rapids: Kregel, 2008), 45–61.

[9] Recall chap. 7's discussion of the preconditions for integrity in the celebration of the ordinances.

both to submit to Jesus and to commit to his church. Second, the church must be able to confidently affirm that the prospective member credibly professes faith in Christ. In other words, the question is not so much about procedure but knowledge. Does the individual know what he or she is signing up for? And does the church know enough about the individual to affirm that person's gospel confession as credible? In a context in which the church is persecuted and nominal Christianity is nonexistent, I think a church needs to know relatively little about a prospective member in order to affirm his profession. In a context featuring nominal Christianity and any degree of social favor toward Christianity, a church needs to know more. All the steps in a sound membership process aim at the simple goal of the Christian knowing what he's doing and the church knowing the Christian.

As we saw in chapter 7, something analogous to a membership class is present in seed form in the teaching that must precede baptism. In addition to preaching the gospel, this teaching must include the nature of baptism as profession of faith in Christ, submission to the authority of Christ, and commitment to the people of Christ. A membership class is simply a standing provision for a prospective member's need to know what he or she is signing up for. Thus membership classes typically major on a church's beliefs and expectations for members, along with whatever other information a church deems prudent to help an individual, and the church, decide whether it would be a good idea for him or her to join.

A membership interview is simply a one-on-one context in which an elder of the church can hear someone's gospel confession and observe some of the fruit of that confession. It allows at least one leader in the church a more intimate acquaintance with the prospective member and provides a low-pressure context in which any issues that may hinder the person from joining the church can surface. It is fitting for elders to conduct these interviews since the elders should lead the church in its exercise of the keys of the kingdom (1 Thess 5:12–13; Heb 13:17). The authority of the keys ultimately rests with the whole congregation, but they should exercise that authority in a manner informed by the leadership of their elders. Smaller churches may decide to have some type of interview before the whole church, as many Baptist churches used to. If they do, the elders should still lead the discussion, since their spiritual maturity and insight are needed for the crucial task of discerning and affirming true gospel confessions and confessors.

Next, some people object to the signing of a statement of faith and church covenant because such documents are "extrabiblical"—they contain words and phrases not found in Scripture. Yet if the documents are faithful to Scripture, they will simply synthesize and summarize Scripture's teaching about what Christians are to believe and do. To synthesize and summarize Scripture's teaching is necessary in order to teach and apply it. Every time we talk about Scripture, we use words not found in Scripture. Further, churches are called not only to confess the gospel but to defend the gospel (1 Tim 3:15). Churches need to be able to confess the truth in such a way as to refute error, which often fills scriptural words with unscriptural meaning.

Every Christian is accountable to confess the truth and walk in the truth. A statement of faith and a church covenant simply specify the basic contours of how we are to believe and live, in order that they may serve as public, accessible standards to which people can be held accountable. Further, in a time and place with a dizzying array of denominations, it is practically necessary to define what you believe as a church. You can't take anything for granted. And in a culture that generally treats church as an optional accessory to faith, a formal church covenant sends the necessary message that to be a Christian is to be committed, both to Christ and to a concrete body of Christians.

Remember that baptism and the Lord's Supper are oath-signs. They are actions which make promises to both Christ and the church. A church covenant and statement of faith make the terms of those promises explicit. The promises are already *there* in baptism and the Lord's Supper; a statement of faith and a church covenant simply name them for the purposes of clarity and accountability.

Finally, what about congregational approval? Congregationalists like me hold that persons should enter and exit the church only by the express consent of the church.[10] But doesn't that mean you actually *become* a member through the congregation's vote, not through partaking of the ordinances? In response, think of it this way: the congregational vote is a little like a basketball team drafting a player, and baptism (for a new Christian) and the Lord's Supper (for every Christian) are like the player signing the contract and showing up at game time. There's a distinction between authorization and execution. As we saw in chapter 5, a church determines to extend membership to a new believer by vote and then confers that status of membership in and through baptism. And there's a sense in which, if an already baptized Christian joins a church,

---

[10] For a full exposition and defense of this position, see Jonathan Leeman, *Don't Fire Your Church Members* (Nashville: B&H, 2016).

his status of membership is first authorized by congregational vote and then executed or fulfilled in his participation in the Lord's Supper.

In some churches this process could take a few months. But if baptism should be into membership, what about a new convert? Shouldn't they be baptized immediately? I'd argue that a church is justified in asking a new convert to work through the membership process before being baptized. This is not a probationary period. Instead, it simply ensures that they know what they're getting into and that the church knows who they are. Further, I would suggest that each of these more elaborate practices is supported by both a biblical and a contextual rationale. If the church must instruct baptismal candidates, then a membership class simply makes that instruction formal and regular. A membership class simply gives regular, institutional shape to a practice implied in Scripture itself. And we've seen that the same is true for these other practices.

But the specific form of these practices is justified by contextual considerations as well and so will take different forms in different contexts. At Pentecost it was pretty clear what you were signing up for: opposition from the Jewish leaders and a whole new life among this persecuted band of the Messiah's followers. Today things aren't always so clear. So, in order to follow the example of the New Testament church, we must adopt a pastoral practice whose procedural details go beyond it, precisely because our context is so foreign to it. We need to take a longer route to arrive at the same destination because of the roadblocks that modernity and nominal Christianity put in our path.[11] And again, the more elaborate process simply cultivates a seed already present in a faithful, biblical practice of the ordinances.

To Picture, Promote, and Preserve the Gospel

The primary purpose of the ordinances and church membership is to picture, promote, and preserve the gospel. How? In part, by building gospel people into a gospel polity.

"The church," Paul says, is "a pillar and buttress of truth" (1 Tim 3:15). Yes, you and I have personal responsibility to image Christ, make disciples,

---

[11] For a fuller discussion of these issues, see chap. 6 of Jonathan Leeman, *The Church and the Surprising Offense of God's Love: Reintroducing the Doctrines of Church Membership and Discipline* (Wheaton, IL: Crossway, 2010).

and contend earnestly for the faith (Phil 2:5; Matt 28:18–20; Jude 3). But the church as a body plays a special role in picturing, promoting, and preserving the gospel. In our love for one another, a church displays the glory of God's self-giving love to the world (John 13:34–35). In our unity a church images the fellowship of the Trinity (John 17:20–21). By living in harmony and singing with one voice, we glorify the God of the gospel, who has made us one (Rom 15:6). In all this a church adorns and thereby promotes the gospel. And as we honor faithful elders, reject false teachers, and instruct one another (1 Tim 5:17; 2 John 10–11; Rom 15:14), we help preserve the gospel in our generation: we uphold its truth, expose counterfeits, and drive it deeper into one another's hearts.

As we've seen, the ordinances and church membership are crucial for the church's work of picturing, promoting, and preserving the gospel. Baptism displays our death to sin and our resurrection to new life in Christ. It seals our commitment to Christ and his people. It draws a line between the church and the world, extending the invitation, "Look, world: see what a gospel people are like!" In the Lord's Supper we enjoy fellowship with Christ and one another on the basis of his blood. As we partake, we experience the gospel anew. As we reratify our covenant commitment to Christ and his church, God's gospel purposes reach ever deeper into our hearts.

Finally, church membership gives a name to the new people who are bound together by this new relation of fellowship in Christ. It ensures that those who should be in are in and those who should be out are out. It shows the church and the world that those who claim the name of Christ but don't submit to his rule have no part in his kingdom and therefore no part in his people. And it testifies that those marked by the obedience of faith are God's people, God's possession, heirs of the world to come.

God's gospel is mighty and magnificent. It frees from guilt, saves from wrath, raises the dead, shatters barriers, reconciles enemies, conforms us to Christ. The word of the gospel creates a gospel people who proclaim and promote the gospel, especially in the new life they now live as one. Baptism, the Lord's Supper, and church membership are there for the gospel. They are prongs for the jewel, a frame for the painting. So when you celebrate the ordinances, remember you're celebrating the gospel. When you live as a church member, giving yourself to the body, remember you're polishing a mirror to reflect the glory of the God who saves.

By constituting a gospel polity, baptism, the Lord's Supper, and church membership make visible a gospel people. They gather up all our flickering little candles into one roaring flame of witness to Christ. Tracing out a biblical theology and practice of the ordinances isn't a distraction from the gospel but a service to the gospel. Certainly the frame is made for the picture, not the picture for the frame. But in order for the frame to fit, it needs the right shape.

Appendix

Explaining Why Baptism Is Required for Membership in Three Minutes

Why must someone be baptized as a believer in order to join a local church? Because church membership is a public affirmation of someone's public profession of faith in Christ, and Jesus has appointed baptism as the means by which his followers publicly profess their faith in him. A church can't affirm the profession of someone who hasn't yet made that profession.

Baptism is how you publicly identify yourself with Jesus and with his people (Acts 2:38–41). It is how you visibly signify that you are united to Christ in his death, burial, and resurrection (Rom 6:1–4). It is how you become identified before the church and the world as one who belongs to the Triune God (Matt 28:19). It is how you publicly embrace Jesus as your Savior and submit to him as Lord (1 Pet 3:21).

Baptism is where faith goes public. It is how you nail your colors to the mast as Jesus' disciple. Therefore baptism is how a new Christian shows up on the whole church's radar as a Christian. Baptism is like a jersey that shows you're now playing for Jesus' team. Because of this purpose Jesus has assigned to baptism, a church may publicly identify itself only with those who have publicly identified with Jesus in baptism.

Baptism is a wordless vow, a symbolic promise to follow Christ in the fellowship of his church. The Lord's Supper is another wordless vow, in which you repeatedly own Christ as your Savior and his people as your people (1 Cor 10:16–17; 11:17–34). On one level church membership is nothing other than ongoing admission to the Lord's Supper. And no one can renew his vow to Christ who has not first made that vow in the form appointed by Christ. No one can be identified with the body of Christ who has not first identified with Christ and his body. Baptism necessarily precedes the Lord's Supper like entering the front door necessarily precedes sitting down at the family meal.

But what about infant baptism? If baptism is where faith goes public, then infant baptism simply is not baptism, and those who have been "baptized" as infants need to be baptized—for the first time—as believers. It's not that the first baptism was somewhat lacking, so there needs to be a do-over. Instead, the first "baptism" wasn't baptism at all, and a believer who has not yet been baptized needs to obey Christ's first command in order to enter his church. We who are convinced of believers' baptism must love our paedobaptist brothers and sisters in Christ. In this case the best way to love them is to help them see that they have not yet obeyed Jesus' first command, and they need to.

NAME INDEX

Easley, Kendell H. *62*
Edwards, Jonathan *113–14, 119, 123–24*

Fee, Gordon *113, 118*
Fesko, J. V. *46, 56*
Forsyth, P. T. *149*
Fowler, Stanley K. *27, 43–44, 99*
Fuller, Andrew *71, 79*

Gaebelin, Frank *69, 87*
Gaines, Darrell Grant *133*
Garland, David E. *121*
Gasque, Ward *116*
Gentry, Peter J. *46, 57–58, 61, 82*
George, Robert P. *78, 122*
Gilbart-Smith, Mike *215*
Girgis, Sherif *78, 122*
Goodwin, Thomas *89, 189*
Goold, William H. *17, 71, 88, 97, 99, 182*
Green, Michael *41*
Grenz, Stanley J. *71, 125*
Grudem, Wayne *155*
Gunton, Colin E. *142*

Hall, Robert *13, 51, 170, 183, 195*
Hammett, John S. *15–16, 182*
Hardy, Daniel W. *142*
Hartman, Lars *41*
Haykin, Michael A. G. *172*
Hays, Richard B. *121*
Heclo, Hugh *18*
Henry, Carl F. H. *62*
Heppe, Heinrich *131*
Holmes, Stephen R. *50, 206*
Horton, Michael S. *71–72, 108, 111, 117*
Howell, R. B. C. *16, 179, 203*
Hubmaier, Balthasar *72, 77, 94–95, 143*

Hugenberger, Gordon P. *57–58, 63–64, 74*
Husbands, Mark *75, 97*

Jamieson, Bobby *11, 201, 215*
Jewett, Paul K. *50*
Jones, Brandon *56, 73, 93*
Jones, Brandon C. *43, 73, 214*

Kantzer, Kenneth S. *62*
Keach, Benjamin *182*
Kiffin, William *16–17, 116, 171–72, 174*
Kinghorn, Joseph *17, 179–80, 183, 185, 197, 201, 204*
Kline, Meredith G. *64, 66*
Köstenberger, Andreas J. *46*

Lee, Jason K. *92, 101, 150*
Leeman, Jonathan *xi, 22, 59, 76, 82, 84, 86–89, 93–94, 105, 129, 132–33, 142, 145, 148–49, 172–73, 189, 220, 222–23*
Lee, Michelle V. *112*
Leonard, Bill J. *200*
Lints, Richard *117*
Lumpkin, William L. *200*

Mabry, Eddie *72, 77*
Macaskill, Grant *69, 75, 111, 114, 142*
Malone, Fred A. *50*
Manton, Thomas *116*
Marsden, George M. *27*
Marshall, I. Howard *111–12*
Martin, Ralph P. *116*
Mather, Richard *144*
McCartney, Dan G. *83, 86*
McClendon, James W. *102*
McCune, Roland *28*
Mendenhall, George E. *116*

SUBJECT INDEX

B

baptism
    effective sign of church member-
        ship *17, 96, 100, 102, 104–5, 138,*
        164–65, 184, 218
    embodies the newness of the new
        covenant *62–63*
    front door of the church *3, 103,*
        109–10, 154, 164–65, 167, 204
    initiating oath-sign of the new
        covenant *15, 82, 94, 101, 110,*
        113, 124, 126, 134, 162–63, 212
    making it meaningful *221*
    mandatory for all believers *49–50,*
        182
    mode of *45–46*
    necessary criterion by which a
        church recognizes a Christian
        164, 166–67
    oath of office for kingdom citizens
        93–95
    part of becoming a Christian
        38–41
    passport of the kingdom of heaven
        163–64

    practice of *213–19*
    proper subjects *8, 56*
    public profession of faith and
        repentance *44–45*
    relation between Spirit baptism
        and water baptism *47–49*
    sign of forgiveness and cleansing
        45–46
    sign of new life in Christ *47–48*
    sign of the dawning new creation
        in Christ *49*
    sign of the gift of the Holy Spirit
        48–49
    sign of union with Christ *46–47*
    synecdoche for conversion *41–44*
    where faith goes public *36–38,*
        40–41, 162

C

church covenant *91–92, 134, 151–53,*
    213
church discipline *23–24*
church membership
    a public, representative statement
        166–67

SCRIPTURE INDEX